The
MYSTERIES
of
MITHRAS

The
MYSTERIES
of
MITHRAS

*The Pagan Belief
That Shaped
the Christian World*

Payam Nabarz, Ph.D.

Inner Traditions
Rochester, Vermont

Inner Traditions
One Park Street
Rochester, Vermont 05767
www.InnerTraditions.com

Library of Congress Cataloging-in-Publication Data
Nabarz, Payam.
  The mysteries of Mithras : the Pagan belief that shaped the Christian world / Payam
Nabarz.
      p. cm.
  Includes bibliographical references (p.   ) and index.
  ISBN-13: 978-1-59477-027-2
  1. Mithraism. I. Title.
  BL1585.N33 2005
  299'.15—dc22

                                                              2005002487

Printed and bound in the United States

11

Text design by Jon Desautels and layout by Priscilla Baker
This book was typeset in Berkeley, with Centaur and Legacy Sans used as display
typefaces

Mighty Anahita with splendor will shine,
Incarnated as a youthful divine.

Full of charm her beauty she will display,
Her hip with charming belt she will array.

Straight-figured, she is as noble bride,
Freeborn, herself in puckered dress will hide.

Her cloak is all decorated with gold,
With precious dress Anahita we shall behold.

ORIGINAL POEM BASED ON KASHANI'S PERSIAN FOLK SONGS,
FROM AN AVESTAN INVOCATION TO ANAHITA

Like grapes, we have always accompanied the vat.
From the view of the world, we have disappeared.
For years, we boiled from the fire of love
Until we became that wine which intoxicated the world.

SUFI PIR AND POET DR. NURBAKHSH

CONTENTS

ACKNOWLEDGMENTS

To Alison Jones for reading this manuscript and her numerous helpful comments, discussions, and especially for her encouragement in the "last mile" of this journey.

To John, Paul, Ivor, Moni, Ruth, Alex, Colin, Pascale, Tony, Mogg, and Sharron for stimulating conversations over the years. A special thanks to Mogg Morgan of the Oxford Golden Dawn Occult Society for his magical encouragement for my work with Mithras.

To Caitlín Matthews for reading the manuscript and for her very helpful comments and especially for encouraging me to finish this book.

To Guya Vichi and Lesley Harris and the other Priestesses and Priests of Mithras who are keeping the flame of Mithras alive.

To all the members of the Mithras e-list who have discussed Mithraism with me, especially Parviz, Omid, Peter, Bradley, John, and Hannah.

To Victoria and Laura for their very helpful editorial comments.

To Sun and Moon Druid Grove of OBOD, and to Andrew and Gillian for the shamanic meetings and for helping me to open the gate to a place I had forgotten.

To Tony and Mani for always being there in friendship.

To Terry Graham for helpful discussions.

To Dr. Nurbakhsh, and the late Mr. Niktab (may he rest in peace), for bestowing the light, and all the Sufis on the Path of Love.

Dedicated to Ali "110."

FOREWORD

As a child, my first introduction to Mithras was courtesy of the Romano-British novels of Rosemary Sutcliff, many of whose characters were Roman soldiers seconded to serve on Hadrian's Wall. What seemed to give them the most strength and support was the spiritual brotherhood of their fellow initiates in the Mithraic mysteries. In those exciting novels, the severe commanders and young legionaries alike bore the initiatic mark of Mithras branded upon their brows. This was deeply impressive and left its own mysterious mark upon me. As a teenager, I longed to know more about Mithras and these rites, soon finding that sources were almost unobtainable but that I, as a woman, was probably not expected to find them anyway, for it seemed that Mithras was solely a god for men, just as the Roman Bona Dea was solely a goddess for women. It wasn't until I was much older that I discovered and read what little there was and realized that Mithras had not left me alone after all. We have continued to encounter one another over the years, and so it was thus a great pleasure and not too much of a surprise to be asked to read a manuscript that gathered the Mithraic material into one book.

What makes *The Mysteries of Mithras* so exciting is that not only has Payam Nabarz presented a clear background to the myth and cult of Mithras, but he has taken this book beyond a theoretical study. While you will find the Zoroastrian hymns to Mithra and his mother, Anahita, you will also find seven initiatory meditations and rituals that open the door to the seven Mithraic grades of Corax, Nymphus, Miles, Leo, Perses, Heliodromus, and Pater. Those who pass through these initiatory portals will be able to forge their own friendship with Mithras, whether they be male or female.

The author reveals that Mithras and his mysteries have not gone away but are relevant to our own times. He locates Mithras authentically as a divine power whose pure love shatters to pieces the delusions of our age and yet still has the ability to bind us together in a much-needed code of honor, truth, and peace. The book's power undoubtedly results from the fact that the author is himself Persian, giving the text a sense of continuity and purpose that doesn't leave Mithras in an historical backwater but makes him available to us all.

The strong simplicity and enlightening power of Mithras permeate these pages, bringing liberation to the darkest caverns of the human spirit. May you "see the doors open and the world of the gods which is within the doors, so that from the pleasure and joy of the sight your spirit runs ahead and ascends."

CAITLÍN MATTHEWS

AN INTRODUCTION TO
THE MITHRAIC MYSTERIES

THE PERSIAN MITHRA

Mithra—the Lord of vast green pastures—we do praise,
To "First Celestial God" our voices raise.
Before the sun shines from hilltops, indeed,
The everlasting sun, Mithra will proceed.

It is the first being with ornaments of gold,
That from mountaintops the earth does behold.

And from there, the powerful Mithra will
Watch the abode of the Magi calm and still.

BASED ON KASHANI'S *PERSIAN FOLK SONGS*,
FROM AN AVESTAN INVOCATION TO MITHRA

Mithra is an ancient Indo-Iranian god who was worshipped in polytheistic Persia at least as early as the second millenium B.C.E., and who was almost certainly related to the Vedic Mitra worshipped in India. The myths of this ancient god contain elements that link him with the mythologies of all the Indo-European peoples. A hymn is dedicated to him in the Rig Veda (3.59); in Hinduism, he is also praised as the binomial Mitra-Varuna. Mitra and Varuna maintain order and justice, as they embody the power that formed the warrior caste in ancient India. Mitra is the lord of heavenly light and the protector of truth, invoked whenever a contract or oath is taken.

In Persia, Mithra was the protector god of many tribal societies for centuries, before Zarathushtra (commonly known in the West by his Greek name of Zoroaster) brought about the reformation of Persian polytheism. Zoroaster formed a new religion out of the old Persian form of worship. Over many more centuries, this religion, Zoroastrianism, slowly gained in popularity and finally became the state religion of the Persian Empire until the rise of Islam.

Zoroaster is thought to have lived in northeastern Iran sometime in the sixth or fifth century B.C.E., though some scholars believe it could have been as early as 1200 B.C.E. Zoroaster is said to have had a miraculous birth: his mother, Dughdova, was a virgin who conceived him after being visited by a shaft of light. Zoroaster's teachings led to the world's first monotheistic religion, in which Ahura Mazda, the "Wise Lord" of the sky, was the ultimate creator. In this reformation Mithra, like the rest of the gods and goddesses of the Persian pantheon, was stripped of his sovereignty and powers and his attributes were bestowed upon Ahura Mazda.

The Avesta is the Zoroastrian holy book. It is a collection of holy texts, which include the *gathas,* the songs and hymns of the prophet Zoroaster, and the *yashts,* the ancient liturgical poems and hymns that scholars believe predated Zoroaster and were modified to reflect the reformation. It also contains rituals, precepts for daily life, and rites of passage for birth, marriage, and death. Because of the Avesta, the Zoroastrians were the first of the "people of the book." *Avesta* probably means "authoritative utterance."[1]

Some of the yashts are hymns to ancient Persian deities, who in Zoroastrianism are demoted to the ranks of archangels or angels, with Ahura Mazda at the top of the hierarchy. In this new format, Ahura Mazda has seven immortal aspects—the Amshaspends or Amesha Spentas—each of whom rules over a particular realm. These are: Vohu Mano (good thought, realm of animals), Asha Vahishta (righteousness, realm of fire), Spenta Armaiti (devotion, realm of earth), Khshathra Vairya (dominion, realm of sun and heavens), Haurvatat (wholeness, realm of water), Ameretat (immortality, realm of plants), and Spenta Mainyu, who is identified with Ahura Mazda (realm of humanity).[2] There are also seven Yazatas, the protective spirits: Anahita (water/fertility), Atar (fire), Homa (healing plant), Sraosha (obedience/hearer of prayers), Rashnu (judgment), Mithra (truth), Tishtrya (the Dog Star/source of rain).

The new religion was, as mentioned, monotheistic, with a strong dualism whereby Ahura Mazda's Amesha Spentas and Yazatas, the forces of

Figure 1.1. Zoroastrian temple in Bombay, India. (Photograph by Payam Nabarz)

light, are faced with the forces of darkness of the Angra Mainyu, or Ahriman. Ahriman—whose symbol is the snake—is called the Great Lie (Farsi *durug*). He and his demons create drought, harsh weather, sickness, disease, poverty, and all forms of suffering. The Zoroastrian dualistic idea of Good versus Evil was inherited by Judaism and then Christianity; indeed, it is possible to trace the axis of evil-versus-good theology and mentality from Zoroaster to all the current monotheistic world religions.

In this Zoroastrian eternal battle of light and darkness, Mithra is the great warrior who, according to his hymn (Yasht 10), carries the hundred-knotted mace or club with a hundred edges, "the strongest of all weapons, the most victorious of all weapons, from whom Angra Mainyu, who is all death, flees away with fear." (Today, Zoroastrian priests still carry the mace of Mithra, which is given to them at their ordination as a symbol of fighting evil.) Even though the old gods were stripped of their power, Mithra had such wide popularity and importance that the Zoroastrians adapted the stories concerning him and gave him a prominent place in their religion. The Zoroastrian fire temple, where great ceremonies take place, is called Dare-e Mehr, which means "Court of Mithra."

Interestingly, "Mithra, it has been suggested in sources from the Sassanian era, is the figure responsible for 'mediating' between Ahura Mazda and Angra Mainyu,"[3] which gives Mithra a unique position within the Persian cosmology as one who stands between light and darkness—the gray middle way, or the liberated third path (see "Mithras as Liberator" in chapter 4). Mithra is seen as almost equal to Ahura Mazda in Yasht 10, when Ahura Mazda says to Zoroaster: "Verily, when I created Mithra, the lord of wide pastures, I created him as worthy of sacrifice, as worthy of prayer as myself, Ahura Mazda." Perhaps this is why he can mediate—because he is as worthy as Ahura Mazda and is also feared by Angra Mainyu.

Due to her popularity, another deity who retained a good deal of her importance in the new religion was the water goddess Anahita, who is sometimes referred to as Mithra's virgin mother or as his partner. We shall take a good look at Anahita in chapter 7.

The question of Mithra, Anahita, and other deities surviving into Zoroastrianism is well addressed by Professor Richard N. Frye:

> One problem has been the difficulty of accommodating the "religion"
> of the Younger Avesta, which is more or less a continuation of the old

Aryan beliefs, with the Gathas of Zoroaster. Why and how could the followers of the prophet accept the worship of Mithra, Anahita and other deities in their religion? This has perplexed many scholars but, in my opinion, the question has not been properly put. The question is not the integration of old Aryan beliefs into the religion of Zoroaster, but the reverse, the acceptance of the teachings of a little known priest in a small principality in eastern Iran by the majority who followed the priests of the old Aryan pantheon. The Magi accepted Zoroaster probably as they had absorbed other teachings, but Zoroaster became the founder and the prophet of the new syncretic religion which we call Zoroastrianism for all Iranians.[4]

The name Mithra (or Mehr, the modern form) has three meanings in Farsi: "love," "sun," and "friend." Here in the name perhaps lies the key to the whole of the Mithraic mystery. The divinity is seen as Sun, or the light of Sun, the ultimate source of energy and life on our planet. Mithra is also the unconditional love that emanates regardless of our existence or thought. Most importantly, he is a friend, one who walks with us, side by side in fellowship. Mithra is the beloved, with whom the Magi seek union. He is seen as the protector of the Aryan nations, giving victory to "those who lie not unto Mithra." He is the warrior deity carrying the "hundred knotted mace," from whom all demons flee in fear. In a Zoroastrian hymn during a prayer to the sun, Mithra is mentioned again and referred to as a friend: "I will sacrifice unto that friendship, the best of all friendships, which reigns between the moon and the sun." The plant called *Mehr giah* (Mithra's plant) is mandrake, one of the best-known magical plants, which was said to be use for love spells. In small doses it's a sedative and in higher doses, a poison.

Mithra is also seen in Chinese mythology, where again he is known as "the Friend." Chinese statues represent him as a military general; he is considered a friend of humanity in this life and its protector against evil in the next.[5] There is also possible influence of Mithra on early Buddhism, an area that is currently being researched by a number of both Western and Iranian scholars. "Maitreya" is the Buddha of the future, or the last Buddha, seen as an embodiment of love, and his name means "Benevolent" or "Friendly One."

The line between myth, legend, and history becomes blurry as we look back through the ages to a time when a man named Mithra the Savior also enters the story. According to Professor Moghdam,

The savior was born in the middle of the night between Saturday and Sunday, 24th–25th December, 272 B.C.E., and according to those who believed in Him from an Immaculate (Anahid) Virgin (Xosidhag) somewhere not far from lake Hamin, Sistan, lived for 64 years among men, and ascended to his father Ahura Mazda in 208 B.C.E.[6]

Thus in addition to the Persian Mithra and Vedic Mitra—the Indo-European deity—we now have a Mithra the Savior who, in the growth of Roman Mithraism, is probably the one referred to as follows: "And you saved us after shedding the eternal blood." We will examine the potential influence of Mithra the Savior on Christianity in chapter 4. However, to create a chronological context here, I'd like to refer again to Professor Moghdam who also mentions:

. . . from Armenia, the last stronghold of the religion of Mithra, we had the testimony of Elise Vardapet to the effect that the Lord Mehr was born of a human mother and he is King and Son of God. I believe all students of Iranian religions are familiar with the story of virgins bathing in Lake Hamun where the seed of Zoroaster is preserved for making the chosen virgin pregnant, who is to give birth to the expected savior, on the model of which the story of the virgin birth of Jesus from the seed of David was constructed. Although no seed of David is in substance present at the appearance of the angel in the Annunciation scene on 25 March, Koranic commentators repeat the story that the angel blew in the sleeves of Mary's dress when she came out of the water.[7]

To create a time line that separates the worship of Mithra into phases is somewhat of an arbitrary division and an oversimplification; but it might begin to allow the Invincible Sun to show its light, illuminating the many aspects of Mithraism.

Phase I: Indo-European Mithra/Mitra, as early as 2000 B.C.E.

Phase II: Mithra the Savior, around 272 B.C.E.

Phase III: Roman Mithras, late 100 B.C.E. to 400 C.E.

Phase IV: Rise of Christianity and Islam as world religions in the Common Era, and the absorption of Mithraism into Christianity, Sufism, Yezidism, and other religions.

Phase V: Rise of Western Secret Societies in the Middle Ages.
Phase VI: Revival of Mithraic mysteries, 1900 onward.

Concerning Phase V, some scholars claim that Mithraism had an influence on the development of the Knights Templar, Freemasonry, and the Rosicrucians. However, despite a number of writers stating this, it remains controversial. In my research, the earliest date I found that mentions Mithras in relation to Freemasonry is in the 1870 "Charter of the Mithras Lodge" based in Washington, D.C. This lodge is also referred to in the *United States Presidential Documents* in the following context:

Garfield, James Abram. Address at the Mithras Lodge of Sorrow, Washington, November 10, 1881.[8]

James Abram Garfield was the twentieth president of the United States, and a Freemason. This lodge is still functioning in Washington, D.C., with numerous offshoot lodges, including the recently opened "Mehr Lodge" (1990).

The revival of the Mithraic mysteries (Phase VI) is of course the ongoing phase that we find ourselves in today. It seems to have begun with the publication of practical books from writers with a connection to the Theosophical Society or American Freemasonry, in 1907 and 1913 (see Bibliography for details).

Now let us move from the East to the West, starting with the Roman Empire and then considering the modern day Mithraic revival, Western style.

THE ROMAN MITHRAS

Fertile Earth Pales who procreates everything.
Rockbound spring that fed the twin brothers with nectar.
This young bull which he carried on his golden shoulders
    according to his ways.
And after which I have received it I have borne on my shoulders
    the greatest things of the gods.
Sweet are the livers of the birds, but care reigns.
That which is piously reborn and created by sweet things.
You must conduct the rite through clouded times together.
And here as the first Ram runs exactly on its course.

And you saved us after shedding the eternal blood.
Accept, O holy Father, accept the incense-burning Lions, through
*   whom we offer the incense, through whom we ourselves are*
*   consumed.*
Hail the lions for many and new years.

MITHRAIC INSCRIPTION AT SANTA PRISCA MITHRAEUM IN ROME,
BASED ON HANS DIETER BETZ'S TRANSLATION
IN PROFESSOR MARVIN MEYER'S *THE ANCIENT MYSTERIES*

Are the Persian Mithra, Indian Mitra, and Roman Mithras the same deity, or independent of one another? Or are they culturally modified versions of the same deity? The field is still split and uncertain on the exact origins of the Roman cult of Mithras. There is almost no written formal documentation of the Western style of Mithraic worship, and this makes any study of the connection between the Eastern (Persian Mithra) and Western (Roman Mithras) forms very difficult. The academic community has been debating for decades and is divided between the "out of Persia" camp, which claims a tradition straight from Persia to Rome, and the "independent Roman" camp, which claims the Roman Mithras began independently of the Persian Mithra and only later incorporated some Persian magical lore. There are also other camps in the middle of the two—all of which means that there is no unifying hypothesis about the origin of the Roman Mithras.

In this book, I avoid entanglement in this contentious issue. When speaking of Persian material and sources I will refer to "Mithra," and when speaking of Roman sources I will refer to "Mithras," the Roman form of the name. This will have the added advantage of helping the reader to distinguish the sources. However, in the revival sections and meditations the line blurs as we enter mystical hyper-reality.

As Mithraism was truly a mystery religion, the exact answers will probably continue to remain occult and hidden. I find myself in agreement with Professor Turcan as he puts it in *The Cults of the Roman Empire:*

> The story of Mithras is remarkable and paradoxical. It is remarkable, because this god, who was alien to the pantheon of the Greeks and Romans, had not been so to their distant Indo-European ancestors. When they welcomed a god of foreign appearance, with Persian trousers and a Phrygian cap, the sons of the she-wolf were in fact linking up again, at least partly, with a very ancient religious genetic inher-

itance; but the cult of Mithras, as it was received by the Latin West, had also incorporated a share of Greek culture. Although the god kept his Asiatic costume, his myth and surroundings of symbolic images, he had taken his place in the syncretic pantheon of the Hellenized Near East. At the same time, the paradox lay in the destiny of this god who, honored in the first instance by Rome's enemies, became (with others) an idol of Roman Legionaries. After inspiring and embodying resistance to the ruling power of Asia Minor, Mithraism two centuries later was to sustain and legitimize certain values of "Roman-ness." But vast shadowy areas surround this story and fragment the vision we have of it today, after over a century of remarkable research and discoveries. In particular, the passage of the Iranian god into the Greek world and the many mutations he must have undergone, both in rituals and in the conception of his worshippers, before becoming the mainspring of a mystery cult, for the present almost entirely elude us. A hiatus of two thousand years separates the Vedic Mithras from the first known representations of Mithras the bull-slayer.[9]

Though the exact origins of Roman Mithraism and its development might remain a mystery, this next passage, written around 350 C.E. by Firmicus Maternus (in his *The Error of Pagan Religions*), speaks volumes about how much the Roman Mithras was perceived in Rome to have Persian roots and connections. Maternus was a recent convert to Christianity at the time of writing.

The Persians and all the Magi who dwell in the confines of the Persian land give their preference to fire and think it ought to be ranked above all the other elements. So they divide fire into potencies, relating its nature to the potency of the two sexes, and attributing the substance of fire to the image of a man and the image of a woman. The woman they represent with triform countenance, and entwine her with snaky monsters. . . . The male they worship is a cattle rustler, and his cult they relate to the potency of fire, as his prophet handed down the lore to us, saying: *mysta booklopies, syndexie patros agauou* (initiate of cattle-rustling, companion by handclasp of an illustrious father). Him they call Mithra, and his cult they carry on in hidden caves. . . . Him whose crime you acknowledge you think to be a god. So you who declare it proper for the cult of the Magi to be carried on by the Persian rite in these cave temples, why

Figures 1.2 and 1.3. Two views of a full-scale reconstruction of the Temple to Mithras at Carrawburgh, at the Museum of Antiquities and the Society of Antiquaries of Newcastle upon Tyne, U. K. Reproduced here by kind permission of the museum. (Photographs provided by the museum)

do you praise only this among the Persian customs? If you think it worthy of the Roman name to serve the cults of the Persians, the laws of the Persians . . . [10]

It is possible to combine a number of current ideas in order to derive a theory that fits the evidence; for example, the Roman cult of Mithras was a fusion of the Greek cult of Perseus with a Persian cult of Mithra. The Perseus cult had originated in Tarsus and at some point became fused with the Persian Mithra, with his Zoroastrian connections, before spilling over into the new empire. As Mithraism spread throughout the Roman army, it changed a great deal from any Persian counterpart. The synergetic result was perhaps the most sophisticated religion in the Roman world. The Roman cult of Mithras was at the forefront of astronomy and philosophical thought, making Mithraism the last pagan state religion in Europe and the most important competitor to early Christianity.

The worship of Mithras, the Invincible Sun God, was practiced all over the Roman Empire. Mithraism had an immense popularity among the

Figures 1.4 and 1.5. *Mitreo dei serpenti* and *Mitreo delle sette sfere*. Both Mithraic temples are in Ostia, Italy. Note the serpent on the left temple. The right temple has seven doors drawn on the floor, which are barely visible now due to weathering. (Photograph by Payam Nabarz)

Roman Legions from late in the first century B.C.E. until around 400 C.E., during which time it came under the influence of Greek and Roman mythologies. Although present in the Persian worship, Anahita and other goddesses are by and large absent from the Roman form of Mithraism. In Rome, Mithras became the ultimate noble warrior, a role model for the Roman Legionnaires among whom Mithraism had most of its adherents. We find the remains of Mithraic temples throughout the former Roman Empire, from Palestine, across the North of Africa, across central Europe, all the way to the British Isles. The Temples along Hadrian's Wall and in London can still be seen today, as well as some remains in Wales and York.

However, like other mystery traditions of that period (the Eleusinian mysteries and the Isis mysteries), the Mithraic cult maintained secrecy and its teachings were only revealed to initiates. As a result, all we have inherited are a number of underground temples and their paintings, some statues, and a few antipagan documents by early Christians. The Roman form evolved to become very occult, heavily linked with astrology, a secret brotherhood order where slaves, freedmen, soldiers, citizens, merchants, and Emperors came together as equals—an amazing achievement for that period!

One key we might have used to unlock the Mithra/Mithras mysteries would have been to look at where they possibly started, in the old land of Persia. But in the same way that Christianity overcame the Mithras mysteries and all paganism in the West, what was left of the original Mithra in the East was dissolved into the rise of Islam. However, we do still have the several hymns to him in the Hindu and Zoroastrian holy texts (see appendix A). These give us insight into the energy of this deity before it became fused with a great deal of Greco-Roman magical ideas. The evolution from god of the green land, wild pastures, and the solar light, to that of Invincible Sun God who moves the cosmos by slaying the constellation Taurus, has been a subject of interest to many historians and magicians alike.

In the end, the magical current of the Invincible Sun God survived despite the rise of Christianity and Islam. In the west, Mithras influenced Christianity, and in the East, Mithra was fused with Islamic lore and became part of the mystical branch of Islam, Sufism. (We will discuss these effects further in chapter 4.)

The Roman Mithraic practice was one of the greatest rivals to early Christianity for many reasons. As well as being a popular pagan religion practiced by the Roman Army, it had many similarities to Christianity. These similarities frightened the Christian forefathers, as it meant that years before the arrival of Christ, all the Christian mysteries were already known. To combat this, certain Christian writers said that the Devil, knowing of the coming of Christ in advance, had imitated them before they existed in order to denigrate them.[11] As Christianity gained in strength and became the formal religion of the Roman Empire, the cult of Mithras was one of the first pagan cults to come under attack. In the fifth century of the Common Era, temples of Mithras—like most other pagan temples—were destroyed, and in some places churches were built on top of them.

THE REVIVAL OF MITHRAS IN THE TWENTIETH AND TWENTY-FIRST CENTURIES

I have to create my own system, otherwise I be trapped by another man's system.

WILLIAM BLAKE

So, the reader might ask, what is the relevance of these ancient mysteries to the magician or pagan practitioner of the twenty-first century? I aim to explore the ways in which this belief system can be used, and how the voices of the gods of ancient lands can speak to us through the rituals we create today. All the ceremonies outlined in this work are suitable for group adaptation or solo practice, and may be of interest to many, for example Sufis, Wiccans, Druids, Greek and Roman Revivalists, Shamanic practitioners, and those who engage open-heartedly with other traditions and systems of belief.

The book is divided into three main sections. This first part is a review of the field of Mithraic enquiry, as well as my own interpretations. The second part presents the Mithras Liturgy and a series of meditations on the graded system of initiation into the mystery. Overall, it took me seven years to write the seven initiation meditations, an average of one grade per year. An initiate should not rush through these grades, but rather, should attend to each one fully before moving on. Finally, the appendixes present the full text of the hymns to Mithra and Anahita as they are contained in the Avesta.

Among the neopagan revivals of the twentieth century, Mithraism is one of the oldest—older, even, than the popular Gardnerian Wiccan revival. The first practical books to surface on the subject were G. R. S. Mead's *The Mysteries of Mithra* (1907), G. R. S. Mead's *A Mithraic Ritual* (1907), and

Kenneth Sylvan Guthrie's fascinating work of restoration, *Mithraic Mysteries Restored and Modernized* (1918). Guthrie's rites were written between 1905 and 1909, and the first completed copy was put together in 1913. This was developed further under the encouragement of the Scottish Rite Freemason leader, Mr. Hall of Nashville, in 1917.

Some of the magical current of Mithraism has survived, perhaps through fusion with Sufism, Christian Gnosticism, and the Catholic Church. The Mithraic influence is evident in several local magical customs in areas where there was a Mithraeum (temple), and in some folk practices. There are Mithraic rites in the Scottish practices of Freemasonry, and its "Mithras Lodge of Perfection" is based in Washington D.C., having obtained its Charter in 1870. The Mithraic influence also can be seen in the Ordo Templi Orientis (OTO). OTO is a semi-secret order established in the late nineteenth century by Freemason Karl Kellner, which combines Eastern tantric ideas with Western ritual magic. In 1922, Aleister Crowley succeeded Kellner as the head of OTO. Numerous OTO groups are still operating worldwide. The seventh degree of OTO is a rite to Mithras, called: "VII Grand councilor of the mystical Templars—Magus of the Light. Graal Comrade and Theoretical Rosicrucian. Brother of the Light of the Seven Congregations in Asia. Mysteries of the Mithras cult."

Now there are even new temples to Mithras in some places, for example, "Sun Center" in Tuscany, Italy.[12]

Figure 1.6. A painting of Mithras slaying the bull, with an altar in front of it in the new Temple of Mithras, Tuscany, Italy. (Photograph by Guya Vichi)

Figure 1.7. A new Temple of Mithras, Tuscany, Italy. This beautifully designed temple contains many symbols of the Mithraic mysteries. (Photograph by Guya Vichi)

As in all the other branches of the neopagan revival, a great deal of reinvention has occurred. There are no hereditary "kitchen initiations" or secret texts herein. Mithra is invoked as lord of the truth; hence it is important to make this clear. The work with the Spirit, or Energy, is what matters, rather than any one theory. The key to entering the tradition is simple. All you need to do is to call with an open heart upon Mithra: the Friend, Love, and Sun. In other words, say "Friend" and enter!

The modern Mithraic revival relies heavily upon the "Mithras Liturgy," from the *Greek Magical Papyri*, which dates from the year 350 C.E. We shall become thoroughly acquainted with this piece of magical writing in chapter 6.

Another text that new revivalists use is "A Song to Mithras," from Rudyard Kipling's *Puck of Pook's Hill* (1906), a poem that beautifully expresses the spirit of Mithraism.*

A Song to Mithras

Mithras, God of the Morning, our trumpets waken the wall!
"Rome is above the Nations, but Thou art over all!"
Now as the names are answered, and the guards are marched
*   away,*
Mithras, also a soldier, give us strength for the day!
Mithras, God of the Noontide, the heather swims in the heat,
Our helmets scorch our foreheads; our sandals burn our feet,
Now in the ungirt hour; now ere we blink and drowse,
Mithras, also a soldier, keep us true to our vows!
Mithras, God of the Sunset, low on the Western main,
Thou descending immortal, immortal to rise again!
Now when the watch is ended, now when the wine is drawn,
Mithras, also a soldier, keep us pure till the dawn!
Mithras, God of Midnight, here where the great bull dies,
Look on thy children in darkness. Oh take our sacrifice!
Many roads Thou has fashioned: all of them lead to the Light,
Mithras, also a soldier, teach us to die aright!

This poem is a great contribution to the path of modern Mithraism. Kipling's poetry has been used in other sectors of the pagan revival as well;

---

*In *Songs from Book and Verse* this poem is subtitled "Hymn of the XXX Legion: Circa A.D. 350." It is reproduced here with the kind permission of A. P. Watt, Ltd., on behalf of the National Trust for Places of Historic Interest or Natural Beauty.

for example, he wrote the "May Eve" song, which is used in the *Wiccan Book of Shadows*.

Mithras has been slowly making his way into the popular culture in the last hundred years, no longer only in the domain of magicians and academics but in the fields of art, music, film, and literature. Picasso used Mithraic symbols in a number of his pieces, symbols such as the seven rugged ladders and Mithras's Phrygian cap. Also, the American art historian Ruth Kaufman identified the use of Mithraic iconography in the 1930 Picasso painting entitled "Crucifixion." Other artists as well have produced a number of postmodern art pieces and exhibitions. There was a brief appearance of Mithraic iconography in the Hollywood movie "Blade II." In England, there is the heavy metal band called "Mithras," and also an English folk music band with the very same name. A few years ago an inspiring CD album entitled *Mysteria Mithrae* was released; it features songs to Mithras by various artists, and is dedicated to him. There are now numerous historical novels with Mithraic initiate characters, among them the *Winter King* trilogy by Bernard Cornwell, Mary Stewart's *Merlin of the Crystal Cave*, Nancy McKenzie's *Queen of Camelot*, and Rosmary Sutcliff's *The Eagle of the Ninth*. Finally, with the growth of the Internet there are now numerous Web sites and newsgroups dedicated to the Mithraic mysteries, which serve to bring interested parties together.

The Mithraic revival reflects social and cultural contexts of the last hundred years—and yet it has remained true to the spirit of Mithraism, as expressed in the words of the "Mithraic Liturgy": "I am a Star, wandering about with you [Mithras], and shining forth out of the deep."

MITHRAIC ICONOGRAPHY

As for you [Emperor Julian] . . . I [Hermes] have granted you to
know Mithras the Father. Keep his commandments, thus securing for
yourself an anchor-cable and safe mooring all through your life, and,
when you must leave the world, having every confidence that the god
who guides you will be kindly disposed.

EMPEROR JULIAN CAESARES, 336 C.E.,
IN MANFRED CLAUSS, THE ROMAN CULT OF MITHRAS

Religious icons tend to act as keys that open our minds to the spiritual
meaning behind visual symbols. Understanding the iconography of a religion affords access to the deeper mysteries of the religion, at levels inac-
cessible through the written word, because symbols act on a much subtler
level than words, bypassing the ego completely. Deciphering the meaning in
the Mithraic paintings and statues that have survived in Europe has been
a challenge for many academics in the field; the work of Speidel and
Ulansey has shed light on much of the iconography.[1] The various interpretations of the icons all point to a deep cosmology within the tradition.
Let us explore the essential symbology of Mithras's life and deeds and their
implications for the believer.

To get a better idea of the place of Mithraic iconography in the temple, I highly recommend an online visit to the full-scale reconstruction of
the Temple to Mithras at Carrawburgh, at the Newcastle University
Museum. The virtual tour is at the museum's Web site.[2]

BIRTH OF THE ROMAN MITHRAS

The Roman myth about the birth of Mithras (Dies Natalis Solis Invicti)
ascribes to him a magical birth at the dawn of time, out of a rock from

Figure 2.1. Mithras being born from the cosmic egg, surrounded by the signs of the Zodiac. He is holding a torch and a sword. The Museum of Antiquities and the Society of Antiquaries of Newcastle upon Tyne, by kind permission of the Museum. (Photograph by Mogg Morgan)

which he formed himself using his will, and holding in his hand a dagger and a torch. One can see the similarities with the image of Hecate, the torchbearer with a dagger that cuts the threads of life and death, and which has supposedly become the witch's athame. A statue from Housesteads in England shows Mithras being born from the rock surrounded by the twelve signs of the zodiac, indicating his status as a stellar god who rules the cosmos even at his birth. A serpent is sometimes shown coiled around Mithras or his birth stone/egg. After his birth, when the world was young, he challenged other forces. His battle with Sol, the Sun, resulted in a friendship, and Mithras was bestowed with a crown made of the rays of the Sun.

According to the Zoroastrian tradition mentioned in chapter 1, Mithra the Savior was born in 272 B.C.E. His birth and that of the Roman Mithras are both at the winter solstice. The Persian Mithra was born of the immaculate virgin Mother Goddess Anahita (see chapter 7). Anahita (Anahid) was said to have conceived the Savior from the seed of Zoroaster, which, legend says, is preserved in the waters of Lake Hamun in Sistan, Iran. This birth took place in a cave or grotto, where shepherds attended him and presented him with gifts at the winter solstice. Mithra lived for sixty-four years and then ascended to heaven in 208 B.C.E.

MITHRAS THE HUNTER

Some images survive with Mithras on horseback with bow and arrow in hand, hunting a stag whose horn is the crescent moon. A lion, a snake, and a dog accompany him. Like the tauroctony considered next, the image might be a star map; however, no one has been able to interpret it yet fully.

THE TAUROCTONY

The central icon, ever present in Mithras temples throughout the Roman Empire, is the tauroctony, or bull-slaying. It is the core icon of the Mithraic community, as important to Mithraists as the crucifixion came to be for Christians. Many of these dynamic reliefs can be seen in museums across Europe. The Roman imagery was probably modeled on the image of Nike, the Greek goddess of victory, killing a bull. It is unclear if this is an artistic influence or if some of Nike's myth was also incorporated into the new religion of Mithras. As we will discuss, in Mithraism the tauroctony can be interpreted as a demonstration that love literally moves the universe!

Interestingly, the central relief in some temples was a rotating relief, one side depicting the tauroctony, the other side showing a different Mithraic iconic scene. The rotation might have been used as a magical technique to reveal a different mystery at a specific time in certain rites.

Figure 2.2. Mithras slaying the bull. Rotating altar panel, side A. Musée du Louvre, Paris. (Photograph by Payam Nabarz with kind permission of the museum)

Figure 2.3. Mithras and Sol sitting behind the bull. A torchbearer is passing a drinking horn to Sol. Rotating altar panel, side B. Musée du Louvre, Paris. (Photograph by Payam Nabarz with kind permission of the museum)

The visual effect of the rotating icon on the initiate, in the middle of a rite, could have been a powerful one.

Now let's examine the details of this core Western Mithraic icon. We shall refer to this imagery again and again. The scene shows that Mithras, while facing away from the bull, has one leg on the back of the bull, one hand holding the bull's head, and the other hand stabbing the bull in the neck, where blood pours forth. Around him are a dog, a raven, a scorpion, a snake, a lion, and a cup. From the tip of the bull's tail, a shaft of wheat is growing. The cloak of Mithras is the night sky with stars; the signs of the zodiac surround the whole scene. The symbols of the seven planets are present; the two torchbearers of Mithras stand at either side of the bull-slaying scene.

Figure 2.4. Mithras slaying the bull. Rotating altar panel, side A. Frankfurt Archaeological Museum, Germany. By kind permission of the museum. (Photograph by Mogg Morgan)

What we find in this central mystery is a representation of the constellations Perseus (Mithras), Taurus (bull), Canis Minor (dog), Hydra (snake), Corvus (raven), Scorpio (scorpion). The wheat is the star Spica (the brightest star in Virgo); the blood is the Milky Way. The two torchbearers, Cautes and Cautopates, symbolize the equinoxes. Cautes' torch is pointing upward: the spring equinox. Cautopates' torch is pointing downward: the autumn equinox.

The meaning of this star map lies within the precession of equinoxes. At the present time, the spring equinox occurs when the sun is in the constellation of Pisces. In a hundred years, the equinox will be in the constel-

Figure 2.5. Mithras and Sol, standing behind the bull. Rotating altar panel, side B. Frankfurt Archaeological Museum, Germany. By kind permission of the museum. (Photograph by Mogg Morgan)

lation of Aquarius (the Age of Aquarius). In Greco-Roman times, the spring equinox was in Aries, and the autumn equinox was in Libra, and before that, in the years around 4000–2000 B.C.E., the spring equinox was in Taurus and the autumn equinox was in Scorpio. This also means that the summer solstice was in Leo (lion) while the winter solstice was in Aquarius (cup). The whole bull-slaying scene is therefore the representation of the "heavens" as we on Earth moved from the Age of Taurus to the

Age of Aries. That is, the constellation Perseus, which is above the constellation Taurus, gives us the image of Mithras killing the bull, bringing an end to the Age of Taurus by moving the entire universe.

In a time when both magic and science were based on a geocentric cosmos, with Earth as a fixed body in space and everything revolving around it, the precession could only be understood as a movement of the entire cosmos, rather than a movement of the Earth. Mithras therefore became the Kosmokrator, the "cosmic ruler." The blood of the bull is the Milky Way, the pathway that souls ascend and descend to genesis. The slaying of the constellation Taurus by the constellation Perseus is perhaps one of the greatest star maps left to us. It gives a whole new dimension to the Gnostic notion of overcoming the ego and uniting with the subconscious, a dimension that can be observed *in the cosmos itself*. Mithras presides over the changing of the seasons and the movement of the heavens. Hence the tauroctony is said to demonstrate that Love literally moves the universe.

Several key images around the central tauroctony scene are important because they contain a creation story. In the beginning Mithras is asked by the Sun to kill the first bull, but he is reluctant to do this. The Raven, messenger of the Sun, comes to him again with the message. Mithras goes into the field and captures the bull, and with his might, lifts the back legs of the bull over his shoulder and drags him to the birth cave. The crescent moon over the bull suggests its connection to the moon. As Mithras kills the bull,

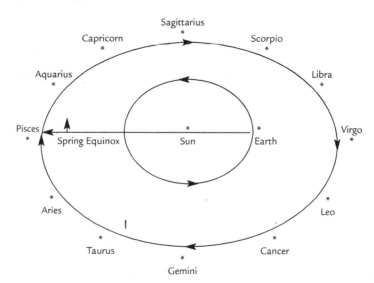

Figure 2.6. The meaning of the tauroctony as a star map lies within the precession of equinoxes.

from his blood come wine and all the plants that cover the earth. The tail becomes wheat, which gives us our bread. The seed and the genitals of the bull are taken to the Moon Goddess and purified, giving rise to all the animals. Hence by this slaying of the first bull, life comes onto the earth.

SOL AND SOL INVICTUS

The new life on Earth is growing very slowly, due to drought. Mithras as the mediator between Heaven and Earth is asked to solve this problem; however, this means a conflict with the Sun, who has been burning the land. The battle between Sol (the sun) and Mithras results in Mithras overcoming the planetary sun and becoming the Invincible Sun. Sol kneels in front of Sol Invictus while Mithras holds the constellation Bear (Ursa Minor) in one hand. This emphasizes his power as the stellar god, one who moves the cosmic pole as well as causing the precession of equinoxes. Mithras and Sol then become friends and shake hands.

Mithras is described as the lord of wide pastures, the lord of truth and contracts. The custom of shaking hands when greeting a friend or after a business deal is said to have originated from the Mithraic mysteries, as a sign of not carrying a weapon, and of trust. The earliest depiction of the act of handshaking in the

Figure 2.7. Bas-relief fragment from Virunum in central Europe. Scenes from Mithras's life, including (from bottom to top): smiting the rock from which the water flowed; holding the leg of the bull in his right hand and placing his left on Sun's head, investiture of the Sun with his halo; Mithras and Sun shaking hands; Mithras and the Sun in the chariot, showing their ascension to the sky. (From *The Mysteries of Mithra*, by Franz Cumont. New York: Dover, 1956)

world is that of Mithra shaking hands (right hands) with the Syrian King Antiochus in the first century B.C.E., a sign of the transfer of divine power from God to his earthly representative and sealing the divine "contract." In the Roman cult of Mithras a number of reliefs show Mithras and Sol shaking their right hands (dexiosis); and Mithraic initiates were termed *syndexioi*, "those who have been united by a handshake"(with the Father). The handshake is also mentioned in Proficentius's poem from Rome, on the occasion of building his Mithraeum:

> This spot is blessed, holy, observant and bounteous:
> Mithras marked it, and made known to
> Proficentius, Father of the mysteries,
> That he should build and dedicate a Cave to him;
> And he has accomplished swiftly, tirelessly, this dear task
> That under such protection he began, desirous
> That the Hand-shaken might make their vows joyfully forever.
> These poor lines Proficentius composed,
> Most worthy Father of Mithras.[3]

It is worth noting that the Freemasons and some Sufis have their own special right-handed handshake, and of course there is the connection with the magical "right-hand path." The act of handshaking is perhaps the most popular sign of a Mithraic act surviving to the modern day. Some even say that the custom of the military salute might have its origins in the Mithraic mysteries, from the Salute to the Sun, which we will take a look at later.

THE MIRACLE OF THE ROCK

Mithras is an archer god, and by firing an arrow into the rock face of a mountain, he causes water to pour forth. The drought ends. The rock may represent the clouds where rain comes from and the clouds may represent the cave or the universe.

THE SACRED MEAL

The remains of the bull are brought by the torchbearers of Mithras—Cautes (dawn, spring equinox) and Cautopates (dusk, autumn equinox)—to a meal where Sol and Mithras sit together. The sacred meal was

Figure 2.8. Mithraic communion and ritual meal. The table is the body of the bull. From left, Corax and Perses initiates approach while carrying a drinking horn. On the right, a Leo and another figure (Miles perhaps) approach. Pater (Mithras) and Sol are at the table. In front is what might be a plate with four round loaves of bread marked with a +. (From *The Mysteries of Mithra*, by Franz Cumont)

enacted by the followers of Mithras during initiation rituals, where Pater represented Mithras, Heliodromus represented the sun, and the other initiates sat around and shared the sacred meal.

THE ASCENSION

After the sacred meal, Mithras gets into Sol's horse-drawn chariot and heads to the sky or the ocean to fulfill his role as the cosmic ruler (Kosmokrator).

LEONTOCEPHALINE (LION-HEADED ONE)

The lion-headed figure found in many Mithraic temples has been something of an enigma. Its statues or paintings have always depicted it with a snake winding around it; it is standing on the cosmic sphere and holding a key in its right hand, and its body is often decorated with the signs of the zodiac and stars. In some mystery religions it is known as Agathodaimon (the good spirit-friend) where it acts as a doorkeeper and door opener.

We can consider the seven grades of the Mithraic mysteries to be symbolized by a ladder or a staircase with seven gates, each associated with

Figure 2.9. The first four images are depictions of the "leontocephalous" from *The Mysteries of Mithra* by Franz Cumont. The image on the lower right is of a leonto-cephaline painting at Sun Center, Tuscany, Italy, a modern-day Temple of Mithras. (Photograph by Guya Vichi)

one of the seven planets, while at the top is an eighth gate associated with the sphere of the fixed stars and leading to the region beyond that sphere. The leontocephaline holds a key to the eight celestial gates, the ways into the realm of fire. Professor David Ulansey has suggested that the leontocephaline functioned partly as a symbol for the ultimate boundary of the universe. In his paper on the "Mithraic Eighth Gate," he first describes the fiery nature of this boundary:

> The idea of a fire at the outermost boundary of the universe later became a commonplace in Stoic thought. Cleanthes, for example, according to Cicero, taught that "the most unquestionable deity is that remote all-surrounding fiery atmosphere called the aether, which encircles and embraces the universe on its outer side at an exceedingly lofty altitude." . . . Among the Middle and Neo-Platonists there was also a widespread belief that the outermost region of reality was a fiery domain. Based on Plato's famous allegory of the cave and of the sun-filled realm outside of it, the doctrine arose that beyond the universe—in the "place beyond the heavens" . . .[4]

Ulansey then goes on to show the link between the leontocephaline and the aetherial cosmic fire:

> The Mithraic leontocephaline, as is well known, is frequently associated with fire-symbolism in a variety of ways, extending even to the existence of statues of the leontocephaline apparently designed so that fire could be sent shooting out of its mouth . . . the leontocephaline is designed to emphasize the concepts of boundary and boundary-crossing. The globe on which the figure stands is located exactly on the arching zodiacal boundary of the universe, while the figure itself extends beyond that boundary as a kind of incarnation of the process of boundary-crossing. The serpent around the leontocephaline symbolizes its role as ultimate boundary.[5]

Interestingly, the Goddess Hecate—goddess of the boundaries and crossroads—is also associated with keys, and her statues have been found occasionally in Mithraic temples. She also, like the leontocephaline, is responsible for the boundary between the cosmos and what is beyond it in the realm of fire.

Chapter 3

THE SEVEN INITIATORY RITES OF MITHRAS

Whether thou wouldst rather bear the bright red name of Titan
In the tradition of the Achaemenid people,
Or of fruitful Osiris, or of him who beneath the rocks of the
Persian Cavern twists the horns of the stubborn bull: Mithras!

COURT POET STATIUS, 92 C.E.

In the Roman mystery cult of Mithras, seven degrees of initiation enabled the neophyte to proceed through the seven celestial bodies, allowing a reversal of the descent of the human soul into the world at birth. To achieve this, the initiate ascended the seven heavens and walked through the Milky Way, returning to the origin of the Soul. The initiates worked with the four elements and seven planetary energies, and the initiations involved the undergoing of purification and "ordeals." The seven sets of symbols on the floor mosaic in the Mithraeum of Felicissimus, in Ostia, Italy, show the emblems for each of the seven grades.

THE RITES

Corax

The first degree was that of Corax (Raven), under the rule of Mercury. This stage symbolized the death of the neophyte. (In ancient Persia, it was the custom to place the bodies of the dead on funeral towers, to be eaten by ravens.) At this first stage the neophyte would die and be reborn into a spiritual path. A mantra was given to him to repeat, and his sins were washed away by baptism in water.

Figure 3.1. Floor mosaic showing seven grades of initiation. Mithraeum of Felicissimus, Ostia, Italy. (Photograph by Payam Nabarz)

The emblems for Grade 1, Corax, appear toward the bottom of the drawing and the grades proceed upward in order to Grade 7, Pater, at the top. The emblems, or tokens, for each grade are shown as follows.

Tokens of Corax under the planet Mercury: a Raven, a Caduceus, and a small beaker.

Tokens of Nymphus under Venus: an oil lamp and a diadem.

Tokens of Miles under Mars: a lance, a helmet, and a soldier's sling bag.

Tokens of Leo under Jupiter: a fire shovel, a rattle (sistrum), and a thunderbolt.

Tokens of Perses under the Moon: a sickle, a Persian dagger, and a crescent moon with a star.

Tokens of Heliodromus under the Sun: a torch, a seven-rayed crown, and a whip.

Tokens of the Pater under Saturn: a Phrygian cap, a libation bowl, a staff, and a sickle.

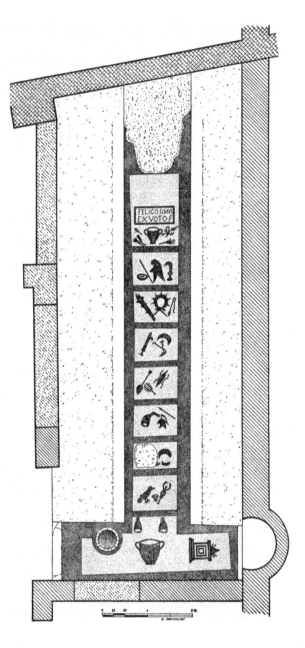

Figure 3.2. Line drawing of the emblems for the seven grades as they appear in the mosaic of the Mithraeum of Felicissimus, Ostia, Italy. (From G. Becatti, *Scavi di Ostia*, II, *I Mitrei*, p. 107)

Ravens have always held a place in mythologies around the world. Their magical significance can be seen today at the Tower of London, which lies within the old Roman city walls. Legend has it that if the ravens leave the tower, the kingdom and the monarchy will fall. This legend is taken very seriously by the British monarchy according to official sources—so much so that during World War II, the ravens came under

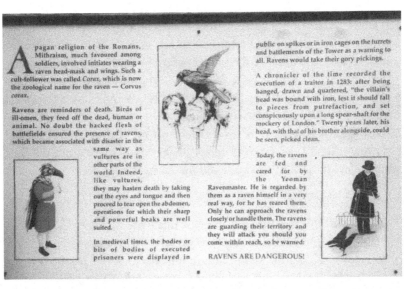

A pagan religion of the Romans, Mithraism, much favoured among soldiers, involved initiates wearing a raven head-mask and wings. Such a cult-follower was called *Corax*, which is now the zoological name for the raven — *Corvus corax*.

Ravens are reminders of death. Birds of ill-omen, they feed off the dead, human or animal. No doubt the hacked flesh of battlefields ensured the presence of ravens, which became associated with disaster in the same way as vultures are in other parts of the world. Indeed, like vultures, they may hasten death by taking out the eyes and tongue and then proceed to tear open the abdomen, operations for which their sharp and powerful beaks are well suited.

In medieval times, the bodies or bits of bodies of executed prisoners were displayed in public on spikes or in iron cages on the turrets and battlements of the Tower as a warning to all. Ravens would take their gory pickings.

A chronicler of the time recorded the execution of a traitor in 1283: after being hanged, drawn and quartered, "the villain's head was bound with iron, lest it should fall to pieces from putrefaction, and set conspicuously upon a long spear-shaft for the mockery of London." Twenty years later, his head, with that of his brother alongside, could be seen, picked clean.

Today, the ravens are fed and cared for by the Yeoman Ravenmaster. He is regarded by them as a raven himself in a very real way, for he has reared them. Only he can approach the ravens closely or handle them. The ravens are guarding their territory and they will attack you should you come within reach, so be warned:

RAVENS ARE DANGEROUS!

Figure 3.3. Ravens at the Tower of London. The tower is within the old Roman London city wall. (Photographs by Payam Nabarz)

special protection. Even now, they are looked after by a "Yeoman Ravenmaster" and have their wings clipped so they won't fly very far away. In preparation against catastrophe, disease, or attack, "reserve" ravens are kept at another location, ready to be brought to the Tower of London if suddenly all the resident ravens were killed, thereby endangering the kingdom.[1] See the photo of Raven degree description in the Tower of London in Figure 3.3.

Ravens have always been the messengers of the Sun, and from antiquity, divine kingship was bestowed by sun gods (e.g. Mithra, Horus); therefore, ravens symbolize the link between the Sun and the king/queen. In Britain, ravens were sacred to Bran, the great protector king whose head was said to be buried under the London Tower, facing Europe to protect Britain—that is, until King Arthur dug it up so as to be sole protector of Britain himself. Ravens were also sacred to King Arthur, and of course, both Arthur and Bran received their "divine king" status from the Sun, which refers us back to sun gods and the raven totem.

Nymphus

The second degree was that of Nymphus (male bride), under the auspices of Venus. Nymphus also means "bee chrysalis," which opens up the neophyte's potential to grow and become a full "bee" later on, at the Leo and Perses levels, by taking part in the honey sacrament. The neophyte wore a veil and carried a lamp in his hand. He was unable to see the "light of truth" until the "veil of reality" was lifted. He was vowed to the cult, and would become celibate for at least the duration of this stage, as he was now a bride (lover) of Mithra. He also offered a cup of water to the statue of Mithra—the cup being his heart, and the water, his love. The ritual greeting for this grade was: "Hail Nymphus, hail New Light."

Miles

On reaching the third degree, Miles (Soldier) under Mars, the neophyte had to kneel naked—casting off his old life—blindfolded and with hands tied (in a similar manner to that of Wiccan initiations). He was then offered a crown on the point of a sword. Once crowned, his bindings were cut with a single stroke of the sword and his blindfold removed. This represented his liberation from the bondage of the material world. He would then remove the crown from his head and, placing it on his shoulder, he would say: "Mithra is my only crown." This vow of loyalty and rejection of ego also symbolizes removing the head itself: allowing Mithra to be the

guide. (The bard Taliesin, in his "Song of the Macrocosm," might be referring to this, and to his own initiation into Mithraism. See the section in
chapter 4 entitled "Mithras in Britain.")

At this stage the neophyte started the real battle against the ego; a soldier is one who actively struggles with the enemy. Indeed, Tertullian, the
early Christian theologian of the second century C.E., records the following comment made to a Christian soldier:

> Are you not ashamed, fellow soldiers of Christ, that you will be found
> wanting, not by him, but by some Soldier of Mithras? At his initiation
> in the cave, in the very camp of darkness, a crown is offered to the
> candidate at the point of a sword, as if in imitation of a martyrdom,
> and put on his head; then he is admonished to put his hand up and
> dash it from his brow onto his shoulder, as it may be, saying: "My
> crown is Mithras!"[2]

At the end of the initiation for the Miles degree, it has been suggested
by some that a mark was branded (or tattooed) on the forehead of the initiate. Of this, Franz Cumont says: "This indelible imprint perpetuated the
memory of the solemn engagement by which the person under vow contracted to serve in that order of chivalry which Mithraism constituted."[3] It is
unclear as to what the mark was; some speculate it might have been an equidistant cross, the symbol of the sun. Robert Turcan writes: "The victorious
horseman who was believed to be Hostilian, the son of Decius Trajan
(249–51), bears on his forehead an X, which H. von Heintze considered to
be a mystery tattoo. Tertullian certainly writes that Mithras marks (signat)
his soldiers on the forehead, but with what 'sign'?"[4] Some writers have even
speculated that this mark was the mark of the "Beast of Revelations," as the
numerological value of the Sun is 666! The image of the brand on the forehead was popularized by Rosemary Sutcliff in her 1954 historical novel for
children, Eagle of the Ninth. The hero is a Mithraic initiate who is branded
on the forehead during his initiation.

The branding might be one reason why initiates did not let their heads
be covered, when the crown was presented—instead, saying "Mithras is
my only crown"—as they would henceforth have the Sun Cross on their
forehead. The similarity to the cross of ashes made on the forehead on the
Christian Ash Wednesday is striking. Some have suggested this to be an
example of the early Christians borrowing from the Mithraic cult; others
suggest that both cults were drawing upon the same prototype.

Leo

The fourth grade, the stage of Leo (Lion), under the guidance of Jupiter, was the first of the senior degrees. The initiate was entering the element of Fire. Therefore, the Lion was not allowed to touch water during the ritual, and instead, he was offered honey to wash his hands and anoint his tongue. Porphyry in the third century C.E. wrote this about the use of honey in the Mithraic rites: "The ancients used to call the priestesses of the Earth-Mother Bees—in that they were initiates of the Earth Goddess—and called the virgin herself Bee-like. They also called the moon Bee, as the Lady of Generation; and especially because the exalted Moon is the Bull, and Bees are Ox-born—that is, souls about to be born are Ox-born."[5]

Porphyry also says: "So in the Lion mysteries, when honey is poured instead of water for purification on the hands of the initiates, they are exhorted to keep them pure from everything distressing, harmful and loathsome; and since he is an initiate of fire, which has a cathartic effect, they use on him a liquid related to fire, rejecting water as inimical to it. They use honey as well to purify the tongue from all guilt."[6]

The Lions carried the food for the ritual meal, which was prepared by the lower grades, to the ritual feast, and took part in it. The ritual feast represented Mithras's "Last Supper" of bread and wine with his companions, before his ascent to the heavens in Sol's chariot. The Lions' duties also included tending the sacred altar flame. In Santa Prisca Mithraeum it is written: "Receive the incense-burners, Father, receive the Lions, Holy One, through whom we offer incense, through whom we offer ourselves consumed!"[7]

They are said to have growled like lions and to move strangely (but this was from the point of view of the Christians, who persecuted them). This emphasizes that the lion or raven masks were not just props, but also acted as part of the shamanistic aspect of the religion. The ordeals of fire, water, heating, and cooling all point to the shamanistic nature of the mysteries. The ordeal pit would have been covered by stone slabs, resulting in the initiate being engulfed by earth. The presence of a potential ordeal pit in the Carrawburgh Mithraeum in the North of England suggests these ceremonies were carried out even in the further reaches of the Roman Empire.

Perses

The fifth degree, Perses (Persian), was under the rule of the Moon. In Greco-Roman mythology Perses is the son of Perseus, and as the cult of Mithras associated the constellation Perseus with Mithras, the ultimate title of *Pater* (Father) for the seventh grade makes sense as Father and Son. The emblem for this stage was a *harpe* (carved sword), the harpe sword that Perseus used to decapitate the Gorgon, symbolizing the destruction of the lower, animal aspects of the initiate. The initiate was again purified with honey, as he was under the protection of the Moon: "Honey is associated with the purity and fertility of the moon, as this was, in ancient Persia, believed to be the source of honey, and thus the expression of 'honey-moon' denotes not the period of a month after marriage, but continued love and fertility in married life."[8]

Heliodromus

In the sixth grade of Heliodromus (Sun Runner) under the influence of the Sun, the initiate would represent the Sun at the ritual banquet. He would sit next to Mithras (Father), and would be dressed in red, the color of sun, fire, and the blood of life. In Figure 2.5, Sun and Mithras are holding the grapes and the drinking horn (bull's horn) while standing behind the slain bull. In Figure 2.3, similarly, we saw Sun reaching for the drinking horn while sitting next to Mithras behind the bull's slain body. The relationship of Mithras and Sun is very close. This close link is also seen between the Persian Mithra and the Sun: the Sun is described as the eye of Mithra.

Pater

The highest grade was that of Pater (Father), under the domain of Saturn. Pater was Mithras's earthly representative, the light of heaven embodied, the teacher of the congregation which he led. Regarding his clothes, according to Charles Daniels in *Mithras and His Temples on the Wall:*

> He wore a red tunic with long sleeves piped with yellow stripes, and a yellow belt (Santa Prisca), or alternatively (in two Roman temples), a white or grey tunic with long sleeves and red piping. His baggy Persian trousers and his cloak were normally red while on his head is a red cap. His symbols were a Persian cap, a patera, or libation dish, a sickle-like sword and his staff of office.[9]

The title of Pater is the most frequently recorded title; his symbols are that of libation bowl and sickle. In congregations where several Paters were present, the title of *Pater Patrum* (Father of the Fathers) was used. Other titles linked to this grade are *Pater Sacrorum* (Father of the Mysteries) and *Pater Nomimus* (Father in Conformity with Custom).

SUFI INTERPRETATION OF THE SEVEN RITES

*The influence of Mithraism, however, remained, coloured by the
spirituality of Islam, to form the "Doctrine of Illumination" in
Sufism (tasavvof), which was compiled by Sohravardi, the
Shaykh of Illumination. It played an important part in preserving
national identity and culture and defending the independence of
Iran, when, under the rule of the Omayyad Caliphs (670–750
A.D.) who acted contrary to the principles of Islam, the Iranians
were subjected to injustice and oppression. Secret national organi-
zations contesting the supremacy of the Arabs appeared in the
guise of the Ayaran, Fetyan, Akhiyan, Javanmardan, Sarbedaran
and Pahlavanan, and organized uprising. Abu Muslim of
Khorasan played an important role in bringing down the
Omayyad Dynasty in the Abbasid Revolution of 750 A.D.*

MASOUD HOMAYOURI, ORIGINS OF PERSIAN GNOSIS

A study of Sufism would allow new insight into Mithraism, and possibly
vice versa. The poetic and metaphorical concepts we observe in Sufi literature can be seen in enacted events during the Mithraic rites. This section
is an attempt to interpret the Mithraic mysteries using Sufi symbolism, and
to show a few parallels between these two esoteric traditions that both
originated in Persia but were separated by several centuries.

While the outer appearance of Mithraism can be detected in
Catholicism, traces of the inner teachings of Mithraism can be found in
Sufism. This could be due to the rise of a series of Persian national organ-
izations around 700 C.E. that were fighting the Arabic Umayyad Dynasty.
These orders included the *Javanmardan* (the chivalrous), the *Sarbedaran*
(headless/hanged from gallows), and the *Pahlavanan* (champion/hero). All
three of these concepts are still seen in modern Persian Sufism, and more
importantly, the ideal of Javanmardan (chivalry) is said to be pre-Islamic,
dating back to Indo-European roots. It is also noteworthy that the
province of Korasan (meaning "place of the sun") in Iran, once an important center of Mithraism, has become associated with the Korasan School
of Sufism, which has the state of *sukr* (intoxication) among its teachings.

The first stage, that of Raven (Corax), represents the rebirth of the
neophyte into a spiritual path (Sufi *Tariqat*); his or her sins are washed
away and a mantra given to each neophyte. This is a common step among
esoteric paths, and not limited to Mithraism or Sufism.

In the stage of the Male Bride (Nymphus), the neophyte offers a cup of water to an image of Mithra. The cup is his heart and the water is his devotional love. Through this offering, he hopes to receive wine—Divine Love—into his cup, later on the path, after many trials. When he reaches the lion stage, he drinks the wine.

The neophyte now sets out to become a bride/lover of Mithra. Remembering that Mithra is Love, the neophyte begins his journey toward the Divine Wedding with the Beloved, as it is known in Sufism. His inability to become united with his Beloved at an early stage of his journey is demonstrated by his carrying a lamp while wearing a veil. This veil needs to be lifted before he can see the light, the source of which he carries in his own hands and is yet unable to see. In the words of the Sufi poet Hafez:

> Between lover and Beloved there is no veil,
> Hafez! Thou thyself art thy own veil
> Rise from this "between."[10]

The degree of Soldier (Miles) is given to those who have taken up the spiritual battle against the ego (nafs in Sufism), the struggle with the lower self. During the rite, the neophyte is crowned: while in the "bondage" of the material world, he is offered the "kingdom" of this world—but he rejects it. In later stages, the significance of removing the crown becomes clearer, as a symbol of attempting to remove the head itself—that is, the intellect—and allowing Mithra to be the guide.

Followers of Mithra came from many different backgrounds. There were normal Centurions, elite Praetorian troops, merchants, slaves, freed slaves, doctors, and even an occasional Emperor. All were equal in this brotherhood despite their social standing elsewhere, and this equality was demonstrated by the nakedness of the neophyte during the initiation at this stage, as well as by the dining arrangement. (See "Mithras as Liberator" in chapter 4.) At the end of the initiation as Miles, the initiate was marked and became part of the brotherhood.

To reach the degree of Lion (Leo) demonstrated one's long-standing commitment to the order and the making of real progress on the path. The Lion's duties included tending the altar flame and setting up the ritual meal (Farsi sofreh). Initiates were now in the element of Fire, and they made no contact with the opposite element. The fire of love engulfed the Lions and no trace remained of the water of intellect. During the ritual meal, they would drink wine; their cup, the heart from which they offered their devotional love at the male-bride stage, was now filled with Divine

Love (Farsi *Esheg*). The bread is the flesh of the bull in whose death there was life.

Interestingly, the great Sufi poet Rumi described all Sufis as lions, but lions on a banner in the wind. And the Hazrat Ali (peace be upon him) himself also bore the title of the "Lion of God" (Arabic *asadollah*).

In the degree of Persian (Perses) the initiate tried to develop a rapport with Persia, or to become part of the chosen people, so to speak. The emblem for this stage is the harpe sword that Perseus (father of Perses) used against the Gorgon. The Gorgon is the ego, which the initiate has been fighting with since the Soldier degree. He drank the wine in the Lion degree, he is ready to face the great monster within, and with the guidance of Perseus (the Father, one who has already decapitated his own Gorgon), the initiate takes the harpe and tries to destroy his ego. This can be likened to Saint George slaying the dragon or Gilgamesh killing Humbaba. Slaying the ego is a common theme on many paths. However, here we see it as a fusion between Eastern and Western mythology.

Symbolizing the break with the worldly ego and movement toward the spiritual realm at this grade is the *barsom* or *baresman* (plural *baresma*), a bundle of twigs tied together with a date-palm cord, which is held by the priest during high liturgies. Current practice is to substitute metal wires. The barsom signifies grass laid out for the spirits to sit on. On the Avesta.org Web site, the baresman is described as an ancient Indo-Iranian emblem of seeking the Holy. In *A Persian Offering*, Feroze Kotwal and James Boyd write that it "establishes a connecting link between this *getig* [material] world and the *menog* [spiritual] realm. The barsom is, as it were, the conduit through which the archetypal principles and powers manifest their presence and receive the offerings."[11] It is also an instrument through which one acquires the sacred power.[12]

In a magical sense, then, the baresman acts as a lightning rod, a magic wand, or a staff. The plant used traditionally was tamarisk; however, the Parsi priests of India substituted metal rods for the traditional twigs due to the unavailability of that plant in India. Some sources say that the twigs may be of the pomegranate tree or of the tree known as the chini. Further details about baresman are available online.[13]

The title of Heliodromus (Sun Runner) would be reserved for one who has seen the sun, and is close to it (sun is another word for love or Mithra in Farsi). In the ritual meal, the initiate of this grade would sit close by Mithras himself (Father). The offering or exchange of wine and grapes that takes place between Mithras and the Sun after the bull is slain parallels the idea of a wine "cup bearer" in Sufism (Farsi *Saqi*), the one who pours divine wine. The mystical wine that comes forth from the Friend intoxicates Sufis into a divine ecstasy (Sufi *Sama*). While the Wine comes from Mithras, the cup comes from the Sun. The Sun becomes the vessel.

The highest grade was of Father (*pir-e moghan*, "Magian Elder" in Sufism), who was Mithras's earthly representative, teacher of all the other grades. He would pour the wine (of love) into the cup (the heart) of the Lions and other grades via the "Sun Runner," and provide the guidance initiates needed to finally "die before you die" and overcome the ego. The symbols of this grade in Roman Mithraism were the staff, bowl, straight sickle, and cap. The libation bowl was for the performance of ceremonies, and the sickle and staff were the symbolic weapons of Saturn. It is worth noting that the symbols of the Persian Sufis are very similar: bowl, cap, and axe (combining a straight sickle with a staff).

In the tauroctony, the central icon of the Western Mithraic cult, all the mystery of this tradition comes together. Its Persian origins and the incorporation of Greek mythology and Roman astrology give rise to an esoteric path that must have had an everlasting impression on those who were prepared to follow it.

The bull that Mithras kills is his ego, the aim of all followers of Mithras. Mithras always looks away from the bull while stabbing him, just as Perseus looked away from the Gorgon when he decapitated her. One who looked upon the Gorgon would turn to stone; that is, the ego would turn the heart and the soul to stone. In order to overcome this ego (*nafs* in Sufism), one must turn the head (the intellect) away, because the intellect is unable to overcome the ego.

Sufism as well as other traditions use a number of techniques to help free the mind, for example dancing, drumming, trance techniques, or yogic eye movement to disorient the everyday self. Also, the use of medicinal plants in rituals might allow the initiate to see the Mithras, the midnight Sun. Homa is the name of a legendary plant with medicinal and spiritual properties that is mentioned in ancient texts from both India and Persia. Actually, it is the name of the spirit presiding over the Homa plant, as the spirit was seen as a deity in its own right: Homa (Sanskrit Soma), lord of harvests. Poets, warriors, and priests drank it. Its juices flowed yellow as the rays of the sun, liquid as the life-giving rain; the drink extracted from the Homa plant had qualities more divine by far than these.[14] It gave bravery to warriors in battle, and visions to priests. No one knows for sure

Figure 3.4. When slaying the bull, Mithras turns his head away. British Museum. (Photograph by Payam Nabarz. © Copyright The Trustees of the British Museum)

what Homa was—some suggest it was hemp based—but Zoroastrians seem to have used an ephedrine for a similar purpose. Drinking Homa resulted in a trancelike state.

Also it is said Homa was stirred together with the fat of a bull to make the drink of immortality. Some academics have suggested another possible candidate for Homa might have been the fly agaric mushroom (*Amanita muscaria*), though the majority believe that *Ephedra* was used in the making of the Homa. According to *The Encyclopedia of Psychoactive Plants* by Christian Rätsch, some traces of the Homa cult still remain in Iran today, where the drink is said to be brewed either from pomegranate juice (*Punica granatum* L.) and ephedra (*Ephedra* spp.) or from rue (*Ruta graveolens* L.) and milk. Some, basing their theories on the Zoroastrian creation story of the white Bull being slayed by Ahriman, have suggested that the Bull is Homa and perhaps the later slaying of the Bull by Mithras is a symbol of the pressing of Homa juice! This is a controversial but interesting view, as Ahura Mazda feeds the white Bull hemp to sedate him so when Ahriman kills him, the Bull wouldn't feel the pain. From the Bull comes all life—both animals and plants.[15]

It is only when we come from our hearts, within which is the truth of "Mithra is my only crown," that the battle can be won. It is only on the path of Love, with the guidance of the Father who has already slain the bull, that we can decapitate our own Gorgon before it turns us to stone.

THE WOMEN'S GRADE

Firmicus Maternus (around 350 A.D.) begins by alluding to a fiery female potency, portrayed with three faces and entwined with snakes. This female figure is paired with a fiery male potency, and the male figure is identified as Mithras himself. The female figure resembles the goddess Hecate but also calls to mind Anahita, the Persian water goddess.

PROFESSOR MARVIN W. MEYER, *THE ANCIENT MYSTERIES*

The Persian god Mithra was worshipped by both genders, and even now in Iran Mithra is a popular girl's name; but the Roman cult of Mithras was said to be a male-only mystery cult. However, there is a brief reference in Porphyry's *De Abstinentia* to male Mithraic initiates being "lions" and female Mithraic initiates being "hyenas." This suggests that occasionally, at least in some of the Roman temples, a special grade for women might have existed. The grade was supposedly that of the Hyena, not too far off from the Lion or Raven grades of the men. As to why it was called Hyena, consider, for a start, that the hyena is a matriarchal pack animal. The female is the one who leads the whole pack, including the males, into the hunt. This seems an appropriate totem animal for the rare women who might have been initiated into the all-male Roman warrior cult.

Tertullian, at the end of the second century C.E., writes that the Mithraic cult had "*virgines et continentes,*" men and women who were celibate in honor of the god; thus we know that a woman could dedicate herself to the deity, even if she was not allowed as an initiate into the mysteries!

Another point worth mentioning: in *The Golden Ass*, written by Lucius Apuleius in the second century C.E. (an active period of Mithraism), the name given to the high priest of Isis is—Mithras. It was an interesting choice of a name for a character. If there was such a grade as Hyena for women initiates, then it was an especially interesting choice, pointing to a potential cross-fertilization of ideas between the Goddess-centered Isis cult and the God-centered Mithras cult, two of the major pagan cults at that time. This becomes even more interesting in light of Bianchi's Lion grade evidence, which we shall see shortly.

Interestingly, the potential participation of women is also seen in the 2003 update of Professor Betz's translation of the Mithras Liturgy, which implies that the rite is possibly being passed from father to daughter. "Be gracious to us, O Providence and Psyche, who writes these mysteries handed down, not for gain, and for an only child I ask for immortality, for an initiate of this our power (furthermore, it is necessary for you, O daughter, to take the juices of herbs and drugs which will be [made known] to you at the end of my sacred treatise), which the great god Helios Mithras ordered to be handed over to me by his archangel so that I alone may go to heaven as an 'eagle' and behold the all."[16]

A quick study of hyena behavior and mythology might help us to speculate on why such a grade might have been used for the rare women who made it into this cult. Here is some background information about hyenas, found on Robin M. Weare's Web site, and reproduced here with her kind permission:

> Lions often take over hyenas' kills; the males will walk right into a clan of feeding hyenas and take the carcass from them. Hyenas will steal kills from lionesses if no male lions are around and they badly outnumber the lionesses. If animals can hate, this is a blood feud of hatred, according to *Eternal Enemies*. Male lions will chase and kill hyenas with no provocation. Hyenas will chase a lioness even after she abandons her kill to them. Hyenas kill and eat sick or injured lions.
>
> It is true that the female hyena's genitals look just like the male's; she has a huge clitoris she can erect at will and even has a sack of fibrous tissue that looks like testicles. This has led to the notion that hyenas can change sex!
>
> The females are dominant but sometimes several males will "bait" a single female, standing around her, barking at and even nipping her. She lies down defensively and takes it, only biting back when they get close. . . . Female hyenas behave very aggressively toward each other. Hyenas from different clans war with one another in pitched mass battles. These fights seldom cause injuries, but occasionally one or even several hyenas are killed. . . . Cubs fight viciously, often quite literally from the moment they're born.[17]

Furthermore, Weare reports:

> The notion that hyenas changed sex from male to female and back
> again and again dates back at least to ancient Greece, although Aristotle
> refuted it. The idea probably comes from the fact that the genitals of the
> two sexes look nearly identical. In fact, Europeans often associated
> hyenas with sexual "perversion," especially homosexuality. Medieval
> Europeans also believed that sometimes a lioness would mate with a
> hyena to produce a strange hybrid called the leucrotta. The leucrotta
> had a human voice and could imitate human speech to lure travelers
> into its clutches. All over the continent (of Africa), there are cultures
> that believe some witches can turn themselves into hyenas.[18]

The possibility that a few women were initiated into the Mithraic mysteries under a special grade is an interesting one. It's also possible that a
few were admitted into the normal grades. A wall painting from North
Africa, dating from around 350 C.E., shows a lady surrounded by mytho-
logical images. The inscription says, "Aelia Arisuth lived to the age of
about sixty." According to Ranuccio Bianchi in *Rome: The Late Empire,
Roman Art A.D. 200–400*:

> The figure of a lioness was painted on the tomb itself, with the
> inscription, *quae lea jacet* ("here lies the lioness"). A corresponding
> inscription, *qui leo jacet* ("here lies the lion"), was found in the locu-
> lus (burial niche) of a tomb dug in the wall that abutted on the sepul-
> chral chamber (her husband's tomb). . . . The use of the words
> "lioness" for the woman and "lion" for the man, shows that the dead
> couple had attained the fourth grade of initiation in the mysteries of
> Mithras. Yet no Mithraic symbols can be identified in the painted dec-
> orations. This looks like a case of religious polyvalence—another
> example, in the same period, being the coexistence of pagan and
> Christian elements in the same decorative painting.[19]

This suggests that either way—Lionesses or Hyenas—occasionally
women might have been admitted to these mainly male mysteries.[20] We
may never be sure, unless some new evidence comes to light, as most of
the existing evidence points toward the male-only membership. However,
it is worth noting that, more like the early mixed-gender Persian worship
of Mithra, in the modern revival there are already a number of Mithraic
women initiates and priestesses.

ECHOES OF MITHRAISM
AROUND THE WORLD

The oldest source of Persian Gnosis is to be found in Mithraism,
an ancient Persian spiritual path, which began in Eastern Iran
many thousands of years ago.

MASOUD HOMAYOURI, ORIGINS OF PERSIAN GNOSIS

We have already touched upon the links between Mithraism and Islamic Sufism. The Mithraic mysteries exerted their influence on other religions and cultures as well. The Mithraic influence on Christianity is the subject of much good historical research; some recommendations are included in the "Further Reading" section at the back of the book. Another religion that was much influenced but is rarely mentioned is Yazidism; nevertheless there is one good book by Taufiq Wahby on the subject (see "Further Reading"). Mithraism has also been suggested to have influenced Greek Hermetic magic. As for the influence of Mithras on Western culture in general, one can see this influence by studying British history. In this chapter we explore some of these connections.

THE ECHO OF MITHRAISM IN CHRISTIANITY

If Christianity had been checked in its growth by some deadly
disease, the world would have become Mithraic.

HISTORIAN JOSEPH RENAN

The assimilation of Mithraism by its rival Christianity resulted in the early decline and loss of true meaning in both religions. The peace-loving message of Christianity, as taught by Christ, was diminished and replaced by the warrior mindset of Mithraism. At the same time, the pagan tolerance of other faiths that Mithraism embodied did not survive the assimilation process. One might say that the emergent religion lost some of the loving, caring Christian aspect and the pagan Mithraic tolerance aspect, resulting in an unhappy marriage of the worst aspects of the two.

The person who stood at the head of this process of systematic assimilation of Mithraism was Paul of Tarsus. Tarsus was one of the hotbeds of the Mithras/Perseus worship. Paul was Jewish, and a full Roman citizen with all the privileges such citizenship held. He never met Jesus in person; his spiritual experience of Christ was in a vision on the road to Damascus, about three years after Jesus' death. The only original Apostles he met were Peter and James. His meeting with them only lasted fifteen days, and occurred after three years of preaching!

Here are a few examples of Paul's possible references to the Mithraic faith: In the first Chapter of Romans he speaks of those who "changed the glory of the incorruptible God into an image like to corruptible man, and to birds and four-footed beasts, and creeping things." This is probably a reference to the Mithraic animal masks used in initiations for the seven degrees.

In Ephesians VI, 10–17 he talks about putting on the armor of god, the shield of faith, the helmet of salvation, the sword of spirit, and so forth. It seems likely that Paul's version of Christianity was influenced by his growing up in a city full of "spiritual warriors of Mithras." This attitude is far away from the nonviolent teaching of Christ in both a spiritual and physical sense.

There are a number of other examples. If you are interested in the role of Paul of Tarsus in the assimilation of Mithraism, I recommend *Mithras: The Fellow in the Cap* by Esme Wynne-Tyson.[1]

Where Paul started, others followed. Later on we see that the Christians adopted the twenty-fifth of December as Christ's birthday, in the fourth century of the Common Era, according to Sir James G. Frazer. In *The Golden Bough*, he writes of

> . . . the festival of Christmas, which the church seems to have borrowed directly from its heathen rival. In the Julian calendar, the 25th December was reckoned as the winter solstice, and was regarded as the nativity of the Sun, because the day begins to lengthen and the power of the Sun increases from that turning point of the year. . . . Mithras was regularly identified by his worshippers with the Sun. The

[Christian] Gospels say nothing of the day of Christ's birth, and accordingly the early church did not celebrate it.[2]

Furthermore, the *New Catholic Encyclopaedia* records:

The birth of Christ was assigned the date of the winter solstice (December 25 in the Julian calendar, January 6 in the Egyptian), because on this day, as the Sun began its return to northern skies, the pagan devotees of Mithras celebrated the Dies Natalis Solis Invicti (Birthday of the Invincible Sun). On December 25, 274, [Roman Emperor] Aurelian had proclaimed the Sun God the principal patron of the Empire and dedicated a temple to Him in the Campus Martius. Christmas originated at a time when the cult of the Sun was particularly strong at Rome.[3]

As Christianity gathered momentum and eventually became the Roman Empire's state religion, Mithraism was not tolerated. According to Cumont, the early church fathers saw it as a "satanic travesty of the holiest rites of their religion."[4] Nevertheless, Catholicism appears to have preserved some of the outer forms of Mithraism. Here is a sampling of the similarities.

Mithras:
- was born on December 25;
- was born of a virgin;
- remained celibate;
- was a savior god, who saved by shedding the eternal blood;
- created water and bread by slaying the bull, and thus created the universe and life on Earth.

His worshippers:
- were baptized;
- viewed wine as sacrificial blood;
- held Sundays sacred;
- called themselves "brothers";
- partook of bread marked with a cross (hot cross buns, some say).

The equidistant cross was a symbol of the sun long before Christianity adopted the crucifix. There are other correspondences:

- The bishops eventually adapted the mitre as a sign of their office. (Mitre is Greek for Mitra; however, this association requires examination by linguists.)
- The Christian priest ultimately became "Father," despite Jesus' specific proscription of such a title (Matthew 23:9). Mithraism also had a "Father of Fathers" (*Pater Patrum*) chosen from among the Fathers.
- "The Mithraic Holy Father wore a red cap and garment and a ring, and carried a shepherd's staff. The Head Christian adopted the same title and outfitted himself in the same manner."[5]
- The Mithraic feast or communion where Mithras, Sol, and the initiates sit around a table of the "slayed bull," before Mithras and Sol ascend to heaven in Sol's chariot, is closely echoed by the motif of Christ's Last Supper and his ascension to heaven.
- Christ is given the Sun God's crown of rays of light, which is even referred to as the "crown of righteousness" (2, Tim, IV, 7, 8).
- Even the design of the church building mirrors that of some Mithraic temples, as Paul Kriwaczek mentions in his book *In Search of Zarathustra:* "Historians of architecture, too, have found a Mithraic residue in the design of Christian churches. Ancient gods, they point out, were worshiped al fresco. But the secret cult of Mithras demanded privacy, so an entirely new kind of sacred building was devised for the purpose. The long, narrow ship shape (nave is the Latin for ship) of the typical early North European church is provocatively similar to that of the structure designed to shelter the devotees of Mithras, with its central aisle and side colonnades dedicated to dining."[6]

It seems there were no copyright concerns back in the years 200 B.C.E to 500 C.E. Otherwise, the competing religions would have been constantly fighting lawsuits. For example, there was much borrowing going on between writers of the new chapters of the Bible and writers of some Mithraic materials; or possibly both religions were drawing upon a common prototype. There are numerous Biblical references to Mithras. The first part of Revelation is almost identical to the *Greek Magical Papyri* text of the "Mithraic Liturgy."* Read the description of Mithras from the "Liturgy" (350 C.E.):

---

*The *Greek Magical Papyri* was a Roman document; in Rome, religious subjects were usually written about in the Greek language. The extracts from the Mithraic Liturgy used here are from Professor Marvin W. Meyer's translation. See www.hermetic.com/pgm/mithras-liturgy.html for the full text of the liturgy and for Meyer's book, *The Ancient Mysteries*.

Mithras having a bright appearance, youthful, golden-haired, with a white tunic and a golden crown and trousers, and holding in his right hand a golden (700) shoulder of a young bull: (seven stars of the Plough) this is the Bear which moves and turns heaven around, moving upward and downward in accordance with the hour. Then you will see lightning-bolts leaping from his eyes and stars from his body.

And now read the description of Christ from Revelation 1 (95 C.E.):

And in the midst of the seven candlesticks one like unto the Son of man, clothed with a garment down to the foot, and girt about the paps with a golden girdle.

14 His head and his hairs were white like wool, as white as snow; and his eyes were as a flame of fire;

15 And his feet like unto fine brass, as if they burned in a fur-nace; and his voice as the sound of many waters.

16 And he had in his right hand seven stars: and out of his mouth went a sharp two-edged sword: and his countenance was as the sun shineth in his strength.

There are many more examples that show the likeness between the "Mithraic Liturgy" and Revelation. Consider these passages from the "Liturgy":

First—origin of my origin, AEEIOYO, first beginning of my begin-ning, spirit . . . of spirit, the first of the spirit (490) in me. . . . Say all these things with fire and spirit, until completing the first utter-ance; then, similarly, begin the second, until you complete the (620) seven immortal gods of the world. When you have said these things, you will hear thundering and shaking in the surrounding realm; and you will likewise feel yourself being agitated. Then say again: "Silence!" (the prayer) Then open your eyes and you will see the doors (625) open and the world of the gods which is within the doors, so that from the pleasure and joy of the sight your spirit runs ahead and ascends. So stand still and at once draw breath from the divine into yourself, while you look intently. Then when (630) your soul is restored, say: "Come, Lord." When you have said this, the rays will turn toward you; look at the center of them. For when

(635) you have done this, you will see a youthful god, beautiful in appearance, with fiery hair, and in a white tunic and a scarlet cloak and wearing a fiery crown. At once, greet him with the fire greeting.
. . .

. . . O Lord, while being born again, I am passing away; while growing and having grown, (720) I am dying; while being born from a life-generating birth, I am passing on, released to death—as you have founded, as you have decreed, and have established the mystery. . . .

The same spirit is abundant in Revelation, to the extent that the names of Mithras and Jesus could be interchangeable!

Revelation 1:

4 John to the seven churches which are in Asia: Grace be unto you, and peace, from him which is, and which was, and which is to come; and from the seven Spirits which are before his throne;

7 Behold, he cometh with clouds; and every eye shall see him, and they also which pierced him: and all kindreds of the earth shall wail because of him. Even so, Amen.

8 I am Alpha and Omega, the beginning and the ending, saith the Lord, which is, and which was, and which is to come, the Almighty.

10 I was in the Spirit on the Lord's day, and heard behind me a great voice, as of a trumpet,

12 And I turned to see the voice that spake with me. And being turned, I saw seven golden candlesticks;

13 And in the midst of the seven candlesticks one like unto the Son of man, clothed with a garment down to the foot, and girt about the paps with a golden girdle.

17 And when I saw him, I fell at his feet as dead. And he laid his right hand upon me, saying unto me, Fear not; I am the first and the last:

18 I am he that liveth, and was dead; and, behold, I am alive for evermore, Amen; and have the keys of hell and of death.

20 The mystery of the seven stars which thou sawest in my right hand, and the seven golden candlesticks. The seven stars are the angels of the seven churches: and the seven candlesticks which thou sawest are the seven churches.

Revelation 2:

1 Unto the angel of the church of Ephesus write; These things saith he that holdeth the seven stars in his right hand, who walketh in the midst of the seven golden candlesticks;

10 Fear none of those things which thou shalt suffer: behold, the devil shall cast some of you into prison, that ye may be tried; and ye shall have tribulation ten days: be thou faithful unto death, and I will give thee a crown of life.

Another Christian example can be found in St. Augustine (John I. Disc. 7.): "I remember that the priests of the fellow in the cap used at one time to say: 'Our Capped One himself is a Christian.'" Interestingly, as Esme Wynne-Tyson points out in *Mithras: The Fellow in the Cap*, "the Mithraic remains found on Vatican Hill and believed to have been part of a former Mithraic temple, become deeply symbolic."[7] Furthermore there are remains of Mithraic temples under the church of Santa Prisca in Rome, under the church of Santa Balbina, under the church of Santo Stefano Rotondo, and underneath a Byzantine church in Hurrarte in Syria.

Despite a tolerant attitude from Mithraists, the early Church got rid of the Mithraic faith along with other pagan religions and built churches on top of the old temples. Toward the end of the fourth century C.E., Jerome wrote a letter to a Christian woman in which he praises the destruction of a Mithraic temple:

Did not your kinsman Gracchus, whose name recalls his patrician rank, destroy a cave of Mithras a few years ago when he was prefect of Rome? Did he not break up and burn all the monstrous images there? . . . Did he not send them before him as hostages, and gain for himself baptism in Christ?[8]

There is perhaps nothing more telling of Christianity's dislike of its main rival than what was found in a Mithraic temple in Sarrebourg, in Lorraine, France. The find was of a human skeleton (a Mithraic priest perhaps) who was chained to the Mithraic altar and the door blocked up. One suspects that the true messages of Christ—love, peace, and goodwill to humankind—were also buried in that temple alongside the nameless Mithraic priest. Perhaps some Christians, in their attempt to survive the age and not be fed to the lions, turned into the very thing they meant to stand against—a valuable lesson here for our own time.

MITHRAS AS LIBERATOR

The initiands hands were tied with chicken's gut, which were then
cut through by a man calling himself his "liberator."
MANFRED CLAUSS, *THE ROMAN CULT OF MITHRAS*

Mithra's Phrygian Cap originated from Phrygia, a centre of
Mithraism in Anatolia, the capital of which was Konya. It was
worn there by manumitted slaves, and Mithra's wearing of the
cap denotes his freedom from slavery of the lower self.
MASSOUD HOMAYOUNI, *THE ORIGINS OF PERSIAN GNOSIS*

The Mithraic faith had fraternity, equality, and liberty at its core, as suggested by Paul Kriwaczek.

> Roman dining rules were clear: in their own home, women sat in chairs, men reclined. In presence of their superiors, the lower classes were only permitted to sit; slaves never reclined to eat. The fact that Mithraic feasts were lectisternia, reclining dinners, rather than sellisternia, sitting meals, had profound implications of equality and freedom. . . . To worshippers of Mithras the Mediator, patron of contracts, of friendship, of courage, probity, honesty, justice and fair dealing, special friend of soldiers, petty traders, freedmen and slaves, the liberty, equality and fraternity hinted at by their dining arrangements may have been among its most important features.[9]

Kriwaczek goes on to say that the use of the Phrygian headgear "to symbolize liberty, equality and fraternity to French revolutionaries of the eighteenth century" could be traced to Mithraism. In ancient Rome, a freed slave wore a Phrygian cap, also called a liberty cap, during the ceremony of his manumission. It is tempting to speculate that Mithras's cap, as well as pointing to his Persian origin might also have been a symbol of the liberated slave, with Mithras a liberator of the initiates as well as their savior. (We'll further consider the heritage of the cap in the upcoming section called "The Liberty Cap.")

Mithras's role as Kosmokrator had to do with the movement of the universe. The discovery of the precession of the equinoxes, in a geocentric world, was big news, a bit like discovering that the Earth is not flat. In such a time, many of the commonly held worldviews and customs were put into question. Mithraism ended up with members from all the social classes: slaves, freed slaves, soldiers, merchants, citizens, officers, some emperors, and maybe even some women. The fraternity that formed cut through the social structure. The idea of a slave initiating an emperor, or an ordinary legionary initiating a senator (or vice versa) speaks volumes about the equality within the brotherhood. Another social taboo broken by the cult followers was that of having a ritual meal, where all ate together. This might seem ordinary now, but in Roman times, gender and social status determined every detail of sitting, reclining, and standing eating arrangements.

The Miles initiate's bindings being cut by the "Liberator," and his refusal to wear a crown, were signs that now, anyone could have the freedom of a king and the connection the king had with the divine. Mithra, like Horus and some other Old-World solar deities, provided a link to kingship, an idea that can be seen right across the Old World countries at different times and eras: from the emperors of Japan's "Land of the rising Sun," to India, Persia, Egypt, Greece, and Rome, to the modern European monarchies, the kings become the Sun God's representatives, all wearing the Sun God's crown. To the Persian kings and queens, Mithra was the bestower of Divine Glory or Kingly Fortune (*Farr* or *Khvarnah*).

In a sense, all Mithraic initiates were now kings, with the same divine connection to Mithras, and no longer bound by social class or consensus reality. The idea of a spiritual people challenging kingship and its authority, and reclaiming it, is nothing new in some magical traditions. For example, some Sufis use the surname Shah (which means king) after their name. This was originally a discordant act, to mock the Shahs. While kings use the title of Shah at the beginning of their name, some Sufis put it at the end, to represent their kingship in the spiritual sense.

The Liberty Cap

So, we might ask, did the model of liberty, freedom, and equality die out with the cult of Mithras? Did his red cap of liberty fall to the ground forever with the rise of the Dark Ages? Much later—some would say by magic, some would say by coincidence, some would say that spirit never dies—the Phrygian cap came to figure heavily in the French Revolution iconography, probably influenced by the Roman goddess Libertas.

The so-called Phrygian cap [in French, *bonnet phrygien*] is also often called the red cap [*bonnet rouge*] or the liberty cap [*bonnet de la liberte*]. The use of the liberty cap started in 1789 during the French Revolution, but the cap became a popular symbol in spring 1790 only. It was initially used to cover the head of the goddesses Liberty and Nation, and became quickly the emblem of Liberty, and then the emblem of men and women who wanted to be citizens instead of subjects. In 1792, it was a normal part of the uniform of the sans-culottes. On 20 June 1792, the king Louis XVI was forced to wear the liberty cap by the crowd who had invaded the palace of Tuileries. After the fall of monarchy, the liberty cap became ubiquitous. . . . [10]

The red liberty cap had also made its appearance in the American Revolution:

The liberty cap as an emblem of liberty was used by the Sons of Liberty as early as 1765. During the American Revolution, particularly in the early years, many of the soldiers who fought for the Patriot cause wore knitted stocking liberty caps of red, sometimes with the motto "Liberty" or "Liberty or Death" knitted into the band. This style of cap was traditional in the North East (having been popular with the French Voyagers) and became immensely popular during the Revolution. [11]

Please note that the cap of the goddess *Libertas* is of indeterminate color, while the Phrygian cap of Mithras is red in color. Hence, the soldiers of the American and French Revolutions wore not just any old liberty cap, but one that was the specific color of the Mithraic tradition.

The symbolic liberty cap, Persian in origin, still surfaces all over the Western world. As a symbol of revolution it carried over into the Latin American revolutions; it is present on a number of national flags. Some have speculated that when the French designed the American Statue of Liberty, they were influenced by the classical designs of the Roman goddess Libertas, who holds a liberty cap and a torch, and wears Mithras-Sol's radiant crown of seven rays. Even the liberty cap mushrooms may well have gotten their name because of the similarity of their shape to the Phrygian cap! (It is worth noting, too, that the cap worn by some Sufi orders resembles a Phrygian cap.)

ECHOS OF MITHRAISM IN THE YEZIDIS
AND THE PEACOCK ANGEL

"The cow driven astray invokes him for help, longing for the stables:
'When will that bull, Mithra, the lord of wide pastures, bring us back, and make us reach the stables? When wilt he turn us back to the right way from the den of the Druj where we were driven?'"

FROM ZOROASTRIAN HYMN TO MITHRA, YASHT 10.86

In addition to the echoes of Mithraic mysteries in Christianity and Sufism, there seem to be lines of connection between Mithraism and Yezidism. The Yezidis are among the Kurdish people of Northern Iraq, and have been the subject of much interest in occult writings.

Yezidis, like the Roman Mithraists, believe in seven heavens and operate a seven-level spiritual system, and this is reflected in their belief of seven *Seihs* (Arabic *Shikh*) through whose intercession they invoke God. These seven sit beside their head saint, Seih Adi. At the festival of Seih Adi, a herd of white bulls are slain and dedicated to Seih Shams. *Shams* translates as "the sun," and these bull sacrifices are made to the sun.

Interestingly, the Yezidis are divided into seven classes; each class has function peculiar to itself. The seven classes are: Shikh, Emir, Kawwal, Pir, Kochak, Fakir, and Mulla. Isya Joseph in *The Sacred Books and Traditions of the Yezidiz,* writes:

> Not only Yezidi, Persian, Moslem, and Christian elements are to be found in the modern Yezidism, but there are many remains of the old pagan religions . . . such as the notion of the sacredness of the number seven, an idea which belongs to the common stock of the ancient inhabitants of Mesopotamia. The Yezidis have seven sanjaks, each has seven burners; their cosmogany shows that god created seven angels or gods; their principal prayer is the appeal to god through seven Seihs (Shikhs); the sceptre engraved on the front of the temple of their great saint has seven branches. This reminds us at once of the Sabians, who adored seven gods or angels who directed the course of seven planets; the seven days of the week were dedicated to their respective deities. Moreover, we note in the Babylonian-Assyrian poem, the seven gates through which Ishtar descends to the land without return.[12]

According to Dr. M. Izady of Kurdish Worldwide Resources (KWR):

Several old, and now extinct, movements and religions also appear to have begun their existence as branches of the Cult of Angels, under circumstances similar to those that gave rise to Alevism. Among these, with due caution and reservation, one may place the Gnostic religions of Mithraism and Zorvânism, and the socio-economically motivated messianic movements of the Mazdakites, Khurramiyya, and the Qarmatites. The Cult also has fundamentally influenced another Gnostic religion, Manicheanism, as well as Ismâ'ili (Sevener) Shi'ism, Druzism, and Bâbism, and to a lesser extent, Zoroastrians, Imâmi Shi'ism, and Bahâ'ism. The Mithraist religious movement seems now to have been a guise under which Cult followers attempted to take over the old Greco-Roman pantheistic religion, with which the Cult had been in contact since the start of the Hellenistic period in the fourth century B.C.E. Mithraism succeeded impressively. By the time of Constantine and the prevalence of Christianity, Mithraism had become so influential in the Roman Empire that it may be that the Roman state observance of the birth of the god Mithras on December 25 inspired the traditional dating of the birth of Christ. This date was the one on which the Universal Spirit first manifested itself in its prime avatar, Lord Creator, whom Mithraism presumed to be Mithras. . . . Is it possible that Malak Tâwus, who created the material world in Yezidi cosmogony by utilizing a piece of the original cosmic egg or pearl that he had dismembered earlier, originally represented Mithras in early Yezidism, and only later Lucifer? The second most important Yezidi celebration points toward this possibility. It is held between middle and late December and commemorates the birth of Yezid. His birthday at or near the winter solstice links him to Mithras. (Mithraism did after all expand into the Roman Empire from this general geographical area in the course of the first century B.C., and Mithras' mythical birth was celebrated on December 25 as already has been discussed.)[13]

The four major celebrations of the Yezidis nearly coincide with the Persian celebrations of the solstices and equinoxes (see chapter 9, "The Four Stations of Mithra"). The Yezidis celebrate the festivals of Nou Ruz, Mithrakan, Tiragan, and the feast of Yezid.

1. Nou Ruz (March 21); spring equinox, also called Nou Roz and celebrated by all Persians: Jews, Muslims, and Zoroastrians. A testament to a common cultural and folk belief in effect along with the orthodox religions of modern Iran.
2. Mithrâkân or Mihrajân at October 6 to October 13. As both forms of the name suggest, this festival is linked to Mithra. The Persian month containing the festival of Mithra, called Mihregan or Mehrgan, begins on September 21 (autumn equinox) and ends on October 21.
3. The feast of Yezid (December 25) is the time of the birth of Mithras, and close to the winter solstice or Yule of December 21 (Persian festival of Yalda).
4. The fourth celebration, observed on the Tiragân by the Yezidis, is in late July. The festival of Tir is a celebration of the star Sirius. The Persian month of Tir begins at the summer solstice on June 21 and lasts until July 21. In Persian cosmology, Tir is the god of rain, who appears as the star Sirius and also fights the demon of draught, Apaosha. The rising of Sirius was also marked in Egypt; this was the time that the Nile flooding began.

Yezidis also believe in a struggle between good and evil, which they represent by the dog and the serpent, and sometimes a chimera of a dog-snake to show the balance between the two forces. In the Roman Mithraic tauroctony, the snake and dog are facing each other (constellations Canis and Hydra) and both facing toward where Mithras's blade stabs the bull: the source of life.

Some Yezidis, during the 1970s, applied to join the Zoroastrian community in Iran and were accepted, and presumably remain Zoroastrians to this day, a sign of the compatibility of their belief systems.

Another interesting parallel between the Yezidis and Roman Mithraism can be seen in the Yezidi ceremony of Qabakh and the legend of Mithras's Bull hunt. The Qabakh ceremony is part of seven days of festivities that take place around the time of the autumn equinox. According to Taufiq Wahby in *The Remnants of Mithraism in Hatra and Iraqi Kurdistan, and Its Traces in Yazidism: The Yazadis Are Not Devil-Worshippers*:

On the 5th day of the communal festival the Yazadis [alternate spelling of Yezidis] perform the rite of Qabakh. A group [of] Yazadis climb to the summit of the mountain overlooking the mausoleum of Shikh Adi where they begin to let off their guns and to celebrate their rejoicing at the beginning of the ceremony. After this they come down to the mausoleum of Shikh Adi [a sacred cave under the temple], where both men and women dance together to the strains of flute and drums. Meanwhile the Mir [Kurdish for Mithra] of Shikhan prepares a large bull and asks those present to protect it from all harm. Armed youths then receive it and take it to the tomb of Shikh Shams [Sun] promising to return it to the mausoleum [cave] of Shikh Adi safe from all harm. While they are repeating a litany and prayers which are unintelligible to non Yazadis, two Yazadis penetrate their ranks secretly and one of them, by stratagem steals the bull. A great wailing goes up and the people recover the bull at once but give no indication of who is the thief, pretending to be ignorant of his name and ignoring his presence. They then lead the bull to the mausoleum of Shikh Adi amidst great cheering and rejoicing. The tribes are then assembled in a place called the Maydan e Jihad [arena of holy battle] and ten brave men come forward to protect the bull. But at this juncture the Mir announces that there is no need for them as the bull has run away. This is because the two men who previously stolen the bull had entered the mausoleum in the guise of being two of Mir's men to protect it. They then ran away with it to the tomb of Shikh Shams which is near the mausoleum of Shikh Adi. There the Yazadis beat the bull soundly with sticks and with whips and slaughter it.*[14]

The format of this Yezidi Bull hunt is very similar to the iconography of the Roman Mithras's hunt for the bull. Mithras is told by the Sun to capture the bull. First he captures the bull and carries it on his shoulders as described in the Santa Prisca inscriptions: "this young bull which he carried on his golden shoulders according to his ways." Later the initiates claim to have carried the bull on their shoulders: "And after I have received it I have borne on my shoulders the greatest things of the gods." The bull, however, escapes from the cave. Mithras has to capture and chase it once again. This time, after riding the bull and engaging in a longer chase, he finally manages to capture it. By hauling the bull's hind legs over his shoulder, he drags it back to his cave and finally slays it.

---

*The words in brackets are my additions/translations. Also note that the final slaughter takes place at the Shikh Shams (Sun) mausoleum.

The Yezidi Qabakh ceremony provides an interesting model and perhaps explains why the poet Commodianus (third century C.E.) described the Roman Mithras as a "cattle thief" god[15] and, even more interesting, why the Christian writer Firmicus Maternus (fourth century C.E.) referred to a Roman follower of Mithras as an "initiate of cattle-rustling, companion by the hand clasp of an illustrious father."[16]

MITHRAS IN BRITAIN

The mysteries of Mithras remained in Britain for some time after the Christianization of Rome. In the "Song of the Macrocosm" (Canu y byd mawr), written in the sixth century C.E., Taliesin the Bard demonstrates his initiatory knowledge of the cult of Mithras.

Song of the Macrocosm

I praise my Father
my God, my strength,
Who infused in my head
Both soul and reason,
Who, to keep guard over me,
Did bestow my seven senses,
From fire and earth, water and air:
The mist and flowers,
The wind and trees,
And much skilful wisdom
Has my father bestowed on me.

One is for instinct,
Two is for feeling,
Three is for speaking,
Four is for tasting,
Five is for seeing,
Six is for hearing,
Seven is for smelling.

As I have said,
Seven heavens there are
Above the astrologer's head,
And three companies (parts) of the sea;

Figure 4.1. The remains of the Temple of Mithras in London. (Photograph by Payam Nabarz)

Figure 4.2. Mithras Wine Bar, next to the remains of the Temple of Mithras in London. (Photograph by Payam Nabarz)

The sea beats on the strand,
The sea is great and wonderful,
The world itself likewise.

On high, God made
The planets:
He made the Sun,
He made the Moon,
He made Mars,
He made Mercury,
He made Venus,
(He made Veneris)
He made Jupiter,
Seventhly, He made Saturn.
The good God made
Five zones of the earth,
For as long as it lasts:
The first is formed cold,
The second is formed cold,
The third is formed hot,
Injurious to flowers,
Unpleasant and hurtful.
The fourth is paradise,
which people shall enter.
The fifth is temperate,
the habitable part of the universe.

Into three it is divided,
Into determined regions:
the first is Asia,
the second is Africa,
the third is Europe,
blessed by baptism,
lasting until doomsday
when everything will be judged.

He made my awen
with which I praise the king.
I am Taliesin,

I have the prophet's voice.
Continuing until the end
For Elffin's deliverance.[17]

Sir James Frazer proposed that indeed Taliesin was a Mithraic initiate. The "Song of the Macrocosm" certainly contains some Mithraic lore; Taliesin was clearly versed in much of the magical lore of the British Isles. Therefore, it is not surprising that he (or a contemporary writing under his name) would be familiar with Mithraic mysteries.*

All of the Indo-European people's pantheons tend to have a similar structure, as well as similar myths; it is therefore of interest to look for a Celtic equivalent of Mithra, even before the Roman introduction of Mithras. There are two possible candidates who, in the realm of comparative mythology, have characteristics similar to Mithra. They are the Celtic deities Ogma and Lugh. A look at these gods turns up some other interesting correlations as well.

Ogma and Mithra

There are a number of correlations between Ogma and Mithras, one being that both have been linked to alphabets with divinatory functions. Ogma is linked to the Ogham tree alphabet, with one of its many possible uses being an Ogham oracle, while Mithras has been linked to a Greek/Roman proto-tarot.

John Matthews, in *Taliesin: The Last Celtic Shaman*, proposes an interesting connection between the Invincible Sun God and Celtic lore: the language of trees. He is referring to the Ogham alphabet, which according to the lore was invented by the god Ogma. But let us back up a bit to explain.

The great god Dagda and goddess Danu had a son, the god variously called Ogma Cermait (Honey-Mouthed), Grain-aineach (Sun-faced), or Trenfher (Strongman, Champion). In Gaul he was called Ogmios and was worshipped as a god of light and learning. "In an inscription found at Richborough, Ogmios is depicted with rays of light coming from his head and holding the whip of Sol Invictus."[18] All three of the names of Ogma certainly echo the titles and characteristics of Mithras, and the inscription

---

*The theme of Mithraic initiates rubbing shoulders with druids and bards is beautifully touched on in these historical novels: *The Winter King* trilogy by Bernard Cornwell, Mary Stewart's *Merlin of the Crystal Cave*, Nancy McKenzie's *Queen of Camelot*, and *The Eagle of the Ninth* by Rosemary Sutcliff.

in Richborough also supports a link. However, what is not clear is whether the link derives from the original Mithra, that is, dating back to the spread of the Indo-European people, several millenia B.C.E., or from the more recent introduction of Mithras with the Roman Empire.

As to the origins of Ogham or Ogam, Philip Carr-Gomm in *The Druid Tradition* says: "It is probably pre-Celtic in origin, although most of the existing inscriptions have been dated to the fifth and sixth centuries."[19] The Ogham alphabet possibly gained some Romano characteristics during the Roman Empire. In Charles Squires' *Mythology of the Celtic People* we read: "The origin of this alphabet is obscure. Some authorities consider it of great antiquity, while others believe it entirely post-Christian. It seems, at any rate, to have been based upon, and consequently to presuppose a knowledge of, the Roman alphabet."[20]

Ogham is not a language, as such, but a method of writing. Each stroke of Ogham represents a letter of the alphabet, and "there has been much controversy as to whether the Ogham really was used as a calendar by druids, linking each tree and letter of the alphabet to a moon month, as suggested by Robert Graves."[21] There are kennings (allusive metaphors), which represent symbols and meanings—it is perhaps the only alphabet to have a "hieroglyphic effect" on the reader.

In short, the original purpose of Ogham is unknown. Its emergence as a way to communicate, rather than to display Celtic symbolism, was during the time when all the Celto-Roman pagan religions including the cult of Mithras were going underground, due to heavy persecution by the Christians. It is tempting to speculate that with the use of some local symbols, a whole new secret language was created, which looked local to some extent but could only be understood by a reader with knowledge of the Roman alphabet. In a similar manner the Christians—during the times when the persecution was aimed at them—were perhaps using their fish symbol to communicate with each other, drawn in part by one and completed by another.

But why the Ogham alphabet? R. A. S. MacAlister suggests that the early form could have been used as a sign language, which would explain its groupings of five. Of the other possible candidates, the Greek Formello-Cervettie alphabet is almost identical to Ogham. Matthews says: "Caesar remarks that druids used Greek letters to record their communications, but not their religious teaching."[22] The symbols were possibly "borrowed by Gaulish druids around the fifth century B.C.E." from the Greek, and no earlier than 500 B.C.E. adapted for their own use. Therefore, the Romans were no stranger to the Ogham symbols, but perhaps were unfamiliar with the Celtic versions or interpretations. They would have been a good choice for a "hidden" language—one that, with knowledge of the Roman alphabet and initiation into secret religions, could be understood, but would still look to the untrained eye like the local Greek/Celtic symbols.

Thus Mithras, like Ogma, has been linked to an alphabet with divinatory function. Use of an early form of Greek had another beneficial aspect. In *Hermetic Magic* by Dr. Stephen Flowers we read: "At some point in the early centuries C.E., a connection was forged between the letters of the Greek alphabet and the lore of Mithraism. Curiously enough, this Mithraic lore in turn seems to be an unmistakable link with the symbolism of the Tarot."[23]

Flowers's reconstruction, shown in Table 4.1, rearranges the tarot order to agree with the esoteric meanings of the Greek letters in the Mithraic tradition. That is, the original tarot or proto-tarot order followed the system of Greek letters. Most interestingly, each of the Roman esoteric names begins with a different letter in the Latin alphabet, and as suggested by Dr. Flowers, when you arrange these in their traditional order,

A B C D E F G H I K L M N O P Q R S T U X Z

The traditional order of the Major Arcana of the tarot is revealed. That is: Fool (Apis), Magician (Bacatus-Typhon), Priestess (Caeles-Isis), Empress (Diana), Emperor (Eon-Aeon), Heirophant (Flamen), Lovers (Gaudium), Chariot (Hamaxa), Justice (Iustitia), Hermit (Kronos), Wheel of Fortune (Libra), Strength (Magnitudo), Hanged Man (Noxa), Death (Orcus), Temperance (Pluvia), Devil (Quirinus), Tower (Ruina), Star (Stellae), Moon (Trina), Sun (Victor-Unus), Judgment (Xiphias), World (Zodiacus). This order differs significantly from what all modern tarot use; it would be interesting to experiment with this format.

This fascinating observation weakens the kabbalistic eighteenth/ nineteenth century theory for the origin of the proto-tarot; but it remains compatible with Chaldean astrology and the Celtic initiation theory, as well as the historical evidence of the tarot in fifteenth-century Italy. According to Dr. Flowers:

> From these materials we can suppose that the symbolism of the Tarot is ultimately based on a syncretized Irano-Hellenic model, not an originally Semito-Hebraic one. Furthermore it points to the possibility

Table 4.1

GREEK ALPHABET AND MITHRAIC CORRESPONDENCE*

Greek name	Number	Arcanum	(Esoteric Roman name)	Mithraic Meaning
Alpha	1	The Fool	(Apis)	the Bull
Beta	2	The Magician	(Bacatus-Typhon)	the Daimonic
Gamma	3	The Priestess	(Caeles-Isis)	the Divine
Delta	4	The Empress	(Diana)	Four Elements
Epsilon	5	The Emperor	(Eon-Aeon)	Aion
Zeta	7	The Hierophant	(Flamen)	Sacrifice
Eta	8	The Lovers	(Gaudium)	Joy, Love
Theta	9	The Chariot	(Hamaxa)	Crystal-Heaven
Iota	10	Justice	(Iustitia)	Ananke
Kappa	20	The Hermit	(Kronos)	Koronos, Death
Lambda	30	Wheel of Fortune	(Libra)	Plants
Mu	40	Strength	(Magnitudo)	Trees
Nu	50	The Hanged man	(Noxa)	Hecate
Xi	60	The Star	(Stellae)	Stars
Omicron	70	The Sun	(Victor-Unus)	Sun
Pi	80	The Devil	(Quirinus)	Serapis-Mithras
Rho	100	The Moon	(Trina)	the Feminine
Sigma	200	The Death	(Orcus)	Bearer of dead
Tau	300	The World	(Zodiacus)	Human
Ypsilon	400	Temperance	(Pluvia)	Water
Phi	500	Judgment	(Xiphias)	Phallus
Chi	600	?		Possessions
Psi	700	The Tower	(Ruina)	Zeus
Omega	800	?		Riches

*Table as proposed by Dr. S. E. Flowers. Excerpted from *Hermetic Magic: The Postmodern Magickal Papyrus of Abaris*, edited and introduced by Stephen Edred Flowers. With permission of the publisher, York Beach, Maine, and Boston: Red Wheel/Weiser.

of there being an original twenty-four Major Arcana, not twenty-two. This would cause the whole body of Tarot arcana, counting the Major and Minor Arcana together, to equal eighty, not seventy-eight.

As far as any connection between the Greek alphabet and the Tarot made through this Mithraic theory, it seems possible that the (proto-) Tarot was indeed shaped by this, or some related tradition. It is also worthy of note that the "Gypsies," so often connected with the Tarot, are actually of Central Asian origin (not Egyptian!). The language they speak, Romany, is closely related to the Iranian that must have been spoken by those original magus. These facts strengthen the connection of the Romany people with Tarot, while placing them in their true Indo-Iranian cultural sphere.[24]

The purpose of all this hypothesizing is to suggest that the Mithraic mysteries and other Romano religious orders may very well have had a broad influence on the magical lore of Europe, and perhaps this influence was not limited to the time of the Roman Empire.

As the Mithraic movement went underground at the end of the fourth century C.E., a special grade was created: that of *Chryfii*, meaning "hidden ones." This is inscribed in a Mithraeum in Rome. This might have been to ensure that the lore was not totally lost, and it is during this time that we see the Mithraic lore return to the Middle East with all of its new Greco-Roman-based knowledge. According to some, the spread, amazingly, went all the way to Korea, and then finally reached Japan in 612 C.E. By modifying to fit local customs and adapting to each new culture, the lore survived, so that Mithras was worshipped from Hadrian's Wall in England in the West all the way to Japan in the East. The Invincible Sun God lived up to his title and survived all his adversaries. The vague possibility of Taliesin the Bard being a Mithraic initiate in the sixth century (and certainly having knowledge of the lore) also gives evidence to the way lore was preserved by fusion with local customs, and could remain hidden by being one with the masses.

Findings of local goddess statues and other Celtic religious artifacts in the Mithraic temples along Hadrian's Wall suggest that the male-only status of the cult had shifted, and that it was again fusing with local customs and deities. It is perhaps a romantic notion and one only found in the pages of novels to think that as Christianity overcame paganism within the Isle, the remaining pagans of the different traditions put aside their differences and gathered in the remaining secret Druid Groves, or Temples of

Figure 4.3. Statues of Cautes and Cautopates from Mithraea along Hadrian's Wall, England. (Photograph by Payam Nabarz)

Isis, or the well-protected walls of the underground Mithraea, to pull together! Pagans alongside one another, invoking their gods to stop the destructions! But what we do know is that, in the years 360–363 C.E., Emperor Julian did make one last-ditch effort to return the Empire to Paganism from Christianity.

Lugh and Mithra

Another name for Lammas is Lughasadh (commemoration of Lugh). Lugh is a Gaelic god of sun and light and is often shown as Lugh, Lord of the Shining Hand of Light. The name Lugh itself comes from the same root as the Latin *lux*, meaning "light."

Lugh, like Christ and Mithras, follows the sacrificial sun god cycle: he dies (is sacrificed) for his people, and gets reborn or resurrected. Lugh carries a magic spear, which is unstoppable in battle. His spear was obtained for him by the "Gaelic Argonauts." Lugh had set them a number of tasks, one of which was to obtain for him a certain magic spear: "The poisoned spear of Pisear, King of Persia; it is irresistible in battle; it is so fiery that the blade must always be held under water, lest it destroy the city in which it is kept." The Gaelic Argonauts use a magic apple, kill the king, and bring the spear from Persia to Eire for Lugh.

The story, as told by Charles Squires in his *Mythology of the Celtic People*, goes like this:

> The three brothers rested for a while after that, and then they said they would go and look for some other part of the fine. "We will go to Pisear, King of Persia," said Brian, "and ask him for the spear."
>
> So they went into their boat, and they left the blue streams of the coast of Greece, and they said: "We are well on when we have the apples and the skin." And they stopped nowhere till they came to the borders of Persia.
>
> "Let us go to the court with the appearance of poets," said Brian, "the same as we went to the King of Greece." "We are content to do that," said the others, "as all turned out so well the last time we took to poetry; not that it is easy for us to take to a calling that does not belong to us."
>
> So they put the poet's tie on their hair, and they were as well treated as they were at the other court; and when the time came for poems Brian rose up, and this is what he said:
>
> "It is little any spear looks to Pisear; the battle of enemies are broken, it is not too much for Pisear to wound every one of them.
>
> "A yew, the most beautiful of the wood, it is called a king, it is not bulky.
>
> May the spear drive on the whole crowd to their wounds of death."
>
> "That is a good poem," said the king, "but I do not understand why my own spear is brought into it, O Man of Poetry from Ireland."
>
> "It is because it is that spear of your own I would wish to get as the reward of my poem," said Brian.
>
> "It is little sense you have to be asking that of me," said the king; "and the people of my court never showed greater respect for poetry than now, when they did not put you to death on the spot."
>
> When Brian heard that talk from the king, he thought of the apple that was in his hand, and he made a straight cast and hit him in the forehead, so that his brains were put out at the back of his head, and he bared the sword and made an attack on the people about him.
>
> And the other two did not fail to do the same, and they gave him their help bravely till they had made an end of all they met of the people of the court. And then they found the spear, and its head in a cauldron of water, the way it would not set fire to the place.[25]

It is unclear what, if any, historical aspects there are to this story. Nevertheless, the very existence of the story is interesting: that Lugh, a solar fire warrior god—like Mithra—obtains his greatest weapon—the spear of fire—from Persia. The connections among the Indo-Europeans, the sharing of similar myths and pantheon structure, is also evident when we look at their languages: for example, Éire (Ireland) and Iran both mean "Land of the Aryans."

SIMORGH—
A MITHRAIC FAIRY TALE

"You didn't need faith to fly, you needed to understand flying.
This is just the same. Now try again." . . . *Then one day*
Jonathan, standing on the shore, closing his eyes, concentrating,
all in a flash knew what Chiang had been telling him. "Why,
that's true! I am a perfect, unlimited gull!" He felt a great shock
of joy.

RICHARD BACH, JONATHAN LIVINGSTON SEAGULL

Nothing ever becomes real until it is experienced—even a proverb
is no proverb to you until your life has illustrated it.

JOHN KEATS

"Simorgh" is one of the great mystical fairy tales in the Persian tradition. The characters and symbolism demonstrate a clear continuity between the ancient, pre-Zoroastrian Persian religion and Sufism. There are several different versions of this tale in the Farsi language, and as they have been orally transmitted from one generation to another, the origin of any one rendering cannot be proven. Some years ago, the Iranian writer Homa A. Garemani began collecting them from the people of different provinces in Iran. What follows is her compilation of six versions of the tale, which *Sunrise* magazine published in 1984.*

---

*Homa A. Garemani, "Simorgh—An Old Persian Fairy Tale," *Sunrise* (June/July, 1984). Copyright © 1984 by Theosophical University Press. Reproduced here by the kind permission of the Press. For more information or to locate the original, please see: www.theosophy-nw.org/theosnw/world/mideast/mi-homa.htm

The text within parentheses is Garemani's explanation of certain phrases and symbols for readers who might be unfamiliar with their traditional meanings. The bracketed numbers correspond to my own interpretations, which are included in the section that follows the story. Note that Prince Khorshid in this story is Mithra.

SIMORGH—AN OLD PERSIAN FAIRY TALE

There was being and nonbeing, there was none but God. (The duality of light and darkness has always existed in the fundamental belief of Iranians; light representing the essence of life, which is consciousness, and darkness representing nonlife, which is form. All Persian fairy tales begin with the sentence "There was being and nonbeing, there was none but God." This may be replaced by "Once upon a time . . .") In the old, old times there was a king (the guardian of the throne of wisdom) who had three sons: Prince Jamshid (king of the golden age of Iranian epics), Prince Mohammed, and the youngest, Prince Khorshid, who had no mother. (Sun, light, divine wisdom. He had no mother because he was self-born—an initiate.) He was the king's favorite because he was the bravest of all. [1]

In the garden of the palace there grew a pomegranate tree (the treasure of secret knowledge) with only three pomegranates; their seeds were fabulous gems that shone like lamps by night. When ripe, the pomegranates would turn into three beautiful girls who were to become the wives of the three princes. Every night, by the king's order, one of his sons guarded the tree lest anyone should steal the pomegranates. [2]

One night when Prince Jamshid was guarding the tree, he fell asleep and, in the morning, one pomegranate was missing. The next night Prince Mohammed was on guard, but he also fell asleep and the next morning another pomegranate was missing. When it came Prince Khorshid's turn, he cut one of his fingers and rubbed salt on it so the burning would keep him awake. Shortly after midnight a cloud appeared above the tree and a hand, coming out of it, picked the last pomegranate. Prince Khorshid drew his sword and cut off one of the fingers. The hand and the cloud hurriedly disappeared.

In the morning when the king saw drops of blood on the ground, he ordered his sons to track them, find the thief, and bring back the stolen pomegranates. The three princes followed the blood drops over mountains and deserts until they reached a deep well where the trail ended. [3] Prince Jamshid offered to be lowered down the well with a rope to investigate.

Less than halfway down he screamed: "Pull me up, pull me up, I am burning." His brothers pulled him up. Next, Prince Mohammed went down
and soon he also cried out that he was burning. When Prince Khorshid
decided to go down he told his brothers that no matter how loudly he
shouted, they should not pull him up but let the rope down farther; and
they were then to wait for him only until dark. If there was no sign of him,
they could go home.

Prince Khorshid entered the well and, in spite of unbearable heat,
went all the way down to the bottom, where he found a young girl, beautiful as a full moon. On her lap lay the head of a sleeping diev (giant:
tyranny of human ignorance and weakness), whose thunderous snores
filled the air with heat and smoke. "Prince Khorshid," she whispered,
"what are you doing here? If this diev wakes up, he will surely kill you as
he has killed many others. Go back while there is still time."

Prince Khorshid, who loved her at first glance, refused. He asked her
who she was and what she was doing there.

"My two sisters and I are captives of this diev and his two brothers. My
sisters are imprisoned in two separate wells where the dievs have hidden
the stolen wealth of almost all the world."

Prince Khorshid said, "I am going to kill the dievs and free you and
your sisters. But I will wake him first; I do not wish to kill him in his
sleep." The prince scratched the soles of the diev's feet until he opened his
eyes and stood up. Roaring, the diev picked up a millstone and threw it at
the prince, who quickly stepped aside, drew his sword, and in the name of
God cut the diev in half. [4] Thereafter he went to the other two wells, finished off the dievs, and rescued the sisters of his beloved. He also collected
the treasure.

As it was not yet dark, his brothers were still waiting for him and when
he called them they started to pull up the rope. The girl whom Prince
Khorshid loved wanted him to go up before her, because she knew that
when his brothers saw the jewels they would be jealous and would not
pull him up. But the prince insisted she go up first. When she saw that she
could not change his mind, she said: "If your brothers do not pull you up
and leave you here, there are two things you should know: first, there are
in this land a golden cock and a golden lantern that can lead you to me.
(The golden cock represents Saroush, or Sarousha in Pahlavi. Sarousha is
a godlike bird who is the most powerful of the gods, since he is the manifestation of righteousness, honesty, and striving. He fights the diev of
frailty and weakness. In some versions of this story, the golden cock in a

chest is a golden nightingale in a golden cage. The golden lantern represents the light of wisdom. In some versions, Prince Khorshid must bring back a golden lantern, in others a golden handmill, which represents the wheel of destiny [or civilization and culture].) The cock is in a chest and when you open it, he will sing for you. And when he sings, all kinds of gems will pour from his beak. The golden lantern is self-illuminated, and it burns forever. The second thing you should know is this: later in the night there will come two oxen that will fight with each other. One is black (terrestrial life leading to darkness), the other white (terrestrial life leading to light). If you jump on the white ox it will take you out of the well, but if, by mistake, you jump on the black one, it will take you seven floors farther down."

As she had predicted, when the princes Jamshid and Mohammed saw the girls and the boxes of gold and silver, they became jealous of their brother's achievements. Knowing that their father would surely give him the kingdom, they cut the rope and let him fall to the bottom of the well. [5] Then they went home and told their father that they were the ones who had rescued the girls, killed the dievs, and brought all the treasure, and that Prince Khorshid had not come back.

Prince Khorshid was heartbroken. He saw two oxen approaching and stood up as they started to fight. In his excitement he jumped on the back of the black ox and dropped with it seven floors down. [6] When he opened his eyes, he found himself in a green pasture with a view of a city in the distance. He started walking toward it when he saw a peasant plowing. Being hungry and thirsty he asked him for bread and water. The man told him to be very careful and not to talk out loud because there were two lions nearby; if they heard him they would come out and eat the oxen. Then he said, "You take over the plowing and I will get you something to eat."

Prince Khorshid started to plow, commanding the oxen in a loud voice. Two roaring lions came charging toward him, but the prince captured the lions, turned the oxen loose, and hitched the lions to the plow. When the peasant returned, he was very much taken aback. Prince Khorshid said, "Don't be afraid. The lions are harmless now and will not hurt you or your oxen. But if you are not comfortable with them, I will let them go." When he saw that the farmer was still reluctant to approach the lions, he unfastened them and they went back where they had come from. [7]

The man had brought food but no water. He explained: "There is no water in the city because a dragon is sleeping in front of the spring. Every Saturday a girl is taken to the spring so that, when the dragon moves to devour her, some water runs through the city's streams and people can collect enough for the following week. This Saturday the king's daughter is to be offered to the dragon." [8]

Prince Khorshid had the peasant take him to the king: "What will be my reward if I kill the dragon and save your daughter's life?" The king replied, "Whatever you wish within my power."

Saturday came and the prince went with the girl to the spring. The moment the dragon moved aside to devour her, Prince Khorshid called the name of God and slew the monster. There was joy and celebration in the city. When Prince Khorshid, asked to name his reward, announced that his one wish was to return to his homeland, the king said: "The only one who could take you up seven floors is Simorgh. She lives nearby in a jungle. Every year she lays three eggs and each year her chicks are eaten by a serpent. If you could kill the serpent, she surely would take you home." [9]

(In Persian literature Simorgh [Saena in Pahlavi] has many manifestations; besides divine wisdom, it may symbolize the perfected human being. According to some Pahlavi texts, Simorgh is a bird whose abode is in the middle of a sea, in a tree that contains all the seeds of the vegetable world. Whenever Simorgh flies up from the tree one thousand branches grow, and whenever she sits on it, one thousand branches break and the seeds fall into the water.

In Ferdowsi's *Shah-Nameh* [Book of Kings]—originally called *Khoday-Nameh* [Book of God]—Simorgh's abode is on top of the mountain Ghaph, by which is meant Alborz mountain.)

Prince Khorshid went to the jungle and found the tree in which Simorgh had her nest. While he was watching, he saw a serpent climbing up the tree to eat the frightened chicks. In the name of God he cut the serpent into small pieces and fed some to the hungry chicks who were waiting for their mother to bring them food. He saved the rest for later and went to sleep under the tree.

Figure 5.1. A replica of a pre-Islamic Persian medallion depicting Simorgh. The original medallion is in the British Museum in London. (Photograph by Payam Nabarz)

When Simorgh flew over the nest and saw Prince Khorshid, she thought he was the one who each year ate up all her chicks. She was ready to kill him, when her chicks shouted that he was the one who had saved them from the enemy. Realizing that he had killed the serpent, she stretched her wings over Prince Khorshid's head to make shade for him while he slept.

When he awoke, the prince told Simorgh his story and asked whether she could help him. Simorgh urged him to go back to the king and ask him for the meat of seven bulls. "Make seven leather bags out of their hides and fill them with water. These will be my provisions for the journey; I need them to be able to take you home. Whenever I say I am hungry you must give me a bag of water, and when I say I am thirsty you must give me the carcass of a bull." [10]

On their way up to the ground, Prince Khorshid did exactly as Simorgh had instructed him until only one bag of water was left. When, instead of saying she was hungry, Simorgh said she was thirsty, Prince Khorshid cut off some flesh from his thigh and put it in Simorgh's beak. Simorgh immediately realized it was human flesh. She held it gently until they reached their destination. As soon as he dismounted, the prince urged Simorgh to fly back at once but, knowing he could not walk without limping, she refused and with her saliva restored the piece of his flesh to his thigh. Having learned how brave and unselfish the prince was, she gave him three of her feathers, saying that if he were ever in need of her he should burn one of them, and she would instantly come to his aid. With that she flew away.

Entering the town, Prince Khorshid learned that three royal weddings were about to take place: for Prince Jamshid, and Prince Mohammed, and the third for the Vizier's son, because the youngest son of the king, Prince Khorshid, had never returned. One day some men came to the shop where Prince Khorshid was [now] apprenticed, saying they had been to all the jewelry stores in town but no one would undertake to make what the king had ordered. Prince Khorshid asked them what it was and was told: "The girl who is to marry the Vizier's son has put forward one condition to the marriage! She will only marry one who can bring her a golden cock from whose bill gems will pour when it sings; she also wants a golden lantern which is self-illuminated and burns forever. But so far no jeweler can build such things."

Prince Khorshid, recognizing the signs, spoke up: "With my master's permission I can build you a chest with such a golden cock and also the golden lantern by tomorrow." The men gave him the jewels needed to build those items and left. Prince Khorshid gave them all to his master, for, he said, he did not need them.

That night Prince Khorshid left the town and burned one of the feathers. When Simorgh came, he asked her to bring him what the girl had demanded, and she did so. In the morning, the astounded men took the precious items to the king, who at once summoned the young man to the court and was overjoyed to discover it was none other than his favorite son. Prince Khorshid told his story but he begged the king not to punish his brothers for the wrong they had done him.

The whole town celebrated his return and there were three weddings indeed. The king made Prince Khorshid his successor to the throne, and all lived happily ever after.

SYMBOLISM OF THE SIMORGH TALE

The word *Naqsh-bandi*, the name of the famed Sufi order, can be translated as "painters or weavers of the pattern, plan, diagram, matrix." This meaning points to the role of the Sufi as, like a shaman, one who sees and is aware of the plan, or the Web of Wyrd. As Rumi puts it: "I am a form-making engraver (Naqsh) each instant I shape an idol." The story of Simorgh is a story with many patterns woven into it, and what follows here is an attempt to bestow some light on this matrix.

All Persian fairy tales begin with the same sentence. In the Farsi, *Yeke bod, Yeke na bod, gir az khoda hechkeye nabod*: "There was being and non-being, there was none but God." In the old, old times there was a king (the guardian of the throne of wisdom), who had three sons:

1. In one version of the story, the three brothers are the princes Kiumars, Jamshid, and Khorshid, while in another version the three brothers are Jamshid, Mohammed, and Khorshid. Let us go back a few generations and trace the lineage of the princes, to see what we can learn. Prince Kiumars was the first human in Ferdowsi's *Shah-Nameh* and also in the ancient Avesta, the Zoroastrian holy text. Kiumars, therefore, in the Avestan tradition, corresponds to Adam in the biblical tradition, as the first human. He was as wide as he was tall and as bright as the sun, and he wore the skins of leopards. He and his people dwelt in the mountains, lived on fruits and roots, wore garments of leaves, and were happy.

This period probably reflects the Stone Age. The paradise was lost not by temptation in this tradition, but by Ahriman sending a black demon (Deav/Div) who killed his son Siamak. Siamak's son Hushang and his army of animals—lions and tigers, all the birds of the air, grass-eating beasts, the ox, and the noble horse—eventually defeated the black demon. It was a time emphasizing the closeness of humans to the rest of the animal kingdom. During another battle with a monster, Hushang discovered fire, the monster fled, and by means of fire Hushang cooked and kept warm.

Prince Jamshid was the grandson of Hushang. In the old epic poems featuring Jamshid we learn that he forged not only tools but weapons of war—swords, spears, arrow heads, and coats of mail—and used these iron weapons to defeat many armies of darkness. His people learned how to spin and weave and wore garments of wool, silk, and linen. Here the society divided into a system of social classes, each with its specific tasks: warrior class, priest class, and farmer class. Jamshid's reign ended due to his excessive pride, seeing himself above God. His army abandoned him, and an era of darkness followed.

The youngest prince, Prince Khorshid—Mithra—had no mother. He was the king's favorite because he was the bravest of all. Mithra or Mehr means sun, light, love, friend. According to one tradition, Mithra had no mother because he was born of a rock, or the cosmic egg, dagger in one hand and burning torch in the other.

The Simorgh story follows the Indo-European tripartite ideology pattern. In any story such as this containing three princes and three princesses, we perceive the Indo-European tripartite of the gods, heroes, and society. In ancient India, the original classes were the Brahmana (priests), Ksatriya (warriors), and Vaisya (producers); these correspond with the gods Varuna, Mithra, and Indra. We can see the pattern not only in India and Iran, but all the way across Europe: the Celts segregated society into the Druids (priests), Flaith (warriors), and Boairig (herders). The story of Simorgh is indeed a very old fable. The hero, like other Indo-European folk heroes, will be expected to face three adversaries, or a monster with three heads, or perhaps, like the Irish hero Cuchulainn, to fight three brothers.

According to some academics, this Indo-European tripartite society format of priests, warriors, and producers still echoes down to modern times, as symbolized in the three-color format of the national flags of numerous Indo-European nations: Afghanistan, Armenia, Azerbaijan, Bulgaria, Belgium, France, Germany, Hungary, India, Iran, Iraq, Ireland, Italy, Lithuania, Luxemburg, Romania, Russia, Syria, Tajikistan, United Kingdom, United States of America, Uzbekistan, and Yugoslavia, to name some.

2. The pomegranate is the tree of knowledge in some myths. In others, it is linked with the underworld, as in the Greek story of Persephone, which lies at the center of the Eleusinian mysteries. Persephone is taken to the underworld by Hades to be his queen. She willingly eats a seed of a pomegranate and is forced to spend every winter with her husband in the land of the dead, symbolizing the yearly decay and revival of vegetation. This seasonal return myth is also found in the Syrian tale of Astarte (Aphrodite) and Adonis; the Phrygian version features Cybele and Attis, and in Egypt, we hear of Isis and Osiris. Our present hero's descent into the underworld is the Persian version of the same story.

The three pomegranates of our tale are becoming ripe and will turn into three princesses; thus in essence the fruit here acts as mediatrix between the two divine worlds of heaven and underworld. In Judaism, the number of seeds in a pomegranate is said to be the exact number of mitzvah, or spiritual duties required of a devout Jew. In Sufism, the pomegranate is an important symbol as well. The Sufi Saint Ali said, "the light of Allah is in the heart of whoever eats pomegranates," and the Prophet Mohammed said, "the pomegranate cleanses you of Satan and from evil aspirations for forty days." This is the fruit still eaten traditionally by Iranians at Shab Yalda (Yule, the winter solstice). On this longest night of the year, the sun/light is at its weakest point. By eating the pomegranate, Iranians symbolically align themselves with the sun while keeping a night vigil, waiting for dawn.

3. The well is an entrance to the underworld; its fires burn the first two princes during their descent, and they bail out. Prince Mithra, on the other hand, makes the leap of faith into the vat and, like the grape, starts his transformation into wine. He continues his journey despite being cooked and burned. At the bottom of the well, Prince Mithra (sun) finds a young girl, beautiful as the moon. The Sun and the Moon meet and immediately fall in love. (There is also a Japanese version of this Sun and Moon falling in love with each other.) In Sufism, the sun represents the Spirit that lights the heavens, while the moon symbolizes the light of this world. Light is seen as divine knowledge; hence, the soul of the mystic is symbolized by the moon, which reflects the light of the sun. When moon and sun meet, love flows between them. Here, the moon warns the sun of the perils of this meeting and of his quest. "Many have come here and the demon has killed them; go back while there is time." But it is too late for Mithra, as he has seen his beloved—perhaps his own soul, his queen to be, or perhaps in this meeting he has caught a glimpse of the ocean of unity.

4. Prince Mithra wakes the demon and faces his demon consciously, and in the name of God. By saying a mantra for the name of God (Sufi *ziker*) he defeats the three demons.

5. The lady tells Mithra to ascend first, knowing how his brothers might react. He ignores her advice: a sign that his journey is not yet complete. She gives him instructions on how to find her. First, there is a golden cock and a golden lantern. Ghahremani has already described how the golden cock represents Saroush, the most powerful of gods, the manifestation of righteousness, honesty, and striving, who fights the diev (or deav) of frailty and weakness. This is the symbolic manifestation that the prince is instructed to bring back with him.

In some versions, Prince Mithra must also bring back a golden lantern, the light of wisdom, while in other versions, he must retrieve a golden handmill, representing the wheel of destiny (or civilization and culture). In some versions of the story, instead of the golden cock in a chest there is a golden nightingale in a golden cage. In Sufi poetry, the nightingale is in love with the rose. The nightingale represents the aspect of self caught in the exterior form of things and thus unable to leave the rose behind.

6. The two oxen represent life that can lead to either light or darkness. According to the Zoroastrian tradition, the first animal in the world was a "uniquely created bull," white in color and as bright as the moon. The bull was killed and its carcass was carried to the moon, and from it came the seeds of many species of animals and plants.

The ox is seen as a symbol of ego (Sufi *nafs*), and by jumping on the back of the white ox, it would carry Prince Mithra up seven heavens (*haft aseman*). But he sits on the black ox and falls seven floors. In order for him to return home, he later has to slay seven bulls. The seven bulls, or the stages of ego (nafs) are:

> *Nafs-i-ammara* (the depraved, commanding ego)
> *Nafs-i-lawwama* (accusing nafs)
> *Nafs-i-mulhama* (the inspired nafs)
> *Nafs-i-mutmainna* (serene nafs)
> *Nafs-i-radiyya* (fulfilled nafs)
> *Nafs-i-mardiyya* (fulfilling nafs)
> *Nafs-i-safiyy wa kamila* (the purified and complete nafs)

The seven stages of development correspond to seven heavens, which in the Sufi tradition are Ether (Moon), Reflection (Mercury), Divine Fantasy (Venus), Light of Heart (Sun), Divine Judgment (Mars), God's Meditation (Jupiter), and Divine Decree (Saturn). We see similar arrangements of divine attributes in the Jewish Kabbalah, with its ten Spheres or Sephiroth upon the Tree of Life. Likewise, we see them in the emanations of the divine within Christian Gnosticism; in the seven chakras of Hinduism; and in the ancient Roman Mithraic mystery cult, where Mithras (Mithra/Mehr/Mitra) ascends seven heavens by killing a bull. Each heaven represents a specific initiatory degree.

The seven valleys of Attar's "Conference of Birds" represent the same journey. Also consider Ursa Major, or the Big Dipper, with its seven stars leading the way to the Northern Lights, a symbol of enlightenment.

7. The lion symbolizes action rather than contemplation in this story. The lion is represented by gold and the sun. Rumi describes Hazrat Ali as the Lion of God; King Richard is given a similar title: Richard the Lion Heart. Lion is also the fourth level in the Mithraic initiatory journey. Another interpretation is the astronomical one. The lion attempting to kill the bull is an old symbol representing the constellation Leo at the summer solstice (the sun and the light at its peak) killing the constellation Taurus (the bull), and moving the world out of the Age of Taurus.

8. Laleh Bakhtiar beautifully describes the mystical significance of the dragon in the Sufi way of understanding:

> In Sufism the dragon relates two astronomical nodes, two diametrically opposed points of intersection between the moon and the sun. Its head is the ascending node, its tail the descending node. An eclipse can only occur when both sun and moon stand at the nodes. To the mystic, the dragon symbolizes the place of encounter between the moon and the sun within. The dragon can either devour the moon, seen symbolically as the mystic's spiritual heart, or it can serve as the place or container of conception. By entering the dragon when the sun is in the nodes, the moon or the heart conceives. Thus, in full consciousness of the perils, one must enter the dragon to await the eclipse in its cosmic womb.[1]

The dragon in this story sits at the source of the waters, and Mithra slays him. In Hindu mythology, Vitra is the dragon of the waters, slain by Indra to release the waters. The Babylonian dragon Tiamat, representative of the primordial waters, chaos, and darkness, was slain by the sun god Marduk. In Egyptian mythology, Apophis, the dragon of darkness, was overcome each morning by the sun god Ra.

9. Simorgh is a fabulous creature having affinities with the Arabian Roc and the Indian Garuda (half man, half eagle, who nests in the wish-fulfilling tree of life). Simorgh is half bird, half mammal, symbolizing the union of heaven and earth; a bird who nevertheless suckles her young. This icon appears in the Persian, Russian, and Caucasian traditions. It is the bird of the Persian tree of life (or tree of seeds); it lives in the land of the sacred Homa (Sanskrit Soma), a plant whose seed can cure all evil. An eagle also nests in Yggdrasil, the Scandinavian world tree, whose branches are said to bind together heaven and hell. According to some fables, the Simorgh lives for seventeen hundred years and then immolates herself like the Phoenix. By the beating of her wings, the seeds on the tree of seeds are scattered and carried away by wind and rain over the earth.

In *Shah-Nameh*, Simorgh plays a prominent role in the greatest of Persian stories, that of Zal and Rustam. Zal was born as an albino child, with hair as white as snow, and because of his unusual features he was thought to be the spawn of darkness. His father, Sam, in great sadness takes the baby Zal to the bottom of Mount Davamad in the Alborz Mountains (also known as Mount Qaf or Mount Hara, the *axis mundi*), where he leaves the child to die in the elements. The Simorgh who resides near the mountain hears the cries of the baby, comes to him, and takes him as prey to her hatched nestlings. But the nestlings will not eat him; instead, they accept him. Simorgh ends up nurturing and rearing the baby Zal.

Zal grows up with the Simorgh in the mountains to become a young man with long white hair. Eventually, Sam hears about him and, realizing it is his son Zal and that he is still alive, returns to the mountain looking for his son. Simorgh flies Zal to the bottom of the mountain, saying: "You are a human and it is fitting you should be with other humans; it is time for us to part. Yet today you are no less my child than you were upon that day when I first found you, weak and helpless, and in the years to come my love and my care will still be yours. If you ever have need of my help, burn this feather of mine and I will know of it and come to you, wherever you may be."

The great Sufi Suhrawardi has elucidated the spiritual meaning of this episode. The bird offers shelter to the Spirit in the other world. The albino is the emblem of the developing soul. Mount Qaf/Davamad is the mountain that the seeker must climb to find himself. At the summit sits the emerald rock, acting as the pole or *qutub* toward which the seeker walks, which sits symbolically at the North. Henry Corbin describes the significance of North to the Sufi:

> In Sufism the quest for the dawning of light in the cosmic North symbolizes the mystic's search for realization. In this spiritual journey, the light arising in man's inner darkness—the Northern Light or Midnight Sun—represents the impartial but brilliant light of Truth, that which sets us free from egotism and from the slavery of material existence.[2]

In our story, the Simorgh even heals the self-inflicted sacrificial thigh wound that Mithra has suffered. Simorgh does not eat the flesh Mithra has cut from his own thigh, but restores the flesh to his thigh. These symbols—the thigh wound and the limping hero—are seen in many stories: the Fisher King, the Greek Adonis, the Phrygian Attis, the Egyptian Osiris, the Christian Jesus, and the Germanic Iron John. Robert Bly, in his study entitled *Iron John,* suggests that the symbolic wound allows the soul to enter the body, and discusses this idea at length.[3]

The enemy of the Simorgh is the serpent who eats her young. In the Hindu tradition, too, the serpent (Sanskrit *naga*) represents the underworld and is in perpetual enmity with the solar Garuda bird. But the serpent is also seen as the guardian of knowledge; so Mithra, after killing the serpent, feeds some to the hungry chicks—giving knowledge to the Simorgh's brood—and saves the rest for later.

10. The Eagle and the Serpent are symbols of an old alchemical formula. For the Simorgh to carry Mithra up seven levels, Mithra must bring the meat of seven bulls. That is, he has to go through the seven stages of the ego (nafs) to ascend seven heavens. Or, as Attar (the twelfth-century Sufi poet) puts it, to reach the king of birds the Simorgh, seven valleys have to be crossed.

In Attar's "Conference of Birds" all the birds gather to begin a quest for the fabulous bird, Simorgh, the king of birds. The hoopoe bird symbolizing inspiration tells all the birds of the existence of the Simorgh, who lives far away, beyond seven valleys. Many of the birds make their excuses and decide not to make the journey, but eventually a group of birds makes their way across the seven valleys, which are: Search, Love, Mystic Apprehension, Detachment, Unity, Bewilderment, and Fulfillment in Annihilation. After many trials and tribulations across the seven valleys, only thirty birds finally reach the court. At first they are turned back, but finally they are admitted. The crucial moment depends on a pun: si means thirty, *murgh* means birds, and hence si-*murgh* literally means thirty birds. Once in the presence of the Simorgh:

> *A new life flowed towards them from that bright*
> *Celestial and ever living light.*
> *Their souls rose free of all they had been before;*
> *The past and all its actions were no more.*
> *Their life came from that close, insistent sun.*
> *And in its vivid rays they shone as one.*
> *There in the Simorgh's radiant face they saw themselves,*
> *the Simorgh of the world with awe. They gazed,*
> *and dared at last to comprehend.*
> *They were the Simorgh and at the journey's end.*
> *They see the Simorgh as themselves they stare,*
> *and see a second Simorgh standing there;*
> *They look at both and see the two are one.*
> *That this is that, that this, the goal won.*
> *They ask (but inwardly; they make no sound)*
> *The meaning of these mysteries that confound.*
> *Their puzzled ignorance—how is it true*
> *That "we" is not distinguished here from "you"?*
> *And silently their shining lord replies:*
> *"I am a mirror set before your eyes,*
> *And all who come before my splendor see,*
> *Themselves, their own unique reality;*
> *You came as thirty birds, and therefore saw*
> *these selfsame thirty birds not less nor more;*
> *If you had come as forty, fifty—here,*
> *An answering forty, fifty would appear;*
> *Though you have struggled, wandered, traveled far,*
> *It is yourselves you see and what you are.*
> *Who see the Lord? It is himself each sees;*
> *What ant's sight could discern the Pleiades?*

What anvil could be lifted by an ant?
Or could a fly subdue an elephant?
How much you thought you knew and saw; but you
Now know that all you trusted was untrue.
Though you traversed the Valley's depths and fought
With all the dangers that the journey brought,
The Journey was in Me, the deeds were Mine—
You slept secure in Being's inmost shrine.
And since you came as thirty birds, you see
These thirty birds when you discover Me,
The Simorgh, Truth's last flawless jewel, the light
In which you will be lost to mortal sight,
Dispersed to nothingness until once more
You find in Me the selves you were before."
Then, as they listened to the Simorgh's words,
A trembling dissolution filled the birds—
the substance of their being was undone,
And they were lost like shades before the sun;
Neither the pilgrims nor their guide remained.
The Simorgh ceased to speak, and silence reigned.[4]

The same spirit is beautifully echoed in the concluding lines of the Wiccan "Charge of the Goddess":

To thou who thinkest to seek Me, know that thy seeking and yearning shall avail thee not unless thou knowest the Mystery. If that which thou seekest thou findest not within thee, thou wilt never find it without. For behold, I have been with thee from the beginning; and I am that which is attained at the end of desire.[5]

THE MITHRAIC LITURGY

I concentrated my attention on the constellation Bear (Ursa Minor) and I observed that it formed seven apertures through which God was showing himself to me. My God! I cried, what is this? He said to me: "These are the seven apertures of the Throne. . . ." Every night, I continued afterward to observe these apertures in Heaven, as my love and ardent desire impelled me to do. And lo! One night, I saw that they were open, and I saw the divine Being manifesting to me through these apertures. He said to me, "I manifest to you through these openings; they form seven thousand thresholds (corresponding to seven principal stars of the constellation) leading to the threshold of the angelic pleroma (malakut). And behold I show myself to you through all of them at once."

"Visions of the Pole," in the Sufi *Ruzbehan of Shiraz*, 1209

The Mithraic Liturgy that follows occupies lines 475–834 of the Greek Magical Papyrus of Paris (350 C.E.). The Mithraic Liturgy contained in the Greek Magical Papyri was discovered in Thebes in Egypt. Its writing has been attributed to work of a magician of the fourth century C.E., but Professor Betz has suggested that two hundred years would be a reasonable estimate for the total time necessary to pull all of its parts together. The estimates by the scholar Dietrerich (1866–1908) is that the Mithraic Liturgy originated in 100 C.E., followed by Egyptian influence 150–200 C.E., and final development by magicians 200–300 C.E. This text is the earliest authenticated complete magical writing in the West that bears a connection to Mithras. It is, in effect, a single spell and only sheds light on the workings of one magician, a Mithraic initiate (one who was perhaps involved with several other cults). The liturgy clearly demonstrates that

Mithras was a deity invoked alongside other deities and was by no means puritan in any way. We see how Ananke (Goddess of Necessity), Pronoia (Providence), and Psyche (Soul) are invoked along with Mithras for the particular magical working of the writer.

This liturgy is used extensively in the modern revival of Mithraism. The version presented here is based on that of G. R. S. Mead, from *A Mithraic Ritual*, published in 1907.*[1] For a very recent and excellent detailed academic analysis of the Mithraic Liturgy, see Professor Hans Dieter Betz's *The Mithras Liturgy: Text, Translation and Commentary* (2003). Supplementary help in gaining insight into the vision of the Mithras Liturgy can be found in Professor Henry Corbin's *Man of Light in Iranian Sufism*, especially Chapter Three, "Midnight Sun and Celestial Pole."[2]

PREPARATION FOR PERFORMING
THE MITHRAIC LITURGY

Create an altar to Mithras, including a statue or drawing of him. Arrange for your altar to include symbols and elements from all different aspects of the Mithraic mysteries. Here are some examples:

Raven or crow feathers for Corax
A lamp and a veil for Nymphus
A sword for Miles
A sistrum (rattle) and some honey for Leo
Honey can also be used for Perses
A large white candle for Heliodromus
A staff and a bowl for Pater

Arrange a time and space in which you will not be interrupted when performing the following ritual. To begin, clap your hands or shake your rattle seven times, and light seven white candles or small lamps; and then place some incense on your incense burner. You can arrange the seven lights in the shape of the seven stars of the Plough/Ursa Minor, to represent the leg of the bull that Mithras holds to move the heavens.

*For the original, unaltered translation of the Mithraic Liturgy, see Hans Dieter Betz, ed., *The Greek Magical Papyri in Translation*, 2d ed. (Chicago: University of Chicago Press, 1996), PGM IV, 475–829. For an online academic analysis of the Mithraic Liturgy see: www.hermetic.com/pgm/mithras-liturgy.html

Figure 6.1. An example of a modern Mithraic Altar. On the altar are statues of Mithras and Anahita, as well as symbols of the seven grades: sistrum; sword; incense burner; raven feather; sun symbol; staff; red and white candles, symbolizing the sun and moon; and so forth. A silver Persian drinking cup in the shape of Simorgh (toward the back) is used for making libations. The round altar table (designed and made by Glyn Wood Kits and Altars) has been decorated with paintings of the constellations at the time of Summer Solstice. There is a hole in the table at each star; when a candle is lit under the table at night one is faced with the glowing constellations. (Photograph by Payam Nabarz)

Alternatively, use fourteen candles—seven white and seven black. Arrange the seven black candles on the left of the altar in the shape of the seven stars of the Plough constellation. On the right of the altar, arrange the seven white candles in shape of the Pleiades constellation. The seven white candles represent the seven Fates or Virgins that are part of the rite. The seven black candles represent the seven Black Bulls or Pole Lords, which are also part of the rite. The seven Fates, which have been described as having the faces of asps, have been suggested by one scholar (Gundel) to be the seven Hathors (Egyptian cow goddesses). This puts forward the interesting vision that the magus, during his ascent in the rite, flies through a corridor or choir of seven black bulls (male) facing seven white cows (female). Mithras descends from the realm of the gods, or the eighth gate, to meet the ascending magus within this sacred bovine conduit, which suggests an additional meaning to the Mithras-Bull symbology.

The ascent of the soul during the rite, according to Professor Meyer in the *Ancient Mysteries,* has seven stages:

1. The four elements;
2. The lower powers of the air;
3. Aion and his powers;
4. Helios, the Sun;
5. The seven Fates;
6. The seven Pole-Lords;
7. The highest god, portrayed as Mithras. Upon meeting Mithras, divine revelation is received.

It is worth noting that in the story of Simorgh (chapter 5), the hero of the story Khorshid (Mithra) descends seven floors by jumping on the black ox by mistake. If he had jumped on the white ox, it would have raised him up seven floors. Later in the story, when finally Prince Khorshid (Mithra) meets Simorgh and asks her for her help, she tells him to ask for the meat of seven bulls, and to make seven leather bags out of their hides, with which to carry water. As they make their ascent, Khorshid gives her a bull's carcass when she asks for water, and one of the seven leather bags when she asks for meat, as she has instructed him to do. Their ascent through seven levels is completed by consuming the bodies of the seven bulls.

During the rite, you declare your name and also your mother's name. Your declaration as a son or daughter of your mother connects you and reminds you that you are born of a Mother Goddess. Regarding the utterance of "Silence," John Matthews, in his version of the liturgy in *Choirs of the God*, writes:

> Silence is a translation of the Greek *Sige*, which represents the supernatural Mother of all things. Thus by invoking her in this way, the candidate is allowing the presence of the divine feminine to enter the ritual as a foundation upon which to build. The "masculine" speech is thus framed by "feminine" silences.[3]

Regarding the "hiss" and "puff," though it is not clear what these involve, they are most likely similar to yogic breathing techniques. One approach is to breathe in deeply with lips almost closed so your breath makes a "hiss," and then breath out with a bellowing "puff." Repeating this in a circular breathing fashion has an interesting effect.

The *Voces Magicae* in the rite are the sounds of ee, o, oe, and so forth, and are to be made according to the Latin pronunciation as follows:

e or ee = ay
o or oo = oh
i or ii = ee
u = oo
a = ah

These chants begin at the top and descend through the scale.

The † symbol in G. R. S. Mead's version of the Mithraic Liturgy, which is used here, refers to various potential magical words from Egyptian, Hebrew, Greek, or glossolalic (speaking in tongues). G. R. S. Mead excluded these words in his 1907 edition (below) presumably for simplification. My recommendation is that once the reader has become comfortable with performing the version here, he or she should move on to one of the editions by Professor Meyer or Professor Betz, which include all the magical sounds and words.

THE RITUAL

I.

[The Father's Prayer]
O Providence, O Fortune, bestow on me Thy Grace—imparting these the Mysteries a Father only may hand on, and that, too, to a Son alone—his Immortality—[a Son] initiate, worthy of this our Craft, with which Sun Mithras, the Great God, commanded me to be endowed by His Archangel; so that I, Eagle [as I am, by mine own self] alone, may soar to Heaven, and contemplate all things.

II.

[The Invocatory Utterance (Logos)]
1. O Primal Origin of my origination; Thou Primal Substance of my substance; First Breath of breath, the breath that is in me; First Fire, God-given for the Blending of the blendings in me, [First Fire] of fire in me; First Water of [my] water. The

water in me; Primal Earth-essence of the earthy essence in me; Thou Perfect Body of me—N.N. [your name], son of N.N. (fem.) [your mother's name]— fashioned by Honored Arm and Incorruptible Right Hand, in World that's light-less, yet radiant with Light, [in World] that's soulless, yet filled full of Soul!

2. If, verily, it may seem good to you, translate me, now held by my lower nature, unto the Generation that is free from Death; in order that, beyond the insistent Need that presses on me, I may have Vision of the Deathless Source, by virtue of the Deathless Spirit, by virtue of the Deathless Water, by virtue of the [Deathless] Solid, and [by virtue of] the [Deathless] Air; in order that I may become re-born in Mind; in order that I may become initiate, and that the Holy Breath may breathe in me; in order that I may admire the Holy Fire; that I may see the Deep of the [New] Dawn, the Water that doth cause [the Soul] to thrill; and that the Life-bestowing æther which surrounds [all things] may give me, Hearing.

3. For I am to behold to-day with Deathless Eyes—I, mortal, born of mortal womb, but [now] made better by the Might of Mighty Power, yea, by the Incorruptible Right Hand—[I am to see to-day] by virtue of the Deathless Spirit the Deathless Æon, the Master of the Diadems in of Fire—I with pure purities [now] purified, the human soul-power of me subsisting for a little while in purity; which [power] I shall again receive transmitted unto me beyond the insistent Bitterness that presses on me, Necessity whose debts can never go unpaid—I, N.N. [your name], son of N.N. (fem.) [your mother's name]— according to the Ordinance of God that naught can ever change.

4. For that it is beyond my reach that, born beneath the sway of Death, I should [unaided] soar into the Height, together with the golden sparklings of the Brilliancy that knows no Death.

5. Stay still, O nature doomed to Perish, [nature] of men subject to Death! And straightway let me pass beyond the Need implacable that presses on me; for that I am His Son; I breathe; I am!

III.
[The First Instruction]
1. Take from the [Sun-]rays breath, inhaling thrice [as deeply] as thou canst; and thou shalt see thyself being raised aloft, and soaring towards the Height, so that thou seem'st to be in midst of Air.

2. Thou shalt hear naught, nor man nor beast; nor shalt thou see aught of the sights upon the earth, in that same hour; but all things thou shalt see will be immortal.

3. For thou shalt see, in that same day and hour, the Disposition of the Gods—the Ruling Gods ascending heaven-wards, the other ones descending. And through his Disk—the God's, my Father's—there shall be seen the Way-of-going of the Gods accessible to sight.

4. And in like fashion also [shall be seen] the Pipe, as it is called, whence comes the Wind in service [for the day]. For thou shalt see as though it were a Pipe depending from His Disk; and toward the regions Westward, as though it were an infinite East Wind. But if the other Wind, toward the regions of the East should be in service, in the like fashion shalt thou see, toward the regions of that [side,] the converse of the sight.

5. And thou shalt see the Gods gazing intently on thee and bearing down upon thee. Then straightway lay thy dexter finger on thy lips and say:

IV.
[The First Utterance]
O Silence! Silence! Silence!
The Symbol of the Living God beyond Decay.
Protect me, Silence! †!

   Next "hiss" forth long: *Sss! Sss!*
   Then "puff" saying: *†!*
   And thereon shalt thou see the Gods gazing benignly on thee, and no longer bearing down upon thee, but proceeding on the proper order of their doings.

V.
[The Second Instruction]
When, then, thou see'st the Upper Cosmos clean and clear, with no one of the Gods (or Angels) bearing down on thee, expect to hear a mighty thunder-clap so as to startle thee. Then say again:

VI.
[The [Second] Utterance (Logos)]
1. *O Silence! Silence!*

I am a Star, whose Course is as your Course, shining anew from out the depth †.

Upon thy saying this, straightway His disk will start expanding.

2. And after thou hast said the second utterance—to wit, twice *Silence* and the rest—"hiss" twice, and "puff" twice; and straightway shalt thou see a mighty host of stars, five-pointed, emerging from His Disk, and filling all the Air.

3. Then say again:

O Silence! Silence!

And when His Disk is opened [fully] out, thou shalt behold an infinite Encircling and Doors of Fire fast closed.

Straightway set going then the utterance that follows, closing thy eyes:

VII.

[The Third Utterance (Logos)]

1. *Hear me, give ear to me—N. N. [your name], son of N.N. (fem.) [your mother's name]—O Lord, who with Thy Breath hast closed the Fiery Bars of Heaven; Twin-bodied; Ruler of the Fire; Creator of the Light; O Holder of the Keys; Inbreather of the Fire; Fire-hearted One, whose Breath gives Light; Thou who dost joy in Fire; Beauteous of Light; O Lord of Light, whose Body is of Fire; Light-giver [and] Fire-sower; Fire-loosener, whose Life is in the Light; Fire-whirler, who sett'st the Light in motion; Thou Thunder-rouser; O Thou Light-glory, Light-increaser; Controller of the Light Empyrean; O Thou Star-tamer!*

2. *Oh! Open unto me! For on account of this, the bitter and implacable Necessity that presses on me, I do invoke Thy Deathless Names, innate with Life, most worshipful, that have not yet descended unto mortal nature, nor have been made articulate by human tongue, or cry or tone of man:*

Ëeö · oëeö · iöö · oë · ëeö · ëeö · oëeö · iöö · oëëe · öëe · öoë · ië · ëö · oö · oë · ieö · oë · öoë · ieöoë · ieeö · eë · iö · oë · ioë · öëö · eoë · oeö · öië · öiëeö · oi · iii · ëoë · öuë · ëö · oëe · eöëia · aëaeëa · ëeeë · eeë · eeë · ieö · ëeö · oëeeoë · ëeö · euö · oë · eiö · ëö · öë · öë · öë · ee · ooouiöë!

3. Utter all these with Fire and Spirit once unto the end; and then begin again a second time, until thou hast completed [all] the Seven Immortal Gods of Cosmos.

When thou hast uttered them, thunders and crashings shalt thou hear in the Surround, and feel thyself a-shake with every crash. Then once more utter *Silence!* [and] the utterance [following it].

4. Thereon open thy eyes; and thou shalt see the Doors thrown open, and the Cosmos of the Gods that is within the Doors; so that for joy and rapture of the sight thy Spirit runs to meet it, and soars up.

Therefore, hold thyself steady, and, gazing steadily into thyself, draw breath from the Divine.

When, then, thy Soul shall be restored, say:

VIII.
[The Fourth Utterance]
1. *Draw nigh, O Lord!*

Upon this utterance His Rays shall be turned on thee, and thou shalt be in the midst of them.

2. When, then, thou hast done this, thou shalt behold a God, in flower of age, of fairest beauty, [and] with Locks of Flame, in a white Tunic and a scarlet Mantle, wearing a Crown of Fire. Straightway salute Him with the Salutation of the Fire:

IX.
[The Fifth Utterance]
1. *Hail Lord! O Thou of mighty Power; O King of mighty Sway; Greatest of Gods; O Sun; Thou Lord of Heaven and Earth; O God of Gods! Strong is Thy Breath; strong is Thy Might!*

O Lord, if it seem good to Thee, make Thou announcement of me unto God Most-high, who hath begotten and created Thee!

2. *For that a man—I,* N.N. [your name], *son of* N.N. (fem.) [your mother's name], *born of the mortal womb* of N.N. (fem.) [your grandmother's name], *and of spermatic ichör, yea, of this [ichör], which at Thy Hands to-day hath undergone the transmutation of re-birth—one, from so many tens of thousands, transformed to immortality in this same hour, by God's good-pleasure, of God transcendent Good—[a man, I say,] presumes to worship Thee, and supplicates with whatsoever power a mortal hath.*

3. Upon this utterance He shall come to the Pole, and thou shalt see Him moving round as on a path.

Then gaze intently, and send forth a prolonged "bellowing," like to a horn-note, expelling the whole breath, with pressure on the ribs, and kiss the amulets, and say first to that upon the right:

X.

[The Sixth Utterance]

Protect me! †!

When thou hast uttered this, thou shalt behold the Doors thrown open, and, issuing from the Depth, Seven Virgins, in byssus-robes, with serpent-faces, and golden sceptres in their hands. These are they who are the so-called Heaven's Fortunes *(Tychai)*.

When thou dost see these things, make salutation thus:

XI.

[The Seventh Utterance]

1. *Hail Heaven's Seven Fortunes, Virgins august and good, ye sacred ones who live and eat with †! Ye holiest Protectors of the Four Supports!*

>*Hail thou, the First, †!*
>*Hail thou, the Second, †!*
>*Hail thou, the Third, †!*
>*Hail thou, the Fourth, †!*
>*Hail thou, the Fifth, †!*
>*Hail thou, the Sixth, †!*
>*Hail thou, the Seventh, †!*

2. There come forth others, too—Seven Gods, with faces of black bulls, in linen loin-cloths, with seven golden fillets on their heads. These are the so-called Heaven's Pole-lords.

And in like fashion unto each of them thou must make salutation with his special name.

XII.

[The Eighth Utterance]

1. *Hail Guardians of the Pivot, ye, sacred sturdy Youths, who all, at once, revolve the spinning Axis of Heaven's Circle, ye who let loose the thunder and the lightning, and earthquake-shocks and thunder-bolts upon the hosts of impious folk, but [who bestow] on me, who pious am and worshipper of God, good-health, and soundness of my frame in every Part, and proper stretch of hearing and of sight, and calm, in the now present good-hours of this day, O mighty Ruling Lords and Gods of me!*

Hail thou, the First, †!
Hail thou, the Second, †!
Hail thou, the Third, †!
Hail thou, the Fourth, †!
Hail thou, the Fifth, †!
Hail thou, the Sixth, †!
Hail thou, the Seventh, †!

2. Now when they [all] are present in their order, here and there, gaze in the Air intently, and thou shalt see lightnings down-flashing, and lights a-quiver, and the earth a-shake; and [then] a God descending, [a God] transcending vast, of radiant Presence, with golden Locks, in flower of age, [clad] in a Robe of brightness, with Crown of gold [upon His Head], and Garments [on His Legs], holding in His Right Hand the golden Shoulder of the Calf.

This latter is the Bear that moves the Heaven[-dome], and changes its direction, now up now down, according to the hour.

Then shalt thou see lightnings leap from His Eyes and from His Body stars.

3. Straightway send forth a "bellowing" prolonged, with belly-pressure, to start thy senses going all together prolonged unto the very end, kissing again the amulets and saying:

XIII.
[The Ninth Utterance]
†, *[O Lord] of me—N. N. [your name]—abide, with me, within my Soul! Oh! Leave me not! For † bids thee [remain].*

And gaze intently on the God, with "bellowing" prolonged, and thus salute Him:

XIV.
[The Tenth Utterance]
Hail Lord, Thou Master of the Water! Hail, Founder of the Earth! Hail, Prince of Breath! O Lord, being born again, I Pass away in being made Great, and, having been made Great, I die.

Being born from out the state of birth-and-death that giveth birth to [mortal] lives, I now, set free, pass to the state transcending birth, as Thou hast stablished it, according as Thou hast ordained and made the Mystery.

Chapter 7

THE GODDESS ANAHITA

Mighty Anahita with splendor will shine
Manifesting Herself as a maiden divine

Girded with Power, in fair robes dight
Her beauty shines forth like Heaven's light

A free-born virgin with healing hand
Chastely loving, with Mithra to stand

Clad in her cloak enriched with gold
The Goddess Anahita we shall behold

A REWORDED VERSION OF "ANAHITA HYMN" BY DICK ENEY*

According to some sources, Mithra's partner and virgin mother is the angel-goddess Anahita. (In Farsi, Mithra and Anahita are also called Mehr and Aban. For the full text of the Avestan hymn to Anahita, "Aban Yasht," see appendix B.) In Persian mythology, Anahita is the goddess of all the waters upon the earth and the source of the cosmic ocean; she drives a chariot pulled by four horses: wind, rain, cloud, and sleet; her symbol is the eight-rayed star. She is regarded as the source of life, purifying the seed of all males and the wombs of all females, also cleansing the milk in the breasts of all mothers. Because of her connection with life, warriors in battle prayed to her for survival and victory. Before calling on Mithra (fiery sun), a prayer was offered to the sea goddess Anahita. In the Avesta she is described as:

---

*This hymn has been reproduced here with the kind permission of Dick Eney.

a maid, fair of body, most strong, tall-formed, high-girded, pure, . . .
wearing a mantle fully embroidered with gold; ever holding the
baresma [sacred plant] in her hand, . . . she wears square golden earrings on her ears . . . a golden necklace around her beautiful neck, . . .
Upon her head . . . a golden crown, with a hundred stars, with eight
rays . . . with fillets streaming down.[1]

To expand upon the mystical and poetic possibilities, she might be further
envisioned as follows: A large silver throne; on either side of it sits a lion
with eyes of blue flame. On the throne sits a Lady in silver and gold garments, proud and tall, an awe-inspiring warrior-woman, as terrifying as
she is beautiful. Tall and statuesque she sits, her noble origins evident in
her appearance, her haughty authority made clear and commanding
through a pair of flashing eyes. A crown of shining gold rings her royal
temples; bejeweled with eight sunrays and one hundred stars, it holds her
lustrous hair back from her beautiful face. Her marblelike white arms
reflect moonlight, and glisten with moisture. She is clothed with a garment
made of thirty beavers, and it shines with the full sheen of silver and gold.
She is prayed to at dawn and dusk. The dove and peacock are said to be
her sacred creatures. The planet Venus is occasionally associated with
Anahita. Some have compared her to the goddesses Ishtar (Babylonian),
Innana (Sumerian), and Sarasvati (Hindu).[2]

The official entry on Anahita by the Embassy of the Islamic Republic
of Iran in Ottawa, Canada, reads:

1. Nearly every ancient religion has preserved the memory of the
   mother goddess in whose person people venerated the very principle of existence. It was a symbol of fertility and abundance, which
   the naïve image represented. These were represented, in varying
   degrees of crudity, in a female personage; and they are found on a
   great number of archaeological sites in the Iranian Plateau. The
   decorative repertory of the pottery of the fourth millennium is
   made up of such elements as the horns of a bull or an ibex, a bird's
   wing, a lion's head, and the foot of some wading birds, to mention
   but a few examples. Her cult was subsequently replaced by that of
   male deities, of whom she remained both wife and mother.

2. In the pre-Zoroastrian Iran, Anahita was the goddess for water,
   rain, abundance, blessing, fertility, marriage, love, motherhood,
   birth, and victory. This goddess was the manifestation of women's

Figure 7.1. A collection of Persian female statues at the British Museum; some may be representations of the goddess Anahita. (Photograph by Payam Nabarz. © Copyright The Trustees of The British Museum)

perfection. Ancient kings were crowned by their queens in Anahita's temple in order to gain her protection and support. Anahita's blessing would bring fertility and abundance to the country.[3]

If the number of children named after her is anything to go by, Anahita's influence is still felt strongly in modern Iran. She was recently depicted in an Iranian war movie in her role as the protector of children.

One can still find Anahita's shrines in the following places. (For more information, see the Web sites included in the "Notes.")

The Temple of Anahita at Kangavar near Kermanshah was built by the Achaemenian Emperor Ardeshir II (Artaxerxes II), 404–359 B.C.E. Full details of this temple are online.[4]

The Pre-Islamic Zoroastrian shrine of Pir e Sabz, or Chek Chek ("drip drip," the sound of water dripping), is in the mountains of Yazd. This is still a functional temple and the holiest site for present-day

Zoroastrians living in Iran, who take their annual pilgrimage to Pir e Sabz Banu, "the old woman in the mountain," also called Pir e Sabz, "the green saint," at the beginning of summer. *Pir* means "elder," and it can also mean "fire." The title of Pir connotes a Sufi master. *Sabz* means green.[5]

Pir e Banoo Pars (Elder Lady of Persia) and Pir e Naraki are located near Yazd. (The dates are unclear.) The Pir Banoo temple is in an area that has a number of valleys; the name of the place is Hapt Ador, which means Seven Fires.[6]

The Temple of Anahita in Bishapur was built during the Sassanian era (241–635 C.E.). The temple is believed to have been built by some of the estimated seventy thousand Roman soldiers and engineers who were captured by the Persian King Shapur (241–272 C.E.), who also captured three Roman emperors: Gordian III, Phillip, and Valerian. The design of the temple is very interesting: water from the river Shapur is channeled into an underground canal to the temple and actually goes under and all around the temple, giving the impression of an island. The fire altar would have been in the middle of the temple, with the water going underground all around it. One might interpret this as a union of water—Anahita—with fire—Mithra.[7]

In addition, the 1100-year-old shrine of Bibi Shahr Banoo, the Islamic female saint, near the 5000-year-old town of Rey (South of Tehran) with its waterfall is believed by some to have been an Anahita shrine at one time. It is also close to the Cheshmeh Ali Hill (spring of Ali Hill), which is dated to 5000 years ago. Perhaps an echo of Mithra-Anahita shrines being close to each other and then becoming linked to Islamic saints, a process seen frequently in Christianized Europe too; for example, sites sacred to the goddess Brigit became sites of Saint Brigit.

As this story by the Iranian writer Jalil Nozari demonstrates, the tradition of Anahita is very much alive.

Tomorrow (21.8.03), I will take part in a ceremony to commemorate a very poor, old woman, a relative of mine, who died recently. Her name was Kaneez. The name in modern Farsi has negative connotations, meaning a "female servant." But, in Pahlavi, the language spoken in central Iran before the coming of Islam, it meant "a maiden," a virgin, unmarried girl. Indeed, it has both meanings of the English "maid."

Figure 7.2. The Temple of Anahita in Bishapur, Iran, on the site of the ancient city built by Shapur I, Sassanian Emperor (241 C.E.–272 C.E.) in celebration of his victory over three Roman Emperors—Gordian III, Phillip, and Valerian. (Photograph by Jamshid Varza, reproduced here with his kind permission)

Anahita, too, means virgin, literally not defiled. But this is not the end of the story. When I was a child, there was a place in Ramhormoz, my hometown, that now is under a city road. In it, there was a small, single-room building with a small drain pipe hanging from it. Women in their ninth month and close to delivery time stood under this pipe and someone poured water through it. There was the belief that getting wet under the drain would assure a safe delivery of the baby. The building was devoted to Khezer (the green one).* Yet, the cult is very old and clearly one of Anahita's. The role of water and safe child delivery are both parts of the Anahita cult. My deceased aunt, our Kaneez, was a servant of this building. The building was demolished years ago to build a road, and Kaneez is no more. I wonder how we will reconstruct those eras, so close to us in time yet so far from our present conditions. It is also of interest that there exist remains of a castle, or better to say a fort, in Ramhormoz, that is called "Mother and Daughter." It belongs to the Sasanides era. "Daughter," signifying virginity, directs the mind toward Anahita. There are other shrines named after sacred women, mostly located beside springs of water. These all make the grounds for believing that Ramhormoz was one of the oldest places for Anahita worshippers.[8]

It has been suggested by some that many of the sacred sites and wells of Anahita were rededicated to Islamic female saints after the arrival of Islam in Persia. On his Web site on sacred sites, Martin Gray writes:

From those (Yazd) holy places only two, Pir-e Sabz and Naraki, have waterfalls at the present time. . . . Waterfalls and springs within such places had functioned as the holy places of Anahita, probably earlier than the Zoroastrian period, under Mithraism's effects. . . . A clue for this idea is that most of these holy places are initiated in relation to the women rather than the men. For example, Banoo in Pir-e Banoo means "lady" or "gentlewoman." Another example is Pir-e Sabz, which is related to Hayat Banoo, a holy woman, although with an inverted Arabic name. There is also a similar story for the initiation of Pir-e Naraki in relation to a holy lady. All of these relationships

---

*There is a folk tradition about Saint Khezer or Khidar (the green one): if one washes (pours water on) one's front door at dawn for forty days, he will appear. Khider is described as friend of the Sufis, and is said to stand at the boundary of sea and land. He is also said to have drunk from the fountain of immortality.

together, according to this theory, could be originated by the effect of Izad Anahita, which then converted to the more acceptable story of Yazdgerd's daughters and later on, due to necessity, converted to the story of those holy ladies with Arabic names.[9]

Furthermore, according to Susan Gaviri in *Anahita in Iranian Mythology* (1993):

. . . it must not be forgotten that many of the famous fire temples in Iran were, in the beginning, Anahita temples. Examples of these fire temples are seen in some parts of Iran, especially in Yazad, where we find that after the Muslim victory these were converted to Mosques.*

The higher social status of women in Iranian society compared to its Arab neighbors has been suggested by some to be due its long respect for Lady Anahita and Hazrat Fatemeh (peace be to her). Indeed, the first woman Muslim to win a Noble Peace Prize (2003) was from Iran; and Iran is one of the few Islamic countries to have numerous female senators and members of Parliament.

According to some academics, in the same way that there are parallels to be drawn between Anahita and Hazrat Fatemeh (peace be to her), similar parallels can be drawn between their respective husbands, Mithra and Hazrat Ali (peace be on him). Here we see another example of the importance of pre-Islamic Iran to the study of religious history. Though the heart of Sufism is rooted in Islam, the cultural influence of Persia can be mined for its rich veins of influence leading back into antiquity. After all, both "Sofreh" and "Deeg Jush" Sufi ceremonies potentially have their precursor in Zoroastrianism.

According to some, the path of Lord Mithra can be viewed as the red path and the path of Lady Anahita as the green path, and that these two paths must be in balance. It is an interesting coincidence that the countries of Iran and Italy—the two countries where Mithra and Anahita enjoyed the greatest devotion in earlier times—both have the same color scheme on their modern national flags: green, white, and red. We might speculate on the significance of these flags' colors: green, the color of Anahita/Venus/female; white, for peace, in the middle; and red, the color of Mithra/Sol/male. (This relates back to the point of the Indo-European

*Note this book is in Farsi—translation here by Payam Nabarz.

tripartite religious and social format that we explored in chapter 5.) It is tempting, also, to speculate that the Indian/Sanskrit words *Anahata* (in yoga, the heart chakra, corresponding to the color green) and *Anahita* might have similar roots; however, this requires confirmation by linguists.

And don't forget there is another interesting observation on relationships of mystical significance, concerning Mehr and Aban. (We already know that Mehr and Aban are the modern Persian names for Mithra and Anahita.) The autumn equinox marks the beginning of the Persian month of Mehr, and the start of the festival of Mehregan. The month of the sun god Mithra is followed by the month of the sea goddess Anahita (according to ancient sources both the partner and mother of Mithra). The month of the sun thus leads into the month of the sea. The sun sets into the ocean. Sunset over the ocean is one of the most beautiful sights there is; as the sun unites with the ocean, the light is reflected upon the water.

Mehr, coming together with Aban, gives rise to a third word: *mehra-ban*, which translates as "kindness," or "one who is kind." Thus, this metaphorical child of light that comes out of the marriage between Sun and Sea is *kindness*. The child of light is the Inner Light, which is in everyone. (This idea is further discussed in chapter 9, "The Four Stations of Mithra," in the section on the autumn equinox.)

The Sun (light of God) and the Sea (divine ocean), united within each person, create perhaps the most important spiritual quality—that of human kindness.

Chapter   8

MEDITATIONS AND INITIATIONS

The soul, having started on its downward course from the inter-
section of the zodiac and the Milky Way to the successive spheres
lying beneath, as it passes through these spheres, not only takes
on the aforementioned envelopment in each sphere by approach-
ing a luminous body, but also acquires each of the attributes that
it will exercise later. In the sphere of Saturn it obtains reason and
understanding, in Jupiter's sphere the power to act, in Mars's
sphere a bold spirit, in the Sun's sphere sense-perception and
imagination. In Venus's sphere the impulse of passion, in
Mercury's sphere the ability to speak and interpret and in the
lunar sphere the function of the molding and increasing bodies.
                    PLATONIST MACROBIUS'S COMMENTARY ON
            CICERO'S "SCIPIO'S DREAM," FIFTH CENTURY C.E.

The seven meditations in this chapter are designed to help the spiritual
seeker develop a deeper understanding of the Mithraic mysteries, an understanding that is based on personal experience, as well as to achieve the
seven degrees of initiation. Each meditation can be used as self-initiation
or as part of a group initiation. It is helpful to orient yourself to the meditations by reading through the text beforehand, so that when you undertake the initiation, you are fully prepared and able to give yourself to the
experience.

If you will be doing the meditation by yourself, you may find it helpful to tape yourself reading the text of the guided visualization out loud so
that stopping to read the directions won't interfere with your experience.

Alternatively, another person can read the text aloud to one or more participants. Note that the italicized comments within the meditation text such as, " . . . [Pause.]" or ". . . [Long pause.]" are there to indicate that the person who is reading the directions out loud should be quiet for a little while to allow participants to fully visualize the last part of the directions.

Each meditation begins and ends with a recitation of the Zoroastrian prayer "Namaz-i chahar nemag" (praise to the four directions).[1] The ideal and concept of Asha (Truth) mentioned in this prayer is similar to the Sufi concept of the divine name Al-Haqq (in Arabic: the Truth). This is the divine truth reflecting an understanding of the nature of reality.

At the beginning of each meditation this praise to the four directions is followed by a slight variation on the "by favor of Ahura Mazda Anahita, and Mithra. . ." prayer from an inscription from Susa by Achaemenian king Artaxerxes II Mnemon (404–359 c.e), which acts here as a protection prayer.

After you have recited the closing prayer for each meditation, you will need to take a few moments to bring yourself back to the here and now and become grounded. You will say your thanks to Mithra, and whatever company you find yourself in, and review the meditation you have just done in reverse, until you are back to where you started. Then you should open your eyes slowly and try eating and drinking something to ground yourself in everyday reality.

Sundays or the sixteenth day of any month would be favorable days for performing any of these meditations. The introductory text for each grade suggests the appropriate time of the day or night, which varies depending on the grade being performed. You should expect to perform each meditation several times before moving on to the next grade. A period of at least one year per grade would be suitable to develop an understanding of the significance of each level and to perfect its imagery. It might also be helpful to make notes afterward about your experiences in each meditation. You might even want to keep a magical diary.

The last four grades fit in well with the four stations of the sun (see chapter 9).

Leo (fire) grade: winter solstice, the birth of the sun and fire

Perses (Persian) grade: spring equinox, Persian New Year (Nou Roz)

Figure 8.1. In a new Mithraeum in Tuscany, the wall panel shows the symbols for the seven grades of Mithraic initiations; in front of it is an altar with a statue of Mithras slaying the bull, and on the left stands the leontocephaline. Temple of Mithras, Tuscany, Italy. (Photo by Guya Vichi)

Heliodromus (Sun Runner) grade: summer solstice, the height of the sun

Pater grade: autumn equinox, festival of Mithra (Mehregan)

I. CORAX MEDITATION AND INITIATION

Die before you die!

SUFI SAYING

In this first stage of Mithraic initiation, the Corax or Raven degree, the initiate falls under the influence of the planet Mercury. The first initiation symbolizes the death of the initiate and his rebirth into the spiritual world. (It was a custom in Zoroastrianism that when a person died, his or her body would be placed on a funeral pyre—the Tower of Silence—and left for the birds to eat. Zoroastrians in Bombay, India, still practice this "air burial.") By entering the first stage you leave the cares of the material world and enter upon a spiritual life.

This is not to suggest that you become a hermit and give all your possessions to charity, or to some guru. On the contrary, the Mithraic system is a very practical system—which is one reason it was so popular among Roman soldiers and merchants. The world is not evil, nor are money and material things. It is the excessive desire for and attachment to the material world that can be destructive to a spiritual path.

Find a place, indoors or outdoors, where you will not be disturbed. An appropriate time would be just before sunrise. An appropriate day would be a Sunday or the sixteenth day of the month, which is a day dedicated to Mithra. Use any paraphernalia that you find to have a helpful effect on your meditation, such as candles, music, or incense.

The more your physical conditions resemble the conditions in the meditation, the better. For example, a real bonfire just before sunrise on the top of a hill would enhance the experience. Stay up the whole night and tell each other stories about Mithra: his fight with the bull, his awesome birth, and other adventures. You might even try making a paper mask of a raven and wearing it.

In preparation for the guided visualization, you begin by imagining yourself as the Raven. Simply let yourself go, and enjoy the sensations of flight and of seeing the world below you from a bird's eye view. In your flight toward the mountain, if you find that you are feeling tired or unable to carry on, return consciousness to your body slowly and concentrate on your breathing. You should continue to work on this stage until you can easily transform yourself into a Raven. You are beginning to explore both the astral and physical worlds in this body.

Early in this meditation participants are asked to welcome Mithra by reciting all or part of the Avestan "Hymn to Mithra." The entire text of this hymn appears in appendix A but it is a very long script, and memorizing it is not easy. If you would rather recite a shortened version, I have transliterated the first section of the Avestan hymn and included it within the text of this meditation. You might try reading from it during the meditation, but this breaks the concentration to some extent. If you are performing the meditation by yourself, it would be better to record either the long or the short version of the hymn so that you can play it back when you reach the "Welcoming of Mithra" part of the meditation. When recording, pause long enough after each line to allow yourself time to repeat the line during your meditation. If performing the meditation as a group, one person can read out the guided visualization and the Hymn to Mithra while the rest of the group joins in to do the chanting (*Ya doust Mithra*) and the transitting.

The technique of transitting is based on one of the Sufi *zeker* (*dhikr*) techniques for putting oneself into a trance state through chanting and head movements.[2] To chant the *Ya doust Mithra*, begin with your head facing toward the left, and start intoning *Yaaa*. Move your head in an arc gently down toward the center of your body and then up toward your right shoulder, intoning *doooussst* at the same time. Next, bring your head down toward the chest, intoning *Miiitt*, and then raise your head up, intoning *raaaa*. You can repeat this a number of times and carry on for a few minutes, inducing a trance state. Move slowly, and be very careful with your neck muscles. Do not do it if you have neck injuries; simply chant.

You are standing at the bottom of a hill. It is very late at night. It is a clear night, and if you look up at the sky you can see the moon having almost completed its night journey into the west. . . . *[Pause.]*

Say in clear loud voice:
Nama (hail) *to Corax, under the protection of Mercury!*

Then recite the "Namaz-i chahar nemag" once facing East, once West, once South, and once North, respectively:
Homage to these places and these lands, and for these pastures, and these abodes with their hay-racks, and for the waters, land, and plants, and for this earth and for your heaven, and for the Asha-owning wind, and for the stars, moon, and sun, and for the eternal stars without beginning, and self-disposing, and for all the Asha-owning creatures of Spenta Mainyu (the bounteous spirit), male and female, the regulators of Asha. . . . [Pause.]

Then face center and say:
By the favor of Ahura Mazda, Anahita, and Mithra, this astral temple I build. May Ahura Mazda, Anahita, and Mithra protect me from all evil, and that which I have built may they not shatter nor harm.

Behind you is a dense pine forest. The grass under your feet is wet, and there are small patches of snow on the ground.

Looking up at the top of the hill, you see there a flicker of light. You start walking up the hill to find the source of this light. It is a long walk, yet you seem not to get tired, and the air becomes even fresher as you ascend. The sounds of the forest begin to fade away. The last sound you hear is the voice of an owl, saying "Hoo."

You are halfway up the hill now, yet still you cannot see the source of the light; so you increase your pace. As you near the top you can hear a chant, the words of which you can't make out, but you feel ever stronger, and you reach the top easily.

A great bonfire is burning, its flames reaching several feet into the air, and you can smell a strange yet pleasant incense. A group of people are sitting around the fire and chanting: *Ya doust Mithra.*

You join the chant. . . . *[Long pause for transitting as outlined above.]*

One of the men stands and faces east, toward a mountain range in the far-off distance. He is welcoming Mithra.*

1. *In the name of the Wise Spirit, who said to Zarathushtra:*
   My Beloved One who emanates celestial light.
   When I created Mithra, the Lord and Spirit of the endless green fields,
   I made Mithra equal to myself, as worthy of song and prayer as myself.

2. *My Beloved One who emanates celestial light.*
   When a person lies, he murders part of the World.
   This is a sin a hundred times worse than any other, always leading to a
       fight.
   Your word is your bond, a sign of Mithra; never break your word.

3. *Mithra—the Lord of vast green pastures—we do praise.*
   To "First Celestial God" our voices raise
   Mithra the Spirit of the endless green fields,
   Gives speed and strength to horses of those that do not lie.
   Atar the element of fire, the child of the Wise Spirit
   Shows them the fastest Way to their celestial soul, without the need
       to die.
   From their pure liberated celestial soul cometh forth
   Worthy offspring, the children of light.

---

*Note: As mentioned above, the entire Avestan "Hymn to Mithra" can be recited here (see appendix A) or you may simply recite this transliteration of the first part of the hymn.

4. A glorious song I will sing to the Spirit of the green pastures and the
      grazed lands.
   May Mithra bring happiness and goodness to the homes of the Magi.
   Come forth for our joy, victory, support, solving of problems, good
      health; ease our heartache and lend us a hand through all of life's tri-
      als and tribulations.

5. I pray to Mithra the unconquerable,
   The essence of the bountiful earth,
   One who, no matter where on earth, is undeceivable,
   One whose name is whispered at every hearth.

6. I raise my cup in offering to the powerful limitless Mithra.
   I sing my song to the Spirit of the Fields; I make an offering of sweet
      meat,
   Milk and blessed magical plants, my good deeds, chants, and mantra.
   Man and woman, who pray in this way, will know good feats.

7. Mithra—the Lord of vast green pastures—we do praise.
   To "First Celestial God" our voices raise.
   Making offering to the green spirit
   With a thousand ears and ten thousand eyes,
   The unseen lord of the skirret
   Sleepless, strong, who flies across the skies.

8. To whom for victory kings and warriors offer sacrifice
   With a cup of wine, song, and Indian spice.
   To whom traders ask for blessing for their merchandise,
   All for his glory and not for some sort of paradise.

9. In battle the side with a purer heart he supports,
   With the glorious lady of the wind.
   They rush forth from their heavenly courts,
   In aid of those with good thoughts and mind.

10. I sacrifice unto Mithra, the Lord of wide green pastures,
    Who is sleepless, ever awake, and makes my soul rapturous.
    (Repeat 7.)

11. Horsemen worship him from their saddles,
    Praying for swiftness and strength for their horses,
    And health for their own bodies and cattle's.
    On their enemies and adversaries, they will come down with full force.

12. I sacrifice unto Mithra, the Lord of wide green pastures,
    Who is sleepless, ever awake, and makes my soul rapturous.
    (Repeat 7.)

13. Mithra—the Lord of vast green pastures—we do praise.
    To First Celestial God' our voices raise,
    Before the sun shines from hilltops, indeed,
    The everlasting sun—Mithra—will proceed.
    It is the first being with ornaments of gold
    That from mountaintops the earth does behold.
    And from there, the powerful Mithra will
    Watch the abode of the Magi, calm and still.

14. Here the valiant knights gather in colored array,
    Where mountains are high and lakes are deep.
    In these green valleys where cattle are plenty
    And all receive the water from one who is never asleep.

15. With a beneficent eye he looks upon the seven continents
    From the north to south, from east to the west,
    And to the middle lands, and worlds of eminence,
    To the green place of cattle, Mithra looks with healing interest.

16. Mithra moves across all countries, as an unseen light.
    Bringing glory, strength, sovereignty, and victory to those with holy
        intent.

17. Unto whom no one must lie,
    Neither lord of the manor nor innkeeper,
    Nor a landlady, nor a child.

18. If lord of the manor, or the innkeeper,
    Or landlady or child lies unto Mithra,
    He will be offended.

19. *Mithra will stand against the side that lies unto him, angry and offended.*

20. *The horses of those who break their contract will fail them,*
    The spell and spears they fling will dart backward at them.

21. *If their spears reach their targets they make no wound,*
    And their spells make no sound.
    The winds blow away the spear and spell that the enemies of Mithra fling.
    (Repeat 4, 5, and 6.)

22. *Mithra—the Lord of vast green pastures—we do praise.*
    To "First Celestial God" our voices raise.
    Who removes obstacles from those who do not lie,
    Who gives and takes away as he should please,
    Who throws down misery on those who lie.
    To truth tellers he brings death with ease.
    We sacrifice unto Mithra, the Lord of wide pastures—sleepless, and
       ever awake.

As the first rays of the sun come over the distant mountain and fall into the vast valley beneath, you see in the distance, heading toward you, a golden chariot driven by four white horses: Mithra rides across the sky, heading toward the hill. You look around and see that the snow patches are all melting away and the grass is growing under your feet. The land is waking up. A withered tree further along on the hill suddenly begins to grow buds, and while you are looking at it, leaves unfurl and the tree blossoms.

The sound of horses brings your attention back to the sky. As you look up, the chariot is almost above the hill now. Mithra looks down and smiles at the gathering. As the chariot passes overhead, all your companions rise into the air, and you too, after vibrating "Mithra" with all your magical will, rise into the air, following Mithra as he rides across the sky. . . . *[Pause.]*

As Mithra's company flies over, the landscape below turns green and all the trees burst into bloom. As you pass over a herd of cows, their udders fill with milk.

Another mountain range lies ahead; before it there is a great lake with flocks of sheep drinking from it. As you fly over the lake you look at your own reflection in the water: you see a Raven. . . . *[Long pause.]*

Finish the rite by reciting the "Namaz-i chahar nemag" again, in reverse order this time, first facing North, then South, West, and East, respectively: *Homage to these places and these lands, and for these pastures, and these abodes with their hay-racks, and for the waters, land, and plants, and for this earth and for your heaven, and for the Asha-owning wind, and for the stars, moon, and sun, and for the eternal stars without beginning, and self-disposing, and for all the Asha-owning creatures of Spenta Mainyu, male and female, the regulators of Asha. . . . [Pause.]*

In your mind review all that you have seen and heard, then return through the meditation until you again find yourself at the starting place at the bottom of the hill. Give thanks to Mithra and to all the guides and fellow travelers you met on your journey. Then open your eyes to return to normal consciousness, and have something to eat and drink to ground yourself in everyday reality.

II. NYMPHUS MEDITATION AND INITIATION

In the second stage, that of Nymphus, or male bride, the initiate is under the influence of the planet Venus. At this point the initiate is prepared to become a bride to Mithra in a spiritual sense, in a similar manner to a nun becoming a bride of Christ (a process of enflaming the heart). The word *nymphus* means "bee chrysalis" as well as "bridegroom"; hence, along with becoming a bride of Mithra, the initiate is seen as one who will one day become a bee. The significance of bees and honey is seen in the Leo and Perses degrees.

In the Roman cult, the idea of celibacy may have been central at this point. This would have been easily practiced in the Roman army: the soldiers would have spent most of their time in the barracks or moving around the empire. Even now most armies allow only a short "shore leave." (If you are stationed on an aircraft carrier for six months at a time, you won't have a chance for sex anyway!) For the followers of Mithras, it would have been rather handy to practice celibacy while spending months fighting an enemy in some remote part of the empire.

These days, the entire modern pagan movement is against the idea of suppressing sexuality. Paganism is at its heart a celebration of life and sexuality. Becoming celibate is neither practical nor likely, and I do not suggest it as a way of life.

What I do suggest, however, is a period without sexual involvement. Another way to think of it is that, while you are away from your partner, on a business trip (or war campaign), Mithra is your partner for that time. Initiates who are married might have some problem explaining to their partner night after night that they have a headache. Therefore, the length of time you refrain from sex—be it a week or a year—is left up to you to decide, depending on your circumstances.

Before starting the next meditation at midday, try fasting for few hours (no food or drink), or just skip breakfast. Have a wash (ritual bath) and dress in clean clothing. Remember this is your wedding day! Investing in a gold wedding ring would be advantageous—wearing it will remind you of Mithra.

As with the previous meditation, the more that your physical surroundings resemble the scene of the meditation, the better. Carrying out this stage in a cave would be great.

Expose a loaf of bread to sunlight for a few hours beforehand. The piece of bread and the ritual drink consumed during this meditation should be the first things an initiate has had for several hours. The drink can be some sort of herbal tea with sugar—representing Homa, the legendary trance-producing drink associated with the cult of Mithra (see chapter 3). As the exact identity of this drink is lost to us, we must use alternatives. I leave the exact choice of alternative up to you. A good one might be milk with honey mixed in or wine or honey mead, if you prefer a drink with alcohol. Another alternative, as mentioned in the Eleusinian mysteries, would be water with grain soaked in it or you could substitute a sun-ripened hops and barley beer.

Technically, all the energy (food) that we consume does come from the sun through the food chain: Plants absorb the sunlight and make sugar, the herbivores eat them, and we eat the plants and the herbivores. Therefore, we already have the sun in us.

Take a few moments and, in your mind's eye, go through your experiences of the first meditation. After you see your reflection as a Raven in the lake, continue your flight toward the distant mountain range.

Say:
Nama to the Bridegrooms, under the protection of Venus!

Then recite the "Namaz-i chahar nemag" once facing East, once West, once South, and once North, respectively:

Homage to these places and these lands, and for these pastures, and these abodes with their hay-racks, and for the waters, land, and plants, and for this earth and for your heaven, and for the Asha-owning wind, and for the stars, moon, and sun, and for the eternal stars without beginning, and self-disposing, and for all the Asha-owning creatures of Spenta Mainyu (the bounteous spirit), *male and female, the regulators of Asha. . . . [Pause.]*

Then face center and say:

By the favor of Ahura Mazda, Anahita, and Mithra, this astral temple I build. May Ahura Mazda, Anahita, and Mithra protect me from all evil, and that which I have built may they not shatter nor harm.

Once you get near the mountain you see a great cave with a river flowing outside of it. You fly toward it, and land in front of it. You now transform back from a Raven into your human body. The cave is dark and all your surroundings are quiet. The river is in front of you.

Are you prepared to step into the cave? Do you have the courage? . . . *[Pause.]*

You walk for a while in the cave and allow your eyes to get used to the darkness. . . . *[Pause.]*

What do you see? What shapes come out of the darkness? Are you afraid? . . . *[Pause.]*

Eventually you see some light ahead and you continue on. You are now standing in a large cavern, and there is a circular opening in the roof that allows a shaft of light to come through. In the middle of the light, there is a loaf of bread and a cup of some herbal drink.

You walk into the shaft of light. Looking up, you see that the sun is directly above the hole and it engulfs you in its light. You pick up the loaf of bread and eat some. This bread has been absorbing the sunlight for many hours and now you, by eating it, are taking this energy of the sun directly into your self. You drink from the cup filled with Homa; it is cooling and sweet, and as you drink you begin to see more clearly. The whole cave is alight now. . . . *[Pause.]*

In one corner, you see a statue of Mithra, which you had not noticed before. It is a large statute made of marble. In front of it stands an altar, on top of which there is a sliver tray, and on that, a golden ring.

You follow your emotion and make your marriage vows as you see fit. . . . *[Long pause.]*

You place the ring on your second finger.

You hear:
Hail Nymphus, hail New Light.

You are now Nymphus. . . . *[Long pause.]*
Finish the rite by reciting the "Namaz-i chahar nemag" in reverse order
again, first facing North, then South, West, and East, respectively:
*Homage to these places and these lands, and for these pastures, and these
abodes with their hay-racks, and for the waters, land, and plants, and for this
earth and for your heaven, and for the Asha-owning wind, and for the stars,
moon, and sun, and for the eternal stars without beginning, and self-disposing,
and for all the Asha-owning creatures of Spenta Mainyu, male and female, the
regulators of Asha. . . . [Pause.]*

In your mind review all that you have seen and heard, then return back
through the meditation until you find yourself once more at the mouth
of the cave with the river flowing by. Give thanks to Mithra and to all the
guides and fellow travelers you met on your journey. When you are ready,
open your eyes slowly to return to the here-and-now and center yourself
as before by having something to eat and drink.

III. MILES MEDITATION AND INITIATION

The third stage, Miles, is that of a soldier, and the initiate is under the
influence of the planet Mars. At this point the initiate is proving his warrior qualities, as in the previous stages he has shown his lack of interest in
materialism and his love for Mithra. A good time for carrying out this
meditation would be at sunset.

If this stage is carried out in a group rather than as a solitary meditation, the following can be added: The initiate should kneel down, be blindfolded and hands tied. Then on the point of a sword, a crown should be
offered for the initiate to wear. He or she will refuse this, saying: "Mithra
is my crown." The bonds are then cut by the sword—very carefully.

At this stage in the ancient cult, the branding of initiates was carried
out. To accomplish the same thing in a less radical and damaging way, you
might choose while at this stage to have a tattoo applied somewhere dis-
creetly, either a henna tattoo or a permanent one, if you so desire.

Begin with the first meditation as you did before. After you see your reflection in the lake, continue your flight toward the distant mountain range and the cave of the Nymphus meditation.

In your mind's eye, revisit the cave with the river flowing by that you entered to become a Nymphus. You are still in the cave, in front of the statue of Mithra. You have finished making your vows and are wearing the gold ring.

Say:
Nama to the Soldiers, under the protection of Mars!

Then recite the "Namaz-i chahar nemag" once facing East, once West, once South, and once North, respectively:
Homage to these places and these lands, and for these pastures, and these abodes with their hay-racks, and for the waters, land, and plants, and for this earth and for your heaven, and for the Asha-owning wind, and for the stars, moon, and sun, and for the eternal stars without beginning, and self-disposing, and for all the Asha-owning creatures of Spenta Mainyu (the bounteous spirit), male and female, the regulators of Asha. . . . [Pause.]

Then face center and say:
By the favor of Ahura Mazda, Anahita, and Mithra, this astral temple I build. May Ahura Mazda, Anahita, and Mithra protect me from all evil, and that which I have built may they not shatter nor harm.

Two torchbearers approach and tell you to follow. Their faces seem familiar, yet you are unable to fully recognize them.
    After following them through the narrow passages of the cave, you reach another cavern, larger than the last one. You can hear the sound of running water.
    In the middle of the cavern, there is a Ring of Fire, about nine feet in diameter. Inside the Ring of Fire, there seem to be some objects; however, you cannot see them clearly from where you are.
    The torchbearers break their silence by telling you: *The exit of the cave lies on the other side of the fire. Go through it and claim your prize.*
    As you approach the fire, you understand where the sound of run-

ning water came from. Around the fire platform is a canal, five feet across, that spirals around the fire. Two steps lead down into the water. You must descend into the canal. . . . *[Pause.]*

The water is very cold, its source a mountain spring higher up. Your body starts shivering. The water reaches up to your chest. Unless you continue moving, you will freeze. You walk in the canal, following its spiral path, getting closer to the center and the fire platform. As you move closer to center, the water depth increases and the canal becomes narrower.

Having made several turns, you reach the three steps that lead out of the water and onto the platform. The flowing water passes through openings on either side of the steps.

You ascend onto the platform, feel the heat of the fire, and walk through the Ring of Fire. Your hair singes, and you can smell the sulfur as you pass through. . . . *[Pause.]*

Within the fire, there is a sword, a helmet, body armor, a spear, and a red shield.

You pick these objects up and dress as a soldier. You are now Miles. . . . *[Long pause.]*

The fire subsides and the water stops flowing; the torchbearers are standing on the other side. You find you are able to jump over the canal to reach the other side. The torchbearers lead you out of the cave and into a clearing. The cool air is refreshing; the sun has already set. . . . *[Long pause.]*

Finish the rite by reciting the "Namaz-i chahar nemag" in reverse order once again, first facing North, then South, West, and East, respectively: *Homage to these places and these lands, and for these pastures, and these abodes with their hay-racks, and for the waters, land, and plants, and for this earth and for your heaven, and for the Asha-owning wind, and for the stars, moon, and sun, and for the eternal stars without beginning, and self-disposing, and for all the Asha-owning creatures of Spenta Mainyu, male and female, the regulators of Asha.* . . . *[Pause.]*

In your mind review all that you have seen and heard, then bring yourself back through the meditation, back to the here-and-now, and center yourself as before. Give thanks to Mithra and to all the guides and fellow travelers you met on your journey. Then open your eyes to return to normal consciousness and have something to eat and drink to ground yourself.

IV. LEO MEDITATION AND INITIATION

In this fourth stage, the initiate is under Jupiter's influence. Draw the symbols of Leo—the fire shovel, the thunderbolt, and the rattle (sistrum)—on a white piece of paper and place it on your altar. Also place a large red candle, a rattle, a jar of honey, an incense burner, and any other fiery symbols on the altar. Jupiter incense can be purchased from a number of occult suppliers both on-line and in shops. This meditation can be performed indoors or outdoors. Try to set the scene as much as possible. If done outdoors it would be great to make a real bonfire; otherwise use candles. Either way, be prepared to burn more incense at the point in your meditation when you enter the bonfire, and to eat a spoonful of honey when visualizing the purification step. This rite should be performed at night.

The "Queen of Heaven" prayer used in this initiation has been borrowed from modern Wicca. In Wiccan rituals it is an invocation used at the winter solstice. Winter solstice is the time of the birth of the sun and the return of fire and light, which fits in with the birth of the initiate, who becomes a "new child of light and fire."

The following line, which is repeated three times, is from the Santa Prisca Mithraeum: "Receive the incense burners, Father, receive the Lions, Holy One, through whom we offer incense, through whom we offer ourselves consumed!" The "incense burner" is the initiate, who is consumed in the fire and passion of Mithras. A similar spiritual idea exists among the Sufis, where the initiate is seen as the moth and God as the candlelight. The moth reaches "enlightenment" as it burns in the flame.

In the wall paintings at the Santa Prisca Mithraeum, masked lion figures bring gifts of food to Mithras at the ritual meal. The Leos appear to be given the role of performing an act of service.

The last passage, "In the lion mysteries . . ." is from the letters of Porphyry, from the third century C.E.

♌

Visualize yourself as you were at the end of the Miles meditation, when you were led by the torchbearers into a clearing, dressed as a soldier. Now you are standing alone in front of a golden door. The area around the door appears dry and you feel warmth emanating from the door. The door has the symbols of the lion grade on it: the fire shovel on the left, the thunderbolt in the middle, and the rattle on the right.

In a loud and clear voice say:
Nama to the Lions, under the protection of Jupiter.

Then recite the "Namaz-i chahar nemag" once facing East, once West, once South, and once North, respectively:
Homage to these places and these lands, and for these pastures, and these abodes with their hay-racks, and for the waters, land, and plants, and for this earth and for your heaven, and for the Asha-owning wind, and for the stars, moon, and sun, and for the eternal stars without beginning, and self-disposing, and for all the Asha-owning creatures of Spenta Mainyu (the bounteous spirit), *male and female, the regulators of Asha.* . . . *[Pause.]*

Then face center and say:
By the favor of Ahura Mazda, Anahita, and Mithra, this astral temple I build. May Ahura Mazda, Anahita, and Mithra protect me from all evil, and that which I have built may they not shatter nor harm. . . . *[Pause.]*

You hear a response from behind the door:
Fire, fire, fire, flames, rays of the sun, warm light, shining stars, and sun.

[Shake your rattle four times and light a red candle, and then place some Jupiter incense or corresponding herb on your incense burner.]
    State the reason why you seek to enter the realm of the Lion. . . . *[Pause.]*
    The door opens, and flying out of it are hundreds of bees, heading for you. Your immediate reaction is to draw your sword and put up your shield. The bees land all over you and begin to sting you. You try to stop them with your shield and sword, but to no avail.
    The two torchbearers come out of the door; they are wearing fiery red cloaks and lion's masks. They say to you:
You the brave warrior, the Miles who picked the flaming sword, who is full of valor and passed through the gates of Mars and its ordeals, are unable to defend yourself against tiny bees!

You are in too much pain to respond; the bees are still stinging you, and the ones that you thought you had killed seem to be alive still. . . . *[Pause.]*
    The torchbearers say:
Miles, did you not say, "My crown is Mithras"? And now you try to fight his bees

and you are failing. To pass through these doors you need more than strength, power, or knowledge.

You become aware that for all your strength, fighting ability, and bravery, you cannot defend yourself against the bees, and their sting, which is burning you. A great bear can be brought down by a pack of wolves. You stop fighting, place your sword back in its scabbard, and say:
I feel the burning stings of the bees on my skin. My body feels like it's on fire. Pater Leonum (Father of Lions), I am here now in humbleness to enter thy mysteries. . . . [Pause.]

The two torchbearers roar like lions and as they approach with their torches, the bees fly back toward the door.

The two torchbearers lead you to the door and you enter. Lined up on either side you see seven lion-masked people, all wearing fiery red cloaks and holding torches. At the end of the line stands a large lion—or is it another masked person? It is difficult to focus on the lion: one moment it appears as a masked person, and the next moment it appears as a full-sized lion. . . . *[Pause.]*

The two torchbearers address the Lion:
Here stands a new lion cub. Pater Leonum, will you take him with you?

The Lion speaks your name as it replies:
[Your name], come and run with me.

You find yourself running very fast with the lion-masked person. You can hear the sound of drums and the roars of lions around you. It feels as if you are running on warm, dry sand. Very soon you can see bright flames on the horizon, and as you approach them you too begin to roar, and your speed increases. How do you see yourself? You are turning into a lion, running with four legs; your senses and awareness are altering. You are running faster, the bright flames are closer now, they come from a large bonfire and around it others dressed as lions are circling, and saying:
Queen of the Moon, Queen of the Sun,
Queen of Heavens, Queen of the Stars,
Queen of the Waters, Queen of the Earth,
Bring to us the Child of Promise,
It is the Great Mother, who giveth birth to him,

It is the Lord of Life, who is born again,
Darkness and tears are set aside,
When the sun shall come up early,
Golden sun of the mountains, illuminate the land,
Light up the world; illuminate the seas and the rivers,
Sorrows be laid, joy to the world,
Blessed be the Great Goddess, without beginning, without end,
Everlasting to eternity, He blessed be.

The Father of Lions looks back and says:
We are jumping through the bonfire.

Moments later, you are faced with the fire. Will you jump through it?

As you jump and feel the flames touch you, for a moment you are certain that you have turned into a lion. Suddenly time stops—all goes quiet—you are at the height of your jump, in mid air above the fire. . . . *[Pause.]*

In the fire you see the figure of the Leontocephaline (lion-headed one), the lord of time. In front of him stands the Father of Lions and as you stand next to him, you see the lightning from the Leontocephaline spreading all around the three of you.

In front of you are two golden incense burners. Engraved on one is your name and on the other the name of the Father of the Lions. The Father of Lions and you say the following:
Receive the incense burners, Father, receive the Lions, Holy One, through whom we offer incense, through whom we offer ourselves consumed!

You repeat it louder:
Receive the incense burners, Father, receive the Lions, Holy One, through whom we offer incense, through whom we offer ourselves consumed!

And now you repeat even louder, full of fire and passion:
Receive the incense burners, Father, receive the Lions, Holy One, through whom we offer incense, through whom we offer ourselves consumed!

You feel yourself being consumed by fire. The Father of Lions faces you and says:
You are becoming a shining beacon. Aim for your acts to be of some help and service

to humanity and the world's creatures. Service is the task of the Lions, and this begins by your taking part in the cooking and serving of the ritual meal. In everyday life, aim to help others. . . . [Pause.]

Time begins to move again, and you land on the other side of the bonfire. All this has taken place in an instant. You are greeted by the two torchbearers, and a huge lion's roar from everyone else. They ask you to stretch your arms forward, palms facing up. They pour honey on your hands and place a spoonful in your mouth while saying:
In the Lion mysteries, honey is poured instead of water for purification on the hands of initiates. You are exhorted to keep yourself pure from everything distressing, harmful, and loathsome; and since you are an initiate of fire, which has a cathartic effect, we use on you a liquid related to fire, rejecting water as inimical to it. We also use honey to purify the tongue from all guilt.

You are then given a lion's mask and a red cloak, to wear as a Leo. . . . *[Long pause.]*

Finish the rite by reciting the "Namaz-i chahar nemag" in reverse order once again, first facing North, then South, West, and East respectively:
Homage to these places and these lands, and for these pastures, and these abodes with their hay-racks, and for the waters, land, and plants, and for this earth and for your heaven, and for the Asha-owning wind, and for the stars, moon, and sun, and for the eternal stars without beginning, and self-disposing, and for all the Asha-owning creatures of Spenta Mainyu, male and female, the regulators of Asha. . . . [Pause.]

In your mind review all that you have seen and heard during this meditation, bringing yourself back through the meditation to the here-and-now, centering yourself as before. Give thanks to Mithra and to all the guides and fellow travelers you met on your journey. Then open your eyes to return to normal consciousness, and have something to eat and drink to ground yourself.

V. Perses Meditation and Initiation

The initiate in this fifth degree is under the protection of the Moon—and the Moon, in every bull-slaying, is depicted as female. The symbols are the harpe (carved sword), the sickle, the crescent moon, and an eight-rayed star. We are certain of little about this grade other than the knowledge that in the ancient cult the initiates were offered honey. Honey was known as a preserver of fruits, and it is this preservative power that is treated symbolically here.

Professor Franz Cumont and Professor David Ulansey both argue that the harpe (carved sword) of this grade connects it to Perseus. The harpe was the weapon used by Perseus to decapitate the Gorgon. Ulansey points out that Perseus had a son named Perses, and that the seventh grade—Father—coincides with Perseus (= Mithras). Ulansey also suggests that the bull-slaying by Mithras is similar to Perseus slaying the Gorgon, with both heroes facing away from their enemies.[3] I have used these ideas as part of the meditation and have added a Gnostic element to it, equating the bull to the ego, as seen in Sufism.

The presence of Luna, a female figure in all bull-slaying scenes, at one of the highest grades, is interesting for a "male mystery" religion and may indicate an initiation to some goddess aspect. I have included my adaptation of the "Hymn to Anahita" (appendix B contains the full hymn), at the point where the initiate is faced with the goddess whose chariot is driven by lions. This image of the goddess is from A. P. Long, *In a Chariot Drawn by Lions: The Search for the Female in Deity*.[4] The description of the goddess I give is that of Anahita as described in *Wise Lord of the Sky: Persian Myth*,[5] and the "Hymn to Anahita." She wears the eight-rayed crown; note that the eight-rayed star is one of the symbols of this grade.

I place this grade at the spring equinox, the Persian New Year, and the lines that begin with "I kindle this fire today . . ." are from a Wiccan spring equinox prayer, which links well to the Persian grade. I have also drawn upon part of the "Mithraic Liturgy."

The tools required for this meditation are a large bowl to fill with water, used to reflect the full moon's light, white candles, a rattle, honey, incense, and a wand, symbolizing the bundle of twigs known as a barsom or baresman (see chapter 3). You can purchase the necessary wand from a variety of staffs and wands that are available from occult suppliers—or even better, make your own.

The rite is to be done at night on or near the time of the full moon, outdoors if possible.

☽

When you are ready to begin, visualize yourself dressed as you were at the end of the Leo meditation, in a red cloak and a lion's mask. It is night, and you are standing under a full moon, in front of a silver curtain. The area around the curtain appears dry, and you feel a gentle, warm breeze emanating from the curtain. The curtain has the symbols of the Perses grade on it: the eight-rayed star on the left, the sickle on the right, and the harpe (carved sword) in the middle.

In a loud and clear voice, say:
Nama to the Persians, under the protection of the Moon!

Then recite the "Namaz-i chahar nemag" once facing East, once West, once South, and once North, respectively:
Homage to these places and these lands, and for these pastures, and these abodes with their hay-racks, and for the waters, land, and plants, and for this earth and for your heaven, and for the Asha-owning wind, and for the stars, moon, and sun, and for the eternal stars without beginning, and self-disposing, and for all the Asha-owning creatures of Spenta Mainyu (the bounteous spirit), male and female, the regulators of Asha. . . . [Pause.]

Then face center and say:
By the favor of Ahura Mazda, Anahita, and Mithra, this astral temple I build. May Ahura Mazda, Anahita, and Mithra protect me from all evil, and that which I have built may they not shatter nor harm. . . . [Pause.]

You hear a response from behind the door:
Blue Fire, silver flames, rays of the moon, moonlight, shining Luna.

[Stare into your silver bowl filled with water; move the bowl until you can see the reflection of the full moon in it. Shake your rattle five times, and light a white candle, and then place some moon incense on your incense burner. . . . Pause.]
    While staring at the reflection of the moon in the water, you state your reason why you seek to enter the realm of the Perses. . . . *[Pause.]*
    The curtains open, and the two torchbearers come out. They are wearing fiery red cloaks and lion's masks, and hanging from their belts are harpe swords. They say to you:

Few enter the realm of Perses, under the Moon. Here you will be faced with things only seen under the light of the Moon. Are you sure you want enter here? And meet Lady Luna?

You answer them, and state your reasons why again. . . . *[Pause.]* Then the two torchbearers lead you in through the silver curtain. You enter a large courtyard, with a large pool in the middle; the whole courtyard and pool is bathed in moonlight, and the full moon above appears much brighter on this side of the curtain.

In one corner of the courtyard you see a great silver chariot, and harnessed to it are two real lions. You look into their eyes, and you can see blue flames glowing out of them.

As you follow the torchbearers toward the temple at the eastern end of the courtyard, you begin to notice the sweet smell of honeysuckle flowers, and you notice that growing up the temple pillars are honeysuckle plants.

In the eastern quarter, you are faced with another silver curtain, an entrance to the inner sanctum. The torchbearers say:

You have traveled far; you flapped your wings and croaked as Raven. You carried the caduceus, and saw the mysteries of Mercury.

You became the bridegroom of Mithras, felt the love of Venus, and fell in love with your Lord Mithras. As a Nymphus we saw you could one day become bearer of fire, and we hailed you as a new light.

You then became his chivalrous soldier, and marched under his blood red Mars banner.

You jumped into the fire and Jupiter, the Father of Lions, and the Leontocephaline transformed you to a burning flame, the first spark of you becoming a light of all worlds.

Now you stand here under the gentle moonlight, no longer flying as a Raven, no longer just in love with your Lord, no longer a battle-driven soldier slaying your inner and outer enemies, and reaching beyond the fiery lion. The next three realms are linked to each other in the way that a nuclear family is linked: Pater, Mater, and child.

They ask you:
Do you have a prayer to offer?

You recite the following:
I kindle this fire today [light another candle]

In the presence of the Holy Ones,
Without malice, without jealousy, without envy,
Without fear of aught beneath the Sun
But the High Gods.
Thee I invoke, O Light of Life,
Be Thou a bright flame before us,
Be Thou a guiding star above us,
Be Thou a smooth path beneath us;
Kindle Thou within our hearts
A flame of love for our neighbors
To our foe, to our friends, to our kindred all,
To all men on the broad earth.
O merciful Son of Anahita,
From the lowliest thing that liveth
To the Name which is highest of all.
O Sun, be thou as armed to conquer the dark. . . . [Pause.]

You hear laughter from beyond, and a female voice says:
Are you really armed to conquer the dark? Are you going to hop on one leg—rather than walking on two? You need both, light and dark.

The curtain opens, and you and the two torchbearers enter the inner sanctum and stand facing a large silver throne; on either side of it sits a lion with eyes of blue flame. On the throne sits a Lady in silver and gold garments, proud and tall, an awe-inspiring warrior woman, as terrifying as she is beautiful. Tall and statuesque she sits, her noble origins evident in her appearance, her haughty authority made clear and commanding through a pair of flashing eyes. A crown of shining gold rings her royal temples, bejeweled with eight sunrays and one hundred stars; it holds her lustrous hair back from her beautiful face. Her white marblelike arms reflect the moonlight and glisten with moisture. She is clothed with a garment made of thirty beavers, and it shines with the full sheen of silver and gold. . . . *[Pause.]*

You feel lightheaded and confused. You—an initiate of a male mystery cult—a warrior, a lion, a raven, and bridegroom, are faced with a goddess. You recall that in all the bull-slaying scenes you have seen, the Lady Luna is facing her brother Sol.

You ask the Lady who she is, and she replies:
I am she who makes the seed of all males fertile, who makes the womb of all females

ripe for bringing forth, who makes all females give birth in safety, who puts milk into the breasts of all females in the right measure and the right quality.

All the waters are my realms. The largest river, known afar, that is as large as the whole of the waters that run along the earth; that runs powerfully from the highest mountain down to the depth of the sea. All the shores of the sea overflow, and all the middle of it overflow, when I run down there, when I stream down there; I, Anahita, have a thousand cells and a thousand channels: the extent of each of those cells of each of those channels is as much as a man can ride in forty days, riding on a good horse. . . . [Pause.]

From this river of mine alone flow all the waters that spread all over the seven continents; this river of mine alone goes on bringing waters, both in summer and in winter. This river of mine vitalizes the seeds in males, the womb in females, the milk in females' breasts. I came forth, lion cub, down from those stars to the earth.

You look at her beautiful white arms, muscular as a horse's shoulder or still stronger; beautiful are her hips, and thus came she, mighty, with strong arms. She says:

Who will praise me? Who will offer me a sacrifice, with libations cleanly prepared and well strained, together with the Homa and meat? To whom shall I cleave, who cleaves unto me, and thinks with me, and bestows gifts upon me, and is of good will unto me?

You reply:

For your brightness and glory, I will offer you a sacrifice worth being heard; I will offer up unto the Goddess Anahita a good sacrifice with an offering of libations. Thus mayest thou advise me when thou art appealed to! Mayest thou be most fully worshipped, O Anahita! With the Homa and meat, with the baresma, with boiling milk, with the wisdom of the tongue, with the holy spells, with the words, with the deeds, with the libations, and with the rightly spoken words. . . . [Pause.]

I offer a sacrifice, to the water springs of Anahita, who is strong and bright, tall and beautiful of form, who sends down by day and by night a flow of motherly waters as large as the whole of the waters that run along the earth, and who runs powerfully. . . . [Pause.]

For your brightness and glory, I offer you a sacrifice. Anahita, you who came from those stars down to the earth. . . . [Pause.]

She says:

I came forth, lion cub and honey mouth, down from the stars to the earth. The men of strength beg of me swift horses and glory.

The wise who read and the students beg of me knowledge and prosperity,
and the victory made by my crushing ascendant.
The maids of barren womb, longing for a man, beg of me a strong
husband;
Women, on the point of childbirth, beg of me a good delivery.
All this I grant unto them, as it lies in my power.

I am keeper of the whole of the holy creation. Through my brightness and glory,
flocks and herds and two-legged men go on, upon the earth: I, forsooth, keeper of
all good things, just as a shepherd keeps his flock. What is it that you seek, my
honey-mouthed child?

You reply:
Secret of secrets that art hidden in the heart of all that lives, Great Goddess, I seek
to enter the realm of Perses and affiliate myself to the people of Magi. . . . [Pause.]

She says:
You seek to become a son of Perseus-Mithras; a child (son or daughter) follows in
its father's footsteps. Are you prepared to seek your inner Gorgon and decapitate
her? She who turns the heart of man to stone. Your ego like a bull keeps you chained
and attached to the world of illusion. Do you have the strength to do it?

You reply:
I who was born from the mortal womb and the fluid of semen, have been trans-
formed into a Raven, Nymphus, Miles, Leo, and now an immortal spirit. Lady, while
born again, I am passing away, while growing and having grown, I am dying; while
born from a life generating birth, I am passing on, released to death—as the wheels
of life turn, as you have founded and decreed, and have established thy mysteries. I
will walk this path to the end and battle with my inner Gorgon. . . . [Pause.]

She says:
Mithras looked away from the Bull while stabbing him; also, Perseus your Father
looked away from the Gorgon when he decapitated her. One who looked upon the
Gorgon would be turned into stone; all those who went to fight her were turned into
stone. That is the ego, which would turn the heart and the soul into stone. In order
to overcome the ego, one has to turn the head (intellect) away, as the intellect is
unable to overcome the ego.
It is only when you look with your heart, which is "Mithra is my only crown,"
that the battle can be fought. It is only on the path of Mithra (love) with the guid-

ance of the Father who has already slain the Bull, that you can decapitate your own Gorgon, before it turns you to stone.

The Tauroctony demonstrates literally that Love moves the Universe. Take this harpe and use it to slay your Gorgon. Eat this honey and act as a preserver of the fruits of knowledge and a helper of the ascent of others to enlightenment.

She hands you a harpe sword. You attach it to your belt, and eat some honey.

You stand as Perses. . . . *[Long pause.]*

Finish the rite by reciting the "Namaz-i chahar nemag" in reverse order once again, first facing North, then South, West, and East respectively: *Homage to these places and these lands, and for these pastures, and these abodes with their hay-racks, and for the waters, land, and plants, and for this earth and for your heaven, and for the Asha-owning wind, and for the stars, moon, and sun, and for the eternal stars without beginning, and self-disposing, and for all the Asha-owning creatures of Spenta Mainyu, male and female, the regulators of Asha. . . . [Pause.]*

Stand in the light of the full moon and review all that you have seen and heard to bring yourself back through the meditation back to the here-and-now, and center yourself as before. Give thanks to Mithra and to all the guides and fellow travelers you met on your journey. Then open your eyes to return to normal consciousness, and have something to eat and drink to ground yourself.

VI. HELIODROMUS MEDITATION AND INITIATION

For this meditation I have drawn heavily upon the "Mithraic Liturgy" and the Zoroastrian "Hymn to Mithra," and the "Hymn to the Sun" (Khorshid). Most passages are taken from one of these three texts, and the gaps are filled in with my own ideas. I have also used the Mithraic iconography of various Sun-Mithras scenes together. The initiates of this grade are under the protection of the sun, so this meditation is best performed during the day, perhaps at midday. The ideal day would be the midday of the summer solstice, the height of power of the sun's light.

The symbols of the grade are Sun's whip, which he uses when driving his chariot; the seven-rayed crown; and a torch. Place a large white candle and large red candle on your altar representing the torches. If you will be performing the meditation outdoors, a garden torch or a bonfire would be appropriate. A crown and whip may also be placed on the altar. If possible, burn some "Sun" incense at the beginning of the rite.

A Persian custom, which forms part of the Nou Roz celebration (see chapter 9), involves placing an orange in a large round bowl of water. The orange represents the sun floating in the cosmic ocean, also the unity of Sun and Sea. Based on this idea I have created the following simple technique, which can be used as part of the meditation for this grade. At dawn, place the bowl with the floating orange in a location where the light of the sun will fall on it during the morning. Then place the bowl on your altar when you are ready to perform the meditation. Once you have finished the meditation, or just before the closing, peel and eat the orange. This eating symbolizes "taking the sun within you," and strengthens your connection to the sun. Remembering that the ritual meal was an important part of the Mithraic mysteries, this is a simple, yet strong, symbolic action.

Visualize yourself dressed as you were at end of the Perses meditation, wearing a fiery red cloak and a lion's mask. Hanging from your belt is the harpe sword that the Goddess handed you as Perses. You are standing in the sunlight in front of a golden door. The area around the door appears dry, and you feel warmth emanating from the door. The door has the symbols of the Heliodromus (Sun Runner) grade on it: the lit torch on the left, the seven-rayed crown in the middle, and a whip on the right.

In a loud and clear voice say:
Nama to the Runner of the Sun, under the protection of the Sun.

Then recite the "Namaz-i chahar nemag" once facing East, once West, once South, and once North, respectively:
Homage to these places and these lands, and for these pastures, and these abodes with their hay-racks, and for the waters, land, and plants, and for this earth and for your heaven, and for the Asha-owning wind, and for the stars, moon, and sun, and for the eternal stars without beginning, and self-disposing, and for all the Asha-owning creatures of Spenta Mainyu (the bounteous spirit), male and female, the regulators of Asha. . . . [Pause.]

Then face center and say:

By the favor of Ahura Mazda, Anahita, and Mithra, this astral temple I build. May Ahura Mazda, Anahita, and Mithra protect me from all evil, and that which I have built may they not shatter nor harm. . . . [Pause.]

You hear a response from behind the door:
Light, light beyond light, the first rays of the sun, warm light, shining star, and sun.

[Shake your rattle six times and light a white and a red candle, and then place some Sun incense on your incense burner.]

State the reason why you seek to enter the realm of the Runner of the Sun. . . . *[Pause.]*

The door opens, and emanating out of it are rays of light, as at dawn; the light falls on you. You feel the warmth of the sun penetrate your skin, and light entering every cell of your body. It is energizing and revitalizing to your body. . . . *[Pause.]*

The two torchbearers come out of the door. They are wearing fiery red cloaks and lion's masks, and hanging from their belts are harpe swords. As you look at them, you can see halos around their heads, in the shape of the seven rays of the sun. They speak to you:
Do you seek to enter the realm of the sun, and to become Mithra's charioteer? To be his comrade?

You answer from your heart. . . . *[Pause.]*

A yellow mist starts to form; light and warmth engulf you. You see in front of you the sun cross, with its equal arms, glowing golden. The cross breaks open; each arm moves away from its point of connection, and from the central point that remains, a most brilliant white light pours forth. You hear the sound of horses. You feel the breath of a horse rush past you, and its sheer energy moves you. Moments later, the yellow mist dissolves and you see a golden chariot, drawn by four horses.

Four stallions draw Mithra's chariot, all of the same white color, undying, living on heavenly food. The hoofs of their forefeet are shod with gold, the hoofs of their hind feet are shod with silver; all are yoked to the same pole, and wear the yoke and the crossbeams of the yoke, fastened with hooks.

Close by him is he who drives the strong cursing thought of the wise man, opposing foes in the shape of a boar, a sharp-toothed he-boar, a sharp-jawed boar, that kills at one stroke, pursuing, wrathful, with a dripping face, strong and swift to run, and rushing all around. . . . *[Pause.]*

Behind him drives Atar (Lord of Fire), all in a blaze, and the lawful kingly Glory. On a side of the chariot of Mithra, the lord of wide pastures, stand a thousand bows well made, with strings of cow gut; they go through the heavenly space, they fall through the heavenly space upon the skulls of the demons. On a side of the chariot of Mithra, the lord of wide pastures, stand a thousand vulture-feathered arrows, with golden mouth, with horn shaft, with brass tail, and well-made. They go through the heavenly space; they fall through the heavenly space upon the skulls of the shadows.

The sun is above your head shining down, the center of our solar system, the source of energy on our planet.

You say:

Hail Mithras-Sol Invictus, bright sun shine ray, bright lightener, founder of earth, master of water, ruler of wind. I, who was born from the mortal womb and the fluid of semen, have now been transformed into an immortal spirit. Invincible Sun, bring me revelation regarding the mysteries of Heliodromus. Lord, while born again, I am passing away, while growing and having grown, I am dying; while born from a life generating birth, I am passing on, released to death—as the wheels of life turn, as you have founded and decreed, and have established thy mysteries. . . . [Pause.]

I sacrifice unto the undying, shining, swift-horsed Sun. When the light of the sun waxes warmer, when the brightness of the sun waxes warmer, then up stand the heavenly stars, by hundreds and thousands: they gather together its Glory, they make its Glory pass down, they pour its Glory upon the earth. They increase of the world of holiness, for the increase of the creatures of holiness, for the increase of the undying, shining, swift-horsed Sun. . . . [Pause.]

And when the sun rises up, then the earth becomes purified; the running waters become pure, the waters of the wells become clean, the waters of the sea become clean, the standing waters become clean; all the holy creatures, the creatures of the world become awake and pure. . . . [Pause.]

Should not the sun rise up, then the shadows would destroy all the things that are in the seven continents, nor would the heavenly stars find any way of withstanding or repelling them in the material world. . . . [Pause.]

I offer up a sacrifice unto the undying, shining, swift-horsed Sun—to withstand darkness, to withstand the demons born of darkness, to withstand the robbers and bandits, to withstand death that creeps in unseen. . . . [Pause.]

I will sacrifice unto Mithra, the lord of wide pastures, who has a thousand ears, ten thousand eyes.

I will sacrifice unto the club of Mithra, the lord of wide pastures, well struck down upon the skulls of the demons.

I will sacrifice unto that friendship, the best of all friendships, that reigns between the moon and the sun. . . . [Pause.]

For his brightness and glory, I will offer unto him a sacrifice worth being heard, namely, unto the undying, shining, swift-horsed Sun. Unto the undying, shining, swift-horsed Sun we offer up the libations, the Homa and meat, the baresma, the wisdom of the tongue, the holy spells, the speech, the deeds, the libations, and the rightly spoken words. . . . [Pause.]

I bless the sacrifice and the invocation, and the strength and vigor of the undying, shining, swift-horsed Sun.

Give unto that man brightness and glory, give him health of body . . . give him the bright, all-happy, blissful abode of the Holy Ones. . . . [Pause.]

You gaze into the air intently, and you see lightning down-flashing, and lights aquiver, and the earth a-shake; and then Mithras. Mithras is descending, transcending vast, of radiant Presence, with golden locks, in the flower of age, clad in a robe of brightness, with a crown of gold upon his head, and garments on his legs, holding in his right hand the golden Shoulder of the Calf. This latter is the Bear that moves the Heavens' dome, and changes its direction, now up now down, according to the hour. Then shall thou see lightning leap from his eyes and from his body stars. . . . [Pause.]

You become aware of the light that is beginning to emanate from yourself. You begin seeing yourself both as a sun and a star. You kneel in front of Mithras as he honors you. He gives you a torch, and a whip, and ignites your aura so you also have a solar halo around your head, the seven rays of the sun shining from you. Mithras "enlightens" you by placing one hand on your head while holding the leg of the bull in his other hand. This is the "investiture." As he moves the heavens by moving the leg of the bull, you become aware of the movements of the stars, the seasons ("Meithras" as 365), the earth, and the passage of time and your life.

You are at the same time a "sun" shining brightly and yet a tiny star among billions of stars (suns) in the star-filled night. Every man and woman is a star. Each person is a star on the cloak of Mithras. You are a star wandering with Mithras, and shining forth out of the deep.

You then stand up, and Mithras shakes your right hand with his right hand. You are now a Runner of the Sun. . . . *[Long pause.]*

Finish the rite by reciting the "Namaz-i chahar nemag" in reverse order once again, first facing North, then South, West, and East, respectively: *Homage to these places and these lands, and for these pastures, and these abodes with their hay-racks, and for the waters, land, and plants, and for this earth and for your heaven, and for the Asha-owning wind, and for the stars, moon, and sun, and for the eternal stars without beginning, and self-disposing, and for all the Asha-owning creatures of Spenta Mainyu, male and female, the regulators of Asha. . . . [Pause.]*

Bring yourself back through the meditation to stand before the golden door and then back to the here-and-now, and center yourself as before. Give thanks to Mithra and to all the guides and fellow travelers you met on your journey. Then open your eyes to return to normal consciousness, and ground yourself by eating and drinking something.

VII. PATER MEDITATION AND INITIATION

In the seventh degree, the initiate is under the influence of Saturn. The symbols of this grade are the libation bowl, Phrygian cap, staff, and sickle. Gather the tools and symbols of this grade on your altar, for example a black candle, a white candle, some "Saturn" incense, a staff, a libation bowl, and a Phrygian cap. It is possible to make a Phrygian cap using red cloth or alternatively buy a Phrygian cap (liberty cap) from one of the re-enactment suppliers' online shops.[5]

This meditation is best performed during the night—at midnight, near the dark of the moon. An ideal night would be at or around the autumn equinox, on September 21, or perhaps on the sixteenth day after the autumn equinox. The month of Mithra (Mehr) begins at the autumn equinox, and the sixteenth day of the month is sacred to Mithra.

For this meditation I have drawn upon the "Mithraic Liturgy," using both ideas and actual excerpts. I have also drawn upon Professor David Ulansey's suggestion about the eighth gate, and his proposition that the leontocephaline functioned partly as a symbol for the ultimate boundary of the universe.[6] The leontocephaline holds a key to the eight celestial gates, the way into the realm of fire. I have also used the Mithraic iconography of various Mithras birth scenes from the cosmic egg, and images of the leontocephaline.

The verse of nine lines quoted in this initiation that begins, "I died from minerality and became . . ." is a poem by Rumi.[7] The long verse that begins with the line, "A new life flows toward you from that bright . . ." is adapted from part of the twelfth-century Sufi poet Attar's "Conference of the Birds." We have already heard this story of the thirty birds who, on a quest to find the fabulous bird Simorgh, the King of Birds, make their way across the seven valleys—searching for Love, Mystic Apprehension, Detachment, Unity, Bewilderment, and Fulfillment in Annihilation. After their many trials and tribulations, the crucial moment depends upon a pun: *si* means "thirty," *murgh* means "birds," and hence, *simurgh* literally means "thirty birds."

The verses that begin with the lines, "To thou who thinkest to seek Me . . ." and "Farewell O Sun . . ." are from modern poems used in Wicca.[8]

♄

You are dressed as you were at the end of the Heliodromus meditation, wearing a fiery red cloak and a lion's mask. Hanging from your belt is the harpe sword, and though it is night, you are shining like a sun and holding a torch. You are standing in front of a golden door. The area around the door appears dry, and you feel warmth emanating from the door. The door has the symbols of the Pater (Father) grade on it: the libation bowl on the left, a Phrygian cap in the middle, and the staff and sickle on the right.

In a loud and clear voice, say:
Nama to the Fathers, under the protection of Saturn.

Then recite the "Namaz-i chahar nemag" once facing East, once West, once South, and once North, respectively:
Homage to these places and these lands, and for these pastures, and these abodes with their hay-racks, and for the waters, land, and plants, and for this earth and for your heaven, and for the Asha-owning wind, and for the stars, moon, and sun, and for the eternal stars without beginning, and self-disposing, and for all the Asha-owning creatures of Spenta Mainyu (the bounteous spirit), male and female, the regulators of Asha. . . . [Pause.]

Figure 8.2. Mithras as the leontocephaline. The head of the lion is at the breast of Mithras. Mithras is surrounded by the signs of the Zodiac and the four gods of winds, the heads in each corner. (From *The Mysteries of Mithra*, by Franz Cumont)

Then face center and say:
By the favor of Ahura Mazda, Anahita, and Mithra, this astral temple I build. May Ahura Mazda, Anahita, and Mithra protect me from all evil, and that which I have built may they not shatter nor harm. . . . [Pause.]

You hear a response from behind the door:
And through his Disk—the God's, my Father's—there shall be seen the Way-of-going to the Gods accessible to sight.

You say:
I am a Star, whose Course is as your Course, shining anew from out of the depth. O thou Star-tamer!

[Shake your rattle seven times and light a white and a black candle and then place some Saturn incense on your incense burner. . . . Pause.]

Now you state the reason why you seek to enter the realm of the Pater. . . . *[Pause.]*

The door opens, and you are faced with the clear, star-filled night. You feel a cool breeze against your skin. The two torchbearers come out through the door. They are wearing fiery red cloaks and lion's masks. Hanging from their belts are harpe swords. As you look at them you can see halos around their heads in the shape of the seven rays of the sun.

They speak to you:
Do you seek to enter the realm of the Pater, and to become one with Mithras?

You answer from your heart. . . . *[Pause.]*

They say:
Step through the door. However, we will not accompany you this time. Each person must complete the final stage of this journey alone.

You step through the door and suddenly you are floating in outer space, among the stars. An intense sense of fear engulfs you and your awareness of the place you are in changes. You are out in space, in front of a gigantic spider web—a web that stretches for thousands of miles in all directions. As you begin to examine the web closely, you realize that each strand is in fact a snake. The Leontocephaline (lion-headed one) stands in the middle of the web. The serpents are winding around it; it is standing on the cosmic sphere and holding a key in its right hand. Its body is decorated with the signs of the zodiac and stars. As you fly closer to the Leontocephaline, you realize that its body is not just *decorated* with the signs of the zodiac—the zodiac *is* part of its body. Every few moments, lightning bolts leave its body, traveling along the web of the millions of serpents to every corner of the cosmos. Billions of suns are connected by this cosmic web. You realize that even as a sun, you are still like a grain of sand on a beach. The Leontocephaline's mouth is open and it is full of fire. The fire extends to the outermost boundary of the universe. However, at the center of its mouth is an immeasurable void like a black hole, darkest dark, and all light disappears into it. . . . *[Pause.]*

Your impulse is to fly away, to run away. Your fear is the fear of being eaten by the Leontocephaline. But no more running away—you fly toward the web. You are flying faster and faster toward it, and then, you are letting yourself get wrapped in the web, the silvery snake threads wrap around you, a snake is choking you. Your heart is beating faster, and you hear the chant *Ya doust Mithra* pulsing in time with your heartbeat. Then the Leontocephaline begins to eat you, biting your body and tearing you—the dismemberment. The pain and the fear is intense; yet you recall the words:

I died from minerality and became vegetable;
And from vegetativeness I died and became animal.
I died from animality and became man.
Then why fear disappearance through death?
Next time I shall die
Bringing forth wings and feathers like angels;
After that, soaring higher than angels—
What you cannot imagine,
I shall be that. . . . [Pause.]

You are boiling and screaming; the "I" is in agony. As the Leontocephaline eats you (or is it Saturn consuming you?), you slowly become part of it. You mind is blurred, you are being consumed by the Leontocephaline fire, and you can hear the following words as you, a Sun Runner, begin to dissolve in the belly of the Leontocephaline.

Farewell O Sun, ever returning Light,
The hidden god who ever yet remains,
Who now departs to the land of Youth,
Through the Gates of Death,

To dwell enthroned. The judge of gods and men,
The shining bright leader of the hosts of Air,
Yet even as he stands unseen about the edge of cosmos,
So dwelt He, within the secret seed,
The seed of the newly reaped grain, the seed of flesh,
Hidden in earth, the marvelous seed of the Stars,
In him is Life and Light is the life of Man,
That which was never born and never dies,
Therefore the wise'ones weep not but rejoice.

You declare with all the strength left in you:
Mithras, while being born again, I am passing away; while growing and having grown, I am dying; while being born from a life-generating birth, I am passing on, released to death—as you have founded, as you have decreed, and have established the mystery. I am a seed and a star. . . . [Pause.]

Time passes, a moment, or hours; the Leontocephaline, the ruler of time, freezes time again. What is left of you is wandering in darkness within the body of the Leontocephaline, as the last of your body and your bones begin to dissolve, and annihilation sets in. You see lightning down-flashing, and lights aquiver, and the earth a-shake; and then Mithras descends, transcending vast, of radiant Presence, with golden locks, in the flower of age, clad in a robe of brightness, with a crown of gold upon his head, and garments on his legs, holding in his right hand the golden shoulder of the Calf. Then you see lightning leap from his eyes, and from his body stars also that fill the firmament. . . . *[Pause.]*
    As he nears you, you feel you recognize him.

A new life flows toward you from that bright
Celestial and ever living light.
Your soul rises free of all you had been before;
The past and all its actions are no more.
Your life came from that close, insistent sun.
And in its vivid rays you shine as one.
There in the Mithra's radiant face you see yourself,
The Mithras of the world, with awe. You gazed,
And dared at last to comprehend.
You are Mithras and at the journey's end.
You see Mithras as at yourself you stare,

And see a second Mithras standing there;
You look at both and see the two are one.
That this is that, that this, the goal won.
You ask (but inwardly; make no sound),
The meaning of these mysteries that confound.
Your puzzled ignorance—how is it true
That "we" is not distinguished here from "you"?
And silently your shining lord replies:
"I am a mirror set before your eyes,
And all who come before my splendor see,
Themselves, their own unique reality,
You came as one with seven parts
(Corax, Nymphus, Miles, Leo, Perses, Heliodromus, Pater),
And therefore saw
These selfsame seven parts, not less nor more;
If you had come as forty, fifty legions—here,
An answering forty, fifty would appear,
Though you have struggled, wandered, traveled far,
It is yourselves you see and what you are.
Who see the divine? It is himself each sees;
What ant's sight could discern the Pleiades?
What anvil could be lifted by an ant?
Or could a fly subdue an elephant?
How much you thought you knew and saw; but you
Now know that all you trusted was untrue.
Though you traversed the Valley's depths and fought
With all the dangers that the journey brought,
The journey was in Me, the deeds were Mine—
You slept secure in Being's inmost shrine.
And since you came as one in seven parts, you see
These one in seven when you discover Me,
The Mithra's, Truth's last flawless jewel, the light
In which you will be lost to mortal sight,
Dispersed to nothingness until once more
You find in Me the selves you were before."
Then, as you listen to Mithra's words,
A trembling dissolution fills you—
The substance of your being is undone,

And you are lost like shades before the sun;
Neither you the pilgrims nor your guides remain.
Then Mithras ceases to speak, and silence reigns.

Time passes (perhaps life times) . . . *[Pause.]* You feel you are slowly growing inside the Leontocephaline—an embryo, to an infant, to a child, within a moment. You begin rising within her and you realize you are breaking through an egg.

You force yourself out of the egg. You can see the zodiac around you and a snake is circling your egg. You are born of Leontocephaline, the guardian of immortal time. As you emerge, your body appears to be made of golden light, rather than of flesh. The egg begins to turn golden in color, too. The egg and the serpent are becoming part you: you become one. You are standing as a human, glowing golden like a star, in the middle of the web, several hundred feet tall, among all the other stars in space. The color of the web begins turning to gold, and finally, a golden web of light runs throughout space. Everything in the universe is connected, and all is one: every man and woman is a Star.

You see in front of you a Phrygian cap, a libation bowl, a staff, and a sickle, items for you to carry as a Pater. On the bowl is written "Anahita," on the staff is written "Mithra." You pick up the staff and place it into the bowl, and instantly, you realize—the union of Mithra (Mehr) and Anahita (Aban) gives birth to their child, MehrAban, which means "kindness." You as Pater, a priest or priestess of Mithras, must bring forth kindness in your actions. . . . *[Pause.]*

As you begin to become of your body again, you hear:
   Remember—To thou who thinkest to seek Me, know that thy seeking and
      yearning shall avail thee not unless thou knowest the Mystery.
   If that which thou seekest thou findest not within thee, thou wilt never find
      it without.
   For behold, I have been with thee from the beginning; and I am that which
      is attained at the end of desire.

As you open your eyes for a moment, you are aware of golden rays that connect everything together. Each person is a sun at the center of his or her own web of light, yet all are connected: Unity.

You feel the cycle of seasons pass one by one, rapidly: leaves falling, buds opening, fire of life running in the veins of the land. You are remembering all of time, all of life in a moment. Everything is so clear, and you suddenly laugh out loud and realize: *Initiation is being let into the cosmic joke—by degrees.*

Light, Life, Love, Liberty. . . . *[Long pause.]*

Finish the rite by reciting the "Namaz-i chahar nemag" in reverse order once again, first facing North, then South, West, and East, respectively: *Homage to these places and these lands, and for these pastures, and these abodes with their hay-racks, and for the waters, land, and plants, and for this earth and for your heaven, and for the Asha-owning wind, and for the stars, moon, and sun, and for the eternal stars without beginning, and self-disposing, and for all the Asha-owning creatures of Spenta Mainyu, male and female, the regulators of Asha. . . . [Pause.]*

Bring yourself back through the meditation to stand before the golden door and then back to the here-and-now, and center yourself as before. Give thanks to Mithra and to all the guides and fellow travelers you met on your journey. Then open your eyes to return to normal consciousness, and ground yourself by eating and drinking something.

Now that you have completed the seventh meditation a long time has passed since you performed the first—perhaps seven years have gone by. The seven valleys have been crossed, you have seen your Simorgh, and now, wearing your Liberty Cap, you stand free! A Zen saying comes to mind: "Nothing happens next. This is it." Let the lessons of your journey settle in; you have arrived. Reread your magical diary if you have kept one since starting these seven rites. You may want to ground your experiences by writing stories or poems about your journey and sharing them with others. Perhaps you will feel moved to set up a group with which you can perform ongoing Mithraic rituals and a working temple in which to perform them. You can manifest the mysteries of Mithras in many ways, Pater. It's up to you!

THE FOUR STATIONS
OF MITHRA

*By the favor of Ahura Mazda, Anahita, and Mithra, this palace I
built. May Ahura Mazda, Anahita, and Mithra protect me from all
evil, and that which I have built may they not shatter nor harm.*

INSCRIPTION FROM SUSA BY ACHAEMENIAN KING
ARTAXERXES II MNEMON (404–359 C.E.)

Mithraism had a "stellar" religious form, with its seven-grade initiation
system under the influence of the planets and its iconography embracing
the precession of the equinoxes. It is therefore natural that both its ancient
and modern forms would include celebration of the four stations of the
sun: winter solstice, spring equinox, summer solstice, and autumn equinox. Marking these four cardinal points in the spiritual landscape allows
one to become aware of the natural flow of life, with its changing seasons,
and of the varying effects that the length and intensity of the sun's light
have both on everyday matters and the deeper life of the spirit.

The festivals that mark these solar events can take the form of rites,
ceremonies, feasting, poetry writing, painting, playing music, parties, and
vigils, to name a few. This chapter provides a number of ideas on how to
observe each of the four events. I highly recommend that you express your
experience around the time of these solar stations in poetry or song, or
any other form that suits you. For example and encouragement, I have
included a poem of my own in each section.

Among the various neo-paganist circles, the nearest thing to a common ground is the custom of celebrating the eight festivals, or sabbats.
There are many resources for beginner pagans describing the sabbats,

which are sorted into the Greater Sabbats—the four fire festivals (Samhain, Imbolc, Beltane, and Lammas)—and the Lesser Sabbats, the sun festivals of solstices and equinoxes. One could argue that the solar festivals are the more significant. For one thing, they are universal: they were celebrated on the same days by most Old World cultures, from the West (as we can see from the ancient Stonehenge solstice alignments in England and Newgrange in Ireland) to various Eastern cultures. Solar festivals are clearly marked by astronomical events and do not change from one year to another; no matter where you are in the Northern Hemisphere, for example, March 20 or 21 will be the spring equinox (autumn equinox in the Southern Hemisphere). In contrast, the agricultural markers for the fire festivals (e.g., the flowering of hawthorn for Beltane) have huge regional variations and also change each year depending on the weather. The effects of global warming will also affect when crops will reach their peak and be ready for harvest, so the timing of future fire festivals will be affected. At any rate, what concern us here are mainly the four solar festivals and their significance to neo-Mithraism (although also included is a subsection on the summer harvest festival, Lammas).

YULE—BIRTH OF THE SUN

At Yule night the clouds are breaking
Pour Old Wine into the cup
Friends celebrate this night
When does god give you a second life?

A TRADITIONAL PERSIAN YULE POEM,
TRANSLATION BY PAYAM NABARZ

Yule is the time of the rebirth of the sun, identified variously as Lugh, Mabon, Arthur, Mithras, Christ, Horus. In the Persian calendar, Yule is called Yalda or Shab-e Yalda and is celebrated on December 21. It is the time of the winter solstice; it is the eve of the birth of Mithra.

According to Massumeh Price, social anthropologist and human ecologist from London University, Kings, and University Colleges,

The Persians adopted their annual renewal festival from the Babylonians and incorporated it into the rituals of their own Zoroastrian religion. The last day of the Persian month Azar is the longest night of the year, when the forces of Ahriman are assumed to be at the peak of their strength. The next day, the first day of the month "Day" known as "khoram rooz" or "khore rooz" (the day of sun) belongs to Ahura Mazda, the Lord of Wisdom. Since the days are getting longer and the nights shorter, this day marks the victory of Sun over the darkness. The occasion was celebrated in the festival of "Daygan" dedicated to Ahura Mazda, on the first day of the month "Day."

Fires would be burnt all night to ensure the defeat of the forces of Ahriman. There would be feasts, acts of charity and a number of deities were honored, and prayers performed to ensure the total victory of sun that was essential for the protection of winter crops. There would be prayers to Mithra (Mehr) and feasts in his honor, since Mithra is the Eyzad responsible for protecting "the light of the early morning," known as "Havangah." It was also assumed that Ahura Mazda would grant people's wishes; especially those with no offspring had the hope to be blessed with children if they performed all rites on this occasion.

One of the themes of the festival was the temporary subversion of order. Masters and servants reversed roles. The king dressed in white would change place with ordinary people. A mock king was crowned and masquerades spilled into the streets. As the old year died, rules of ordinary living were relaxed. This tradition persisted till the Sassanian period, and is mentioned by Biruni and others in their recordings of pre-Islamic rituals and festivals. Its origin goes back to the Babylonian New Year celebration. These people believed the first creation was order that came out of chaos. To appreciate and celebrate the first creation, they had a festival and all roles were reversed. Disorder and chaos ruled for a day and eventually order was restored and succeeded at the end of the festival.[1]

Furthermore, according to the Web site iranheritage.com:

It was said that Mithra was born out of the light that came from within the Alborz Mountains. Ancient Iranians would gather in caves along the mountain range throughout the night to witness this miracle together at dawn. They were known as "Yar-e Ghar" (Cave Mates). In Iran today, despite the advent of Islam and Muslim rituals, Shab-e Yalda is still celebrated widely. It is a time when friends and family gather together to eat, drink and read poetry (especially Hafiz) until well after midnight. Fruits and nuts are eaten, and pomegranates and watermelons are particularly significant. The red color in these fruits symbolizes the crimson hues of dawn and the glow of life, invoking the splendor of Mithra. Because Shab-e Yalda is the longest and darkest night, it has come to symbolize many things in Persian poetry: separation from a loved one, loneliness and waiting. After Shab-e Yalda a transformation takes place—the waiting is over, light shines and goodness prevails.

> The sight of you each morning is a New Year
> Any night of your departure is the eve of Yalda (Sa'adi)
> With all my pains, there is still the hope of recovery
> Like the eve of Yalda, there will finally be an end (Sa'adi).[2]

Some years ago I tried to capture the spirit of Yule and its essence as a global festival by writing this Yule poem:

Yule

> The sun is setting low on the western horizon.
> Sky serpent swallowing him once more
> Yule night has arrived; sun's longest slumbers.
>
> We eat and drink all that is red
> Wine, pomegranate, and watermelon,
> The color of dawn, reminders of what we eagerly wait for.
>
> Shamash, Marduk, Sekhmet,
> Descending immortals, you'll rise again
> Apollo, Ra, salutations to you.
>
> Good night Osiris, weak and tired lying in your coffin,
> Enclosed by darkness, tricked by Seth again!
> An infant sun is born, Horus soaring up into the sky.
>
> Mithras, born of a rock and out from the cave,
> Becoming Sol Invictus and turning the wheel
> Darkness, now a fading memory.
>
> The Oak king sings outside, as the Holly king lays slain

Dawn has arrived, Yule has ended.
Drink up your wine.

The birth of the sun can be enacted in the form of a "ritual drama": The participants if they like can divide into two groups, depending on the energy to which they feel connected: one group will represent the infant sun god, and the second group will represent the goddess mother giving birth to the sun. The suns lie in the center of the room in fetal position, and all are covered by a blanket, while they meditatively identify with being the sun and emerging from the darkness of the longest night. Those in the second group, having covered the suns, form a circle around them and meditate upon helping the sun at its weakest point, and giving birth to it. After a while, the goddess group begins the chant: *Father, brother, consort, sun/son rise.* Slowly they remove the blankets, and the newborn suns arise. The participants of both groups then stand holding hands in a circle, all united. This simple rite can be finished by doing a slow circle dance until everyone feels grounded.

SPRING EQUINOX—NOU ROZ

This is the time to come together to celebrate the arriving spring, the time of balance between day and night, a time for reaching equipoise within as well as with the world around us. At this season, though of equal length the night is waning and the day is waxing, for nothing remains without change, in the tides of earth and sky. Know and remember that whatever sets must also rise, and whatever rises must also set.

Nou Roz is the Persian New Year. The oldest archaeological record of a Nou Roz festival dates from the Achaemenian (Hakhamaneshi) dynasty over 2,500 years ago; and it is still celebrated as a national holiday. The first phase of the celebration takes place on the last Tuesday of the year, after spring cleaning is finished and the homes are clean and ready to welcome the new year. The celebration on Tuesday night is called "Chehar Shainbeh Suri" (eve of red Wednesday).[3] In a purification by fire, people jump over a bonfire, or a series of seven bonfires. While doing so, they chant a simple chant: *Zarde man be to, sorghie to be man,* which means "I give you (the fire) my yellow color and you give me your red color." There are also lots of fireworks to mark the occasion.

In the streets, singers and troubadours, referred to as *haji firuz,*[4] paint their faces black and wear bright red clothes made of satin. The "sacred fool" figures of the haji firuz parade through the streets with tambourines, kettledrums, and trumpets, spreading goodwill and cheer. They are manifesting the spirit of the coming new year.

One of the highlights of the Persian spring equinox celebration is the setting of the New Year altar, the *haft seen*, with seven sacred items.[5] In this custom, handed down from an old Zoroastrian custom, each item corresponds to one of the seven worlds, or creations, and the seven holy immortals protecting them. The Zoroastrians also have the ritual of growing seven seeds. They use wheat or lentil sprouts to represent new growth, and cultivate them in a flat dish a few days before the New Year; these are called *sabzeh* (green shoots). They are decorated with colorful ribbons and kept until Sinzeh Beeh Dar, the thirteenth day of the new year, and then placed into a river.

According to the Web site Farsinet.com (and produced here with their kind permission), the symbolic seven dishes are:[6]

Sabzeh, or sprouts—usually wheat or lentil—representing rebirth.

Samanu is a pudding in which common wheat sprouts are transformed and given new life as a sweet, creamy pudding; it represents the ultimate sophistication of Persian cooking. (Samanu, a thick brownish paste, is eaten today. It is a nutritious meal and could have been part of the feasts. It is also possible that it has replaced Homa, the sacred healing herbal mix that we discussed earlier.)

Seeb means "apple" and represents health and beauty.

Senjed, the sweet, dry fruit of the lotus tree, represents love. It is said that when the lotus tree is in full bloom, its fragrance and its fruit make people fall in love and become oblivious to all else.

Seer, which is garlic, represents medicine.

Somaq, or sumac berries, represent the color of sunrise; with the appearance of the sun, light conquers darkness.

Serkeh, or vinegar, represents age and patience.

To reconfirm all the hopes and wishes expressed by the traditional foods, other elements and symbols are also placed on the *sofreh* (the large white cloth where the food is placed):

A few coins placed on the sofreh represent prosperity and wealth.

A basket of painted eggs represents fertility. The egg is a universal symbol of fertility corresponding to Sepanta Armaiti, or Mother Earth.

An orange floating in a bowl of water represents Earth floating in space (or Sun floating in space and sea).

A goldfish in a bowl represents life and the end of the astral year Pisces.

A flask of rose water, known for its magical cleansing power, is included on the tablecloth.

A pot of flowering hyacinth or narcissus is also set there.

Nearby is a brazier for burning wild rue, a sacred herb whose smoldering fumes ward off evil spirits.

A mirror represents the images and reflections of Creation, as we celebrate anew the ancient Persian tradition and belief that the Creation took place on the first day of spring.

On either side of the mirror are two candlesticks, each holding a flickering candle for each child in the family. The candles represent enlightenment and happiness.

According to some sources, the haft seen altar was called a "haft sheen" in the pre-Islamic period and included wine (Sharab), which later was prohibited under Islam and replaced by vinegar (serkeh). The *haft sheen* (seven items starting with the letters *SH*) became *haft seen* (seven items starting with the letter *S*). In regards to the original haft sheen, Dr. Paul Kriwaczek writes:

> We put seven things beginning with *Sh—Sharab* (wine) for celebration, *Shir* (milk) for nourishment, *Sharbat* (sherbet) for enjoyment, *Shamshir* (sword) for security, *Shemshad* (box) for wealth, *Sham* (candle) for illumination, and *Shahdaneh* (hemp seeds) for enlightenment—so these things could be ours during the coming year.[7]

The last of the festivities is the outdoor picnic day on the thirteenth day of the New Year, the Sinzeh Beeh Dar. In order to dispel the omen of the thirteenth day, it must be spent outdoors, close to nature in the fields or parks, or by the rivers. (It is also called a national picnic or environment day.) This day was devoted in earlier times to the Persian deity Tishtrya (Tir), the bringer of rain. Most people take part in a picnic and offer prayers to Tir for rain and a successful harvest. (Tir is also celebrated at the time of the heliacal rising of the star Sirius at the summer solstice, as we see in the next section.) Sinzeh Beeh Dar is a day for competitive games. As Tir is depicted as a horse, games involving horses were traditionally chosen, with a victory of a horse representing a victory for Tir.

The picnic ends with the setting of the sun. An interesting ritual performed at the end of the picnic day is to throw away the sabzeh (wheat, lentil, or barley shoots) grown for the New Year. The sabzeh is supposed to have collected all the sickness, pain, and ill fate hiding on the family's path for the year ahead. The sabzeh is thrown into a flowing river, which carries the troubles away.

For help in attaining goals, there are other customs to perform on the thirteenth day. In one, unmarried girls can cast a spell to find a husband. They do this by going into the fields and tying a knot between green shoots, the knot representing the marriage knot. Another custom involves planting the seeds of your inspiration for the coming year. A good metaphor is that you might pull the bow of your will and fire the arrow of your inspiration; letting it travel in an arc whose height is the summer solstice, it will land at the autumn equinox.

The spring equinox heralds the coming of new life, as plants begin to grow new leaves and days become warmer and longer. You can feel the excitement of spring affecting everyone. The new-grown green leaves then start their photosynthesis: using the light of the sun they make food—the simple sugars that plants and all other life forms in the food chain (including us) rely on. For me, the process of photosynthesis is one of great beauty, a great example of the circle of life, and a metaphor for the spiritual journey. I once tried to describe the poetry of photosynthesis while, like Merlin in the stories, I was wandering madly in a forest. Merlin saw "dryads," the tree spirits; faced with the same magnificence I saw something no less amazing: Light and Life.

Soul's Journey

I, a rain drop.
Falling down rapidly.
The ground approaches,
the green grass so inviting.
Falling on the soil, slowly sinking in;
Is this the end?
Tentacles reaching out in the dark,
one caresses me.
I enter, the inevitable osmosis.
Journeying rapidly along the dark tunnel.
Then an upward rush, joining the xylem.

Surrounded by others like myself,
Up and up we go,
The walls giving off a faint green glow.
Becoming engulfed by green light.

The end is in sight,
we journey upwards, our soul's delight,
A bright light.
I slowly transform, becoming solid.
A food for others?
Photosynthesis.

Called "Soul's Journey" or "Through the Xylem" (the plant structure that allows water and minerals to travel from the root to the leaves), the poem describes the events that occur as a rain drop (the soul) comes down to earth from the clouds (heaven) and changes through its journey through the roots of a tree, joining other souls in the trunk of the tree (society) and finally reaching the leaves. By the process of photosynthesis (self-sacrifice leading to metamorphosis), it becomes something useful that nurtures all others. The light allows the raindrop to combine with the carbon dioxide to make simple sugars and release oxygen. The light (Mehr) and water (Aban) become the food we eat and the air we breathe.

SUMMER SOLSTICE—TIR

The twenty-first day of June is the midsummer and, in the Persian calendar, the first day of the month of Tir (named after the god Tishtrya). Tir is the god of rain and is personified as the star Sirius (or Dog Star, of the constellation Canis Major). He fights "bad harvest" and drought. There is an entire hymn to Tir in the Zoroastrian Avesta, called "Tishtrya Yasht." Tir is described as a beautiful white horse with golden ears and golden caparison. He fights and overcomes the black horse of drought, and rain pours from the heavens onto the fields. In the past, the Persian festival of Tiragan was celebrated as a water festival.[8] Among the customs of this festival was the tying of rainbow-colored bands on wrists, which were worn for ten days and then thrown into a stream, and of course, there were the water fights among the children and merrymaking among the young people.

The star Sirius (Tir) and Mithras and the summer solstice are all closely linked. According to Phaeded Harmani:

> The Avestan hymn to Sirius is known as the *Tishtrya Yasht*. In this *yasht* we find several elements paralleled in the Roman Tauroctony and its side panel reliefs: control of water/rains, fruitfulness of the earth in connection with bovines, a climactic animal sacrifice and most intriguingly, Mithras who *opened a wide way unto him* (i.e., Sirius, *Tishtrya Yasht* 4.7). The orientation of the large ceremonial altar at Nemrud Dagh to the summer solstice sunrise, a seasonal event heralding the closely related event of Sirius' heliacal rising, also points to this star's relevance at this site.[9]

In the United Kingdom these days, many people go to big open gatherings at places like Avebury and Stonehenge, where all-night vigils take place. People meditate and "party"; carnival folks and musicians perform and make music. The summer solstice is a time for walking the land, enjoying the light and warmth, and having fun. The Mabon, "child of light," was born at the winter solstice; the light and dark are equal at the spring equinox; and now at the summer solstice the Mabon is victorious, at the height of his power. (Of course, this is also when he begins his downfall, as the days start getting shorter.) With the sun at its peak, this is also a good time to shed light on hidden matters, for example looking into the mysteries of Tir. Try laying out candles or small lanterns as a star map of the summer stars and mark the heliacal rising of Sirius; and connect with Tir by meditating and/or reciting the hymn to Tir (*Tishtrya Yasht*).

The summer solstice festival can be divided into three parts: The first is the night vigil, which includes the meditation, poetry, and music. The second is the dawn ceremony, the hailing and welcoming of the sun. The third is the noon ceremony, that of marking the sun's peak of light and strength. The message: Enjoy the summer while it lasts.

As the sun is at the height of its power, so we are shining brightly at the summer solstice. We should all try to create a personal statement, invocation, or celebration of ourselves and our qualities and gifts and focus on being a shining beacon like the sun, so we can illuminate the life of all. For example, one year around the time of the summer solstice, I wrote the following poem, inspired by A. Crowley's "Liber O" and Katy Jenison's "Affirmation" (and also by the Borg in Star Trek, "The Prisoner," and much more). My point was to emphasize that each of us is a sun/star shining forth at the height of the sun and able to break through all social conditioning; or as the "Mithras Liturgy" puts it: "I am a star wandering about with thee, and shining forth out of the deep."

Every Man and Woman Is a Star

I will not be filed, labeled, or categorized.
I am not a number, and will not be assimilated,
I am a free spirit and not part of a cube.

I am not just your father, brother, husband, consort, son, or lover.
I am not just your king, prophet, your knight in shining armor; a
Warrior-bard: destroyer-creator.
I am not an organically fueled dildo, or a pillar of strength, I am not
    here to die in a battlefield defending our cave,
Or to hang from a cross to save the world.

I am not just your mother, sister, wife, daughter, or lover.
I am not just your queen, a wise crone, midwife, artist, teacher.
I give birth or abort, as I wish; from my temple: creator-destroyer.
I am not a cook, a mistress, a virgin, or a whore.
I don't have childbearing hips! I will not stay at home or cover my hair.
I am not your drunken snog or breast feeder, and I get vertigo from
    being on a pedestal.

I am beyond my individual components and traits,
exceeding the total sum of my programming,
seeing past the veil of separation.

I am a dividing cell, meiosis and mitosis manifest.
I am the beat of the heart, sound of a drum, a note on a fiddle,
I am a drop of rain on your face, the wind in your hair.
I am a liberating orgasm, a smile to a stranger.
I am laughter and tears,
the joy of a bird in mid-flight,
the bliss of a sleeping cat.

I am a reflection in a mirror,
the food you eat,
the forbidden fruit on the tree.

I am young and old,
wise and foolish,
yoni and lingam,
earth, sun and moon, dead and alive,
plant, animal and mineral.

I behold all opposites, and all possibilities, until nothing remains.
From that silence, everything burst forth, like spring flowers.
I was a hidden treasure, and I wanted to be known.
with a big bang I have become every atom of the universe.
A star child, a rainbow across the sky.

Yet I am only one point of light in the star-filled night,
shining forth from the deep.
Being Awen, Om and Hu, with every breath.

After the Summer Solstice, the Harvest

After the power of the sun has reached its height and begins its descent, we enjoy the ripening and harvesting of the fruits of the earth. The time of harvest differs from one country to another; it is not universally set like the four stations of the sun. Therefore, one has to work with the harvest time of the land of one's residence and its local customs. For example, in Northern Europe, early August is a good time for the harvest. The neo-pagan Celtic festival Lammas (first of August) marks the beginning of harvest in many countries.

Of course, not many of us work in the cornfields these days, so the relevance of the harvest is questionable on a personal level. Given a sickle and dropped off in a cornfield, I would probably do more damage to myself than cut any corn. So I tend to focus on Lammas more as a person living in the city in the third millennium, seeing it as a time of personal harvest—a time to observe the harvest of our creative work, jobs, families, projects, exam results, and so on. This is a time to look at what we have accomplished in our lives, a time to open ourselves up to our potential for our own harvest.

Another name for Lammas is Lughnasadh (commemoration of Lugh). Lugh is the Gaelic god of sun and light, a sacrificial sun god who (like Christ and Mithras) dies and is reborn. He is the one who sent the Gaelic Argonauts to Persia, to obtain the magic spear; we heard his story earlier.

A good magical site to go to for this festival would be one with links to bulls or oxen. Instead of Lugh (the Corn King), the focus is the great bull of creation being sacrificed by Mithras. The rest of the image/myth cycle is the same. From the bull's blood come the wine and all the plants that cover the earth. The tail becomes the wheat, which gives our bread; the bull is reborn in all life. Offerings of Hungarian "bull's blood" wine, wheat, corn, and bread are appropriate at this time of year, as are barbecue parties and, of course, water fights to cool down.

The images to visualize and get in touch with are the Sun, Mithras, and the Bull. The bull (harvest) transforms to other living forms, like grain and corn—from seed, to ripe corn, to flour and water, to bread. We humans also transform and change like grapes to wine in the vat.

The Rumi poem recited in its entirety in the Pater meditation is quite relevant here. The first few lines read:

> *I died from minerality and became vegetable;*
> *And from vegetativeness I died and became animal.*
> *I died from animality and became man.*
> *Then why fear disappearance through death?*

To capture the spirit of Lammas, I wrote following poem after what was a very rainy and stormy 2002 harvest gathering:

Lammas at RollRights Stone Circle

Who will make it through the storm?
Frantic phone calls, are we still going?
Yep

Torrential rain flooded roads, how many will make it to the
*   RollRights?*
Except seven, none returned from Caer Sidi, but twenty-one made it to
*   RollRights.*
From Leicester, Didcot, Oxford, and London, the clans gathered,
*   braving the storm.*

Thrice that made it back from Caer Sidi were we,
Not in Prydwen, but in cars and on bikes, floating on momentary
*   flood and sea.*
Lightning overhead, thunder drowning our voices, but for Lugh we
*   went.*

Mithras, Zeus, and Thor beckoning and challenging us simultaneously
Will you make the sacrifice of Lammas?
Will you go with the flow?

The fire is a flame, the elements dance,
West takes charge, We are drenched
Despite our attempts at protection.

We call upon Lugh, the shining Hand of Light
Thunder and Lightning all around
Time for our harvest.

Eating sun-colored saffron bread, and taking the sun inside.
Drinking red wine, blood of the vineyards.
To the chorus of Indian and Irish flutes.

Spiraling in the circle, everyone shining, eyes full of light.
Stones whispering, talking in a thousand tongues. Who's dancing,
    them or us?
Watching them, watching us, watching them.
A hall of mirrors reaching infinity in time and space.

Rain falling, softening the skin of the land
Feeding it, nourishing it,
The first sparks of next year's harvest.

AUTUMN EQUINOX—FESTIVAL OF MITHRA

The Sun is said to be the eye of Mithra.

PERSIAN PROVERB

The autumn equinox celebrations begins at sunset of September 21, as the yellowish, bright barley moon wanes and we approach the autumn equinox. The end of the harvest at the Harvest Moon awaits us at the time of this solar festival. It is another time of balance and equilibrium; day and night, light and darkness are again the same length. The arrows of light that we fired at the spring equinox reached their arc's height at the summer solstice and now come down to their earthly home to roost. The symbols of this festival are similar among several magical systems. Here are a few examples of this festival's myths from Thelema, Wicca, Druidry, and Mithraism.

In Thelemic terms, this is the time of the sunset of Liber Resh: "At sunset, facing west, giving the sign of water: the goddess Auramoth (both hands forming a triangle, thumbs touching, forefinger touching). Hail unto thee, who art Tum in Thy setting, even unto Thee who art Tum in Thy joy, who travels over the Heavens in Thy barc at the Down-going of the Sun. Tahuti standeth in his splendor at the prow, and Ra-Hoor abideth at the helm. Hail unto Thee from the Abodes of Day!"[10]

The Wiccan incantation, "Farewell O Sun, ever returning Light" (see Pater meditation) beautifully captures the spirit of this festival. In Druidry the autumn equinox is referred to as Alban Elued, which means "Light of Water." In the Old-World view of a flat world surrounded by water, the sunset in the west is where the sun descends to the ocean and then disappears. The west has often been seen as the place where the dead go. The days become shorter; the waters of the ocean become darker and darker, sooner each day; the world of the dead is slowly approaching the land of the living. Water is the sphere of the autumn equinox, as the year descends into the ocean. This is when the Druids drink the wine of the wisdom of Life, Light, Love, and Liberty. And this is what the Thelemites refer to as "current 93." It is also at this time of Alban Elued that the initiates of the Eleusinian mysteries were shown an ear of grain and were told: "In silence is the seed of wisdom gained."

While meditating on the inner mystery of this station in the context of the Mithraic mysteries, I have found apt connections among the many shared symbols. Consider that the autumn equinox marks the beginning of the Persian month of Mehr and the start of the festival of Mehregan. Remember that the month of the sun god Mithra (Mehr) is followed by the month of the sea goddess Anahita (Aban). The month of the sun leads into the month of the sea, as the Celtic-Druid sun being sets into the ocean. The ocean sunset is a metaphor of the sun uniting with the water. Consider the resultant light reflected upon the water. Mehr comes together with Aban, giving rise to *mehraban*, "one who is kind," the child of light.

Now consider the Mabon, the Celtic child of eternal light, who needs to rise after being hidden in the sea. The Mabon, also known as the Great Prisoner or the Great Son, was taken away from his mother Modron three nights after his birth. The Mabon has been the goal of many spiritual quests; he is the Inner Light within us all. While the child is born at the winter solstice, the time of the autumn equinox belongs to him, as we say farewell to him. As he goes through the gates of death and harvest, he is within the seed of plants and the seed of light in us. The Mabon is fire and water, sun and sea, in their union creating perhaps the most important spiritual quality, that of human kindness.

According to Dr. Taqizadeh (1938):

> The feast of Mithra or baga was, no doubt, one of the most popular if not the greatest of all the festivals in ancient Iran, where it was cele-brated with the greatest attention. This was originally a pre-Zoroastrian and old Aryan feast consecrated to the sun god, and its place in the Old-Persian calendar was surely in the month belonging to this deity. This month was called Bagayadi or Bagayadish and almost certainly corresponded to the seventh Babylonian month Tishritu, the patron of which was also Shamash, the Babylonian sun god. This month was, as has already been stated, probably the first month of the Old-Persian year, and its more or less fixed place was in the early part of the autumn. The feast was in all probability Old Persian rather than Old—or Young—Avestan, and it was perhaps the survival of an earlier Iranian New Year festival dating from some pre-historic phase of the Aryan calendar, when the year began at the autumnal equinox. It was connected with the worship of one of the oldest Aryan deities (Baga-Mithra), of whom traces are found as far back as in the fourteenth century B.C.E.[11]

In Persia the two most significant festivals were Norouz (Nou Roz) and Mehregan, which divided the year into two equal parts. According to Massumeh Price:

> One of the oldest historical records about Mehregan refers back to the Achaemenian times. The historian Strabon (66–24 B.C.E.) has mentioned that the Armenian Satrap presented the Achaemenian king with 20,000 horses at the Mehregan celebrations. Ahura Mazda, Anahita and Mithra were the three major deities during this period. By this time the seventh month (Mitrakana) and the six-teenth day of the same month were dedicated to Mithra and named after him (Mehr Mah and Mehr Rouz in moden Persian). Mithra's temples are discovered from the Parthian period as well. There is a

temple in present day Ashkabad in Turkmenistan with the inscription "mehriyan" or "place of Mithra."

Other Greek sources mention that the kings would dress in purple, dance, drink, and this was the only occasion they could get drunk in public. The celebration is also mentioned in the Talmud, the ancient Jewish text. The festival is not specific to Iranians and has been celebrated by many cultures in Asia Minor and throughout ancient Mesopotamia. However, what has been celebrated in Iran with its uniquely Iranian characteristic is based on the ancient Zoroastrian texts. . . . Kings would wear a crown shaped like a sun with actors wearing masks and musicians playing music. Ancient Iranians believed that it was on Mehr day that humans were given urvan (*ravan* in modern Persian, meaning soul), and the earth was enlarged on this day to provide more land for the growing population. Moon (Mah), which was a cold and dark object, for the first time received light from the sun on this day and began illuminating at night. . . .[12]

In the autumn of 1999, I wrote the following poem to capture the sinking into the ocean and dying into the west aspect of this festival.

Ocean of Light

How I pine for you, I miss you,
my tears for you, stop me from seeing you.
Who are you? I don't know you
yet I seek you, hoping to know you
to hold you, to love you
to be with you, to be one with you.
As a raindrop seeks the Ocean.

According to the Web site Iranonline.com:

For this celebration, the participants wear new clothes and set a decorative, colorful table. The sides of the tablecloth are decorated with dry wild marjoram. The holy book Avesta, a mirror and Sormeh Dan (antimony cellar) are placed on the table together with rose water, sweets, flowers, vegetables and fruits, especially pomegranates and apples. A few silver coins and senjed seeds (fruit of the lotus tree) are placed in a dish of pleasant smelling wild marjoram water. Almonds and pistachio are also used.

A burner is also part of the table setting for kondor (frankin-cense) and espand (rue seeds) to be thrown on the flames.

At lunchtime when the ceremony begins, everyone in the family stands in front of the mirror to pray. Sherbet is drunk and then as a good omen, antimony is rubbed around the eyes. Handfuls of wild marjoram, senjed seeds and noghl (sugar plum) are thrown over each other's heads while they embrace one another.

In some of the villages in Yazd, Zoroastrians still sacrifice sheep for Mehr. These sacrifices are done on the day of Mehregan and for three days afterwards. The sacrifice should be done during the hours of sunlight. The sheep is placed on three stones in the furnace, rep-resenting the good words, good deeds and good thoughts, and barbe-cued. After this special ritual, the sheep, including the skin and fat, is taken to the fire temple. The fat is thrown on the fire to make the flames burn fiercely and then the participants pray. This celebration continues for the next five days.[13]

EPILOGUE

A note of caution: when pursuing a spiritual life it is important to have a good sense of humor. Indeed, one of the differences between enlightened mystics and religious fundamentalists is that mystics can make jokes about their god and laugh, while fundamentalists take everything so seriously that if you make a joke about their god they get offended and might even try to kill you! Therefore, I'd like to finish the text with a comical poem that I wrote as a parody of Rudyard Kipling's excellent poem, "A Song to Mithras." Mine is called "The Marching Song of the Ninth Legion," and it is about the old Roman legion that was said to have disappeared mysteriously in Scotland. Let this be a reminder that the spiritual life is meant to be full of joy, fun, and love. One has to be able to laugh at oneself, and follow the comical Sufi Master Mulla Nasrudin's school of thought.

To Mithras
(Marching Song of the Roman Ninth Legion)

As the sun rises
And we soldiers march to "meet Ra"
We sing; hail to the sun god
He's a real fun god, mit ra ra ra

As our loins feel the heat of the midday sun,
As Lions we roar, and run for a shade, a glade, a pool.
We swim across rivers, to cool our heated leather pouch,
We brave and cocky soldiers of "Sol Invictus."

The afternoon siesta ends, and we march home.
Rome's sons have defended the Wall with honor again.
Like their Lord, hope to get their "leg over" a bull tonight.
So much wine will we drink, at dusk, for our Friend.

As the bars shut, we get thrown out, at the midnight hour.
We compete for a place to sleep in the ordeal pit.
'Cause we are hard, we soldiers of Mithras.
O Lord, please clear our hangovers by dawn.

ZOROASTRIAN HYMN TO MITHRA (MEHR YASHT 10)

> *Baba Yaga: "Are you here of your own free will or by compulsion, my*
> *good youth?"*
> *Ivan: "Largely of my own free will, and twice as much by compulsion!"*
> ROBERT BLY AND MARION WOODMAN, *THE MAIDEN KING*

The following "Hymn to Mithra" was translated from the Avesta by James Darmesteter and printed in *Sacred Books of the East*, American Edition, 1898, part of Oxford University Press's Sacred Books of the East (SBE) series. Copyright permission has been kindly given by Joseph H. Peterson. I have made a comparison to the Persian text and have made some changes and updates.

The original hymn is from the Yasht section of the Avesta, and is estimated to date back to around 500 B.C.E., though some parts of the hymn are thought to be much older.

> *May Ahura Mazda be rejoiced! . . .*
> *Ashem Vohu: Holiness is the best of all good. . . .*
> *I confess myself a worshipper of Mazda, a follower of*
>   *Zarathushtra, one who hates the Daevas, and obeys the laws of*
>   *Ahura;*
> *For sacrifice, prayer, propitiation, and glorification unto [Havani],*
>   *the holy and master of holiness. . . .*
> *Unto Mithra, the lord of wide pastures, who has a thousand ears, ten*
>   *thousand eyes, a Yazata invoked by his own name, and unto*
>   *Rama Hvastra,*

Be propitiation, with sacrifice, prayer, propitiation, and glorification.
Yatha ahu vairyo: The will of the Lord is the law of holiness. . . .

I.

1. *Ahura Mazda spake unto Spitama Zarathushtra, saying: "Verily, when I created Mithra, the lord of wide pastures, O Spitama! I created him as worthy of sacrifice, as worthy of prayer as myself Ahura Mazda.*

2. *"The ruffian who lies unto Mithra brings death unto the whole country, injuring as much the faithful world as a hundred evil-doers could do. Break not the contract, O Spitama! neither the one that thou hadst entered into with one of the unfaithful, nor the one that thou hadst entered into with one of the faithful who is one of thy own faith. For Mithra stands for both the faithful and the unfaithful.*

3. *"Mithra, the lord of wide pastures, gives swiftness to the horses of those who lie not unto Mithra.*
   "Fire, the son of Ahura Mazda, gives the straightest way to those who lie not unto Mithra.
   "The good, strong, beneficent Fravashis of the faithful give a virtuous off-spring to those who lie not unto Mithra.

4. *"For his brightness and glory, I will offer unto him a sacrifice worth being heard, namely, unto Mithra, the lord of wide pastures.*
   "We offer up libations unto Mithra, the lord of wide pastures, who gives a happy dwelling and a good dwelling to the Aryan nations.

5. *"May he come to us for help! May he come to us for ease! May he come to us for joy! May he come to us for mercy! May he come to us for health! May he come to us for victory! May he come to us for good conscience! May he come to us for bliss! he, the awful and overpowering, worthy of sacrifice and prayer, not to be deceived anywhere in the whole of the material world, Mithra, the lord of wide pastures.*

6. *"I will offer up libations unto him, the strong Yazata, the powerful Mithra, most beneficent to the creatures: I will apply unto him with charity and prayers: I will offer up a sacrifice worth being heard unto him, Mithra, the lord of wide pastures, with the Homa and*

meat, with the baresma, with the wisdom of the tongue, with the holy spells, with the speech, with the deeds, with the libations, and with the rightly spoken words.

"Yenhe hatam: *All those beings of whom Ahura Mazda* . . .

II.

7. "We sacrifice unto Mithra, the lord of wide pastures, who is truth-speaking, a chief in assemblies, with a thousand ears, well-shapen, with ten thousand eyes, high, with full knowledge, strong, sleepless, and ever awake;

8. "To whom the chiefs of nations offer up sacrifices, as they go to the field, against havocking hosts, against enemies coming in battle array, in the strife of conflicting nations.

9. "On whichever side he has been worshipped first in the fullness of faith of a devoted heart, to that side turns Mithra, the lord of wide pastures, with the fiend-smiting wind, with the cursing thought of the wise. For his brightness and glory, I will offer him a sacrifice worth being heard. . . .

III.

10. "We sacrifice unto Mithra, the lord of wide pastures, . . . sleepless, and ever awake.

11. "Whom the horsemen worship on the back of their horses, begging swiftness for their teams, health for their own bodies, and that they may watch with full success those who hate them, smite down their foes, and destroy at one stroke their adversaries, their enemies, and those who hate them,

"For his brightness and glory, I will offer him a sacrifice worth being heard. . . .

IV.

12. "We sacrifice unto Mithra, the lord of wide pastures, . . . sleepless, and ever awake;

13. "Who first of the heavenly gods reaches over the Hara, before the undy-
    ing, swift-horsed sun; who, foremost in a golden array, takes hold of
    the beautiful summits, and from thence looks over the abode of the
    Aryans with a beneficent eye.

14. "Where the valiant chiefs draw up their many troops in array; where
    the high mountains, rich in pastures and waters, yield plenty to the
    cattle; where the deep lakes, with salt waters, stand; where wide-
    flowing rivers swell and hurry towards Ishkata and Pouruta, Mouru
    and Haroyu, the Gava-Sughdha and Hvairizem;

15. "On Arezahi and Savahi, on Fradadhafshu and Vidadhafshu, on
    Vourubareshti and Vourujareshti, on this bright Karshvare of
    Hvaniratha, the abode of cattle, the dwelling of cattle, the powerful
    Mithra looks with a health-bringing eye;

16. "He who moves along all the Karshvares, a Yazata unseen, and brings
    glory; he who moves along all the Karshvares, a Yazata unseen, and
    brings sovereignty; and increases strength for victory to those who,
    with a pious intent, holily offer him libations.
    "For his brightness and glory, I will offer him a sacrifice worth being
    heard. . . .

V.

17. "We sacrifice unto Mithra, the lord of wide pastures, . . . sleepless, and
    ever awake;
    "Unto whom nobody must lie, neither the master of a house, nor the lord of
    a borough, nor the lord of a town, nor the lord of a province.

18. "If the master of a house lies unto him, or the lord of a borough, or the
    lord of a town, or the lord of a province, then comes Mithra, angry
    and offended, and he breaks asunder the house, the borough, the
    town, the province; and the masters of the houses, the lords of the
    boroughs, the lords of the towns, the lords of the provinces, and the
    foremost men of the provinces.

19. "On whatever side there is one who has lied unto Mithra, on that side
    Mithra stands forth, angry and offended, and his wrath is slow to
    relent.

20. "Those who lie unto Mithra, however swift they may be running, cannot overtake; riding, cannot overtake; driving, cannot overtake. The
spear that the foe of Mithra flings, darts backwards, for the number
of the evil spells that the foe of Mithra works out.

21. "And even though the spear be flung well, even though it reach the body,
it makes no wound, for the number of the evil spells that the foe of
Mithra works out. The wind drives away the spear that the foe of
Mithra flings, for the number of the evil spells that the foe of Mithra
works out.
"For his brightness and glory, I will offer him a sacrifice worth being
heard. . . .

VI.

22. "We sacrifice unto Mithra, the lord of wide pastures, . . . sleepless, and
ever awake;
"Who takes out of distress the man who has not lied unto him, who
takes him out of death.

23. "Take us out of distress, take us out of distresses, O Mithra! as we have
not lied unto thee. Thou bringest down terror upon the bodies of the
men who lie unto Mithra; thou takest away the strength from their
arms, being angry and all-powerful; thou takest the swiftness from
their feet, the eyesight from their eyes, the hearing from their ears.

24. "Not the wound of the well-sharpened spear or of the flying arrow
reaches that man to whom Mithra comes for help with all the
strength of his soul, he, of the ten thousand spies, the powerful,
all-seeing, undeceivable Mithra.
"For his brightness and glory, I will offer him a sacrifice worth being
heard. . . .

VII.

25. "We sacrifice unto Mithra, the lord of wide pastures, . . . sleepless, and
ever awake;
"Who is lordly, deep, strong, and weal-giving; a chief in assemblies,

pleased with prayers, high, holily clever, the incarnate Word, a warrior with strong arms;

26. "Who breaks the skulls of the Daevas, and is most cruel in exacting pains; the punisher of the men who lie unto Mithra, the withstander of the Pairikas; who, when not deceived, establisheth nations in supreme strength; who, when not deceived, establisheth nations in supreme victory;

27. "Who confounds the ways of the nation that delights in havoc, who turns away their Glory, takes away their strength for victory, blows them away helpless, and delivers them unto ten thousand strokes; he, of the ten thousand spies, the powerful, all-seeing, undeceivable Mithra.

    "For his brightness and glory, I will offer him a sacrifice worth being heard. . . .

VIII.

28. "We sacrifice unto Mithra, the lord of wide pastures, . . . sleepless, and ever awake;

    "Who upholds the columns of the lofty house and makes its pillars solid; who gives herds of oxen and male children to that house in which he has been satisfied; he breaks to pieces those in which he has been offended.

29. "Thou, O Mithra! art both bad and good to nations; thou, O Mithra! art both bad and good to men; thou, O Mithra! keepest in thy hands both peace and trouble for nations.

30. "Thou makest houses large, beautiful with women (soft pillows and large beds), beautiful with chariots, with well-laid foundations, and high above their groundwork; thou makest that house lofty, beautiful with women, beautiful with chariots, with well-laid foundations, and high above its groundwork, of which the master, pious and holding libations in his hand, offers thee a sacrifice, in which thou art invoked by thy own name and with the proper words.

31. "With a sacrifice, in which thou art invoked by thy own name, with the proper words will I offer thee libations, O powerful Mithra! With a

sacrifice, in which thou art invoked by thy own name, with the
proper words will I offer thee libations, O most beneficent Mithra!
"With a sacrifice, in which thou art invoked by thy own name, with
the proper words will I offer thee libations, O thou undeceivable
Mithra!

32. "Listen unto our sacrifice, O Mithra! Be thou pleased with our sacrifice,
O Mithra! Come and sit at our sacrifice! Accept our libations!
Accept them as they have been consecrated! Gather them together
with love and lay them in the Garo-nmana!

33. "In the name of the covenant between you and ourselves, grant us these
boons which we beg of thee, O powerful God in accordance with the
words of revelation: namely, riches, strength, and victory, good conscience and bliss, good fame and a good soul; wisdom and the knowledge that gives happiness, the victorious strength given by Ahura, the
crushing Ascendant of Asha Vahishta, and conversation (with God)
on the Holy Word.

34. "Grant that we, in a good spirit and high spirit, exalted in joy and a
good spirit, may smite all our foes; that we, in a good spirit and high
spirit, exalted in joy and a good spirit, may smite all our enemies;
that we, in a good spirit and high spirit, exalted in joy and a good
spirit, may smite all the malice of Daevas and Men, of the Yatus and
Pairikas, of the oppressors, the blind, and the deaf.
"For his brightness and glory, I will offer him a sacrifice worth being
heard. . . .

IX.

35. "We sacrifice unto Mithra, the lord of wide pastures, . . . sleepless, and
ever awake;
"Victory-making, army-governing, endowed with a thousand senses;
power-wielding, power-possessing, and all-knowing;

36. "Who sets the battle a going, who stands against (armies) in battle,
who, standing against (armies) in battle, breaks asunder the lines
arrayed. The wings of the columns gone to battle shake, and he
throws terror upon the center of the havocking host.

37. "He can bring and does bring down upon them distress and fear; he
    throws down the heads of those who lie to Mithra, he takes off the
    heads of those who lie unto Mithra.

38. "Sad is the abode, unpeopled with children, where abide men who lie
    unto Mithra, and, verily, the fiendish killer of faithful men. The graz-
    ing cow goes a sad straying way, driven along the vales of the
    Mithradrujes: they stand on the road, letting tears run over their
    chins.

39. "Their falcon-feathered arrows, shot from the string of the well-bent
    bow, fly towards the mark, and hit it not, as Mithra, the lord of wide
    pastures, angry, offended, and unsatisfied, comes and meets them.
    "Their spears, well whetted and sharp, their long spears fly from their
    hands towards the mark, and hit it not, as Mithra, the lord of wide pas-
    tures, angry, offended, and unsatisfied, comes and meets them.

40. "Their swords, well thrust and striking at the heads of men, hit not the
    mark, as Mithra, the lord of wide pastures, angry, offended, and
    unsatisfied, comes and meets them.
    "Their clubs, well falling and striking at the heads of men, hit not the
    mark, as Mithra, the lord of wide pastures, angry, offended, and
    unsatisfied, comes and meets them.

41. "Mithra strikes fear into them; Rashnu strikes a counter-fear into them;
    the holy Sraosha blows them away from every side towards the two
    Yazatas, the maintainers of the world. They make the ranks of the
    army melt away, as Mithra, the lord of wide pastures, angry,
    offended, and unsatisfied, comes and meets them.

42. "They cry unto Mithra, the lord of wide pastures, saying: 'O Mithra,
    thou lord of wide pastures! here are our fiery horses taking us away,
    as they flee from Mithra; here are our sturdy arms cut to pieces by
    the sword, O Mithra!'

43. "And then Mithra, the lord of wide pastures, throws them to the ground,
    killing their fifties and their hundreds, their hundreds and their thou-
    sands, their thousands and their tens of thousands, their tens of thou-

sands and their myriads of myriads; as Mithra, the lord of wide pastures, is angry and offended.

"For his brightness and glory, I will offer him a sacrifice worth being heard. . . .

X.

44. "We sacrifice unto Mithra, the lord of wide pastures, . . . sleepless, and ever awake;

"Whose dwelling, wide as the earth, extends over the material world, large, unconfined, and bright, a far-and-wide-extending abode.

45. "Whose eight friends sit as spies for Mithra, on all the heights, at all the watching-places, observing the man who lies unto Mithra, looking at those, remembering those who have lied unto Mithra, but guarding the ways of those whose life is sought by men who lie unto Mithra, and, verily, by the fiendish killers of faithful men.

46. "Helping and guarding, guarding behind and guarding in front, Mithra, the lord of wide pastures, proves an undeceivable spy and watcher for the man to whom he comes to help with all the strength of his soul, he of the ten thousand spies, the powerful, all-knowing, undeceivable god.

"For his brightness and glory, I will offer him a sacrifice worth being heard. . . .

XI.

47. "We sacrifice unto Mithra, the lord of wide pastures, ... sleepless, and ever awake;

"A god of high renown and old age, whom wide-hoofed horses carry against havocking hosts, against enemies coming in battle array, in the strife of conflicting nations.

48. "And when Mithra drives along towards the havocking hosts, towards the enemies coming in battle array, in the strife of the conflicting nations, then he binds the hands of those who have lied unto Mithra, he confounds their eye-sight, he takes the hearing from their ears; they can no longer move their feet; they can no longer withstand

those people, those foes, when Mithra, the lord of wide pastures, bears them ill-will.

"*For his brightness and glory, I will offer him a sacrifice worth being heard. . . .*

XII.

49. "*We sacrifice unto Mithra, the lord of wide pastures, . . . sleepless, and ever awake;*

50. "*For whom the Maker, Ahura Mazda, has built up a dwelling on the Hara Berezaiti, the bright mountain around which the many (stars) revolve where come neither night nor darkness, no cold wind and no hot wind, no deathful sickness, no uncleanness made by the Daevas, and the clouds cannot reach up unto the Haraiti Bareza;*

51. "*A dwelling that all the Amesha Spentas, in one accord with the sun, made for him in the fullness of faith of a devoted heart, and he surveys the whole of the material world from the Haraiti Bareza.*

52. "*And when there rushes a wicked worker of evil, swiftly, with a swift step, Mithra, the lord of wide pastures, goes and yokes his horses to his chariot, along with the holy, powerful Sraosha and Nairyosangha, who strikes a blow that smites the army, that smites the strength of the malicious.*

"*For his brightness and glory, I will offer him a sacrifice worth being heard. . . .*

XIII.

53. "*We sacrifice unto Mithra, the lord of wide pastures, . . . sleepless, and ever awake;*

54. "*Who, with hands lifted up, ever cries unto Ahura Mazda, saying: 'I am the kind keeper of all creatures, I am the kind maintainer of all creatures; yet men worship me not with a sacrifice in which I am invoked by my own name, as they worship the other gods with sacrifices in which they are invoked by their own names.*

55. "'If men would worship me with a sacrifice in which I were invoked by my own name, as they worship the other Yazatas with sacrifices in which they are invoked by their own names, then I would come to the faithful at the appointed time; I would come in the appointed time of my beautiful, immortal life.'

56. "But the pious man, holding libations in his hands, does worship thee with a sacrifice, in which thou art invoked by thy own name, and with the proper words.
"With a sacrifice, in which thou art invoked by thy own name, with the proper words will I offer thee libations, O powerful Mithra!
"With a sacrifice, in which thou art invoked by thy own name, with the proper words will I offer thee libations, O most beneficent Mithra!
"With a sacrifice, in which thou art invoked by thy own name, with the proper words will I offer thee libations, O thou undeceivable Mithra!

57. "Listen unto our sacrifice, O Mithra! Be thou pleased with our sacrifice, O Mithra! Come and sit at our sacrifice! Accept our libations! Accept them as they have been consecrated! Gather them together with love and lay them in the Garo-nmana!

58. "Grant us these boons which we beg of thee, O powerful god! in accordance with the words of revelation, namely, riches, strength, and victory, good conscience and bliss, good fame and a good soul; wisdom and the knowledge that gives happiness, the victorious strength given by Ahura, the crushing Ascendant of Asha-Vahishta, and conversation (with God) on the Holy Word.

59. "Grant that we, in a good spirit and high spirit, exalted in joy and a good spirit, may smite all our foes; that we, in a good spirit and high spirit, exalted in joy and a good spirit, may smite all our enemies; that we, in a good spirit and high spirit, exalted in joy and a good spirit, may smite all the malice of Daevas and Men, of the Yatus and Pairikas, of the oppressors, the blind, and the deaf.
"For his brightness and glory, I will offer him a sacrifice worth being heard. . . .

XIV.

60. "We sacrifice unto Mithra, the lord of wide pastures, . . . sleepless, and ever awake;

"Whose renown is good, whose shape is good, whose glory is good; who has boons to give at his will, who has pasture-fields to give at his will; harmless to the tiller of the ground, . . . beneficent; he, of the ten thousand spies, the powerful, all-knowing, undeceivable god.

"For his brightness and glory, I will offer him a sacrifice worth being heard. . . .

XV.

61. "We sacrifice unto Mithra, the lord of wide pastures, . . . sleepless, and ever awake;

"Firm-legged, a watcher fully awake; valiant, a chief in assemblies; making the waters flow forward; listening to appeals; making the waters run and the plants grow up; ruling over the Karshvares; delivering; happy; undeceivable; endowed with many senses; a creature of wisdom;

62. "Who gives neither strength nor vigor to him who has lied unto Mithra; who gives neither glory nor any boon to him who has lied unto Mithra.

63. "Thou takest away the strength from their arms, being angry and all-powerful; thou takest the swiftness from their feet, the eye-sight from their eyes, the hearing from their ears.

"Not the wound of the well-sharpened spear or of the flying arrow reaches that man to whom Mithra comes for help with all the strength of his soul; he of the ten-thousand spies, the powerful all-knowing undeceivable god.

"For his brightness and glory, I will offer him a sacrifice worth being heard. . . .

XVI.

64. "We sacrifice unto Mithra, the lord of wide pastures, . . . sleepless, and ever awake;

"Who takes possession of the beautiful, wide-expanding law, greatly
and powerfully, and whose face looks over all the seven Karshvares
of the earth;

65. "Who is swift amongst the swift, liberal amongst the liberal, strong
amongst the strong, a chief of assembly amongst the chiefs of assemblies; increase-giving, fatness-giving, cattle-giving, sovereignty-
giving, son-giving, cheerfulness-giving, and bliss-giving.

66. "With whom proceed Ashi Vanguhi, and Parendi on her light chariot,
the awful Manly Courage, the awful kingly Glory, the awful sovereign Sky, the awful cursing thought of the wise, the awful Fravashis
of the faithful, and he who keeps united together the many faithful
worshippers of Mazda.
"For his brightness and glory, I will offer him a sacrifice worth being
heard. . . .

XVII.

67. "We sacrifice unto Mithra, the lord of wide pastures, . . . sleepless, and
ever awake;
"Who drives along on his high-wheeled chariot, made of a heavenly
substance, from the Karshvare of Arezahi to the Karshvare of
Hvaniratha, the bright one; accompanied by the wheel of sovereignty, the Glory made by Mazda, and the Victory made by Ahura;

68. "Whose chariot is embraced by the great Ashi Vanguhi; to whom the
Law of Mazda opens a way, that he may go easily; whom four heavenly steeds, white, shining, seen afar, beneficent, endowed with
knowledge, swiftly carry along the heavenly space, while the cursing
thought of the wise pushes it forward;

69. "From whom all the Daevas unseen and the Varenya fiends flee away
in fear. Oh! may we never fall across the rush of the angry lord, who
goes and rushes from a thousand sides against his foe, he, of the ten
thousand spies, the powerful, all-knowing, undeceivable god.
"For his brightness and glory, I will offer him a sacrifice worth being
heard. . . .

XVIII.

70. "We sacrifice unto Mithra, the lord of wide pastures, . . . sleepless, and ever awake;

"Before whom Verethraghna, made by Ahura, runs opposing the foes in the shape of a boar, a sharp-toothed he-boar, a sharp-jawed boar, that kills at one stroke, pursuing, wrathful, with a dripping face; strong, with iron feet, iron fore-paws, iron weapons, an iron tail, and iron jaws;

71. "Who, eagerly clinging to the fleeing foe, along with Manly Courage, smites the foe in battle, and does not think he has smitten him, nor does he consider it a blow till he has smitten away the marrow and the column of life, the marrow and the spring of existence.

72. "He cuts all the limbs to pieces, and mingles, together with the earth, the bones, hair, brains, and blood of the men who have lied unto Mithra.

"For his brightness and glory, we offer him a sacrifice worth being heard. . . .

XIX.

73. "We sacrifice unto Mithra, the lord of wide pastures, . . . sleepless, and ever awake;

"Who, with hands lifted up, rejoicing, cries out, speaking thus:

74. "O Ahura Mazda, most beneficent spirit! Maker of the material world, thou Holy One!

"'If men would worship me with a sacrifice in which I were invoked by my own name, as they worship the other gods with sacrifices in which they are invoked by their own names, then I should come to the faithful at the appointed time; I should come in the appointed time of my beautiful, immortal life."

75. "May we keep our field; may we never be exiles from our field, exiles from our house, exiles from our borough, exiles from our town, exiles from our country.

76. *"Thou dashest in pieces the malice of the malicious, the malice of the men of malice: dash thou in pieces the killers of faithful men!*
"Thou hast good horses, thou hast a good chariot: thou art bringing help at every appeal, and art powerful.

77. *"I will pray unto thee for help, with many consecrations, with good consecrations of libations; with many offerings, with good offerings of libations, that we, abiding in thee, may long inhabit a good abode, full of all the riches that can be wished for.*

78. *"Thou keepest those nations that tender a good worship to Mithra, the lord of wide pastures; thou dashest in pieces those that delight in havoc. Unto thee will I pray for help: may he come to us for help, the awful, most powerful Mithra, the worshipful and praiseworthy, the glorious lord of nations.*
"For his brightness and glory, I will offer him a sacrifice worth being heard. . . .

XX.

79. *"We sacrifice unto Mithra, the lord of wide pastures, . . . sleepless, and ever awake;*
"Who made a dwelling for Rashnu, and to whom Rashnu gave all his soul for long friendship;

80. *"Thou art a keeper and protector of the dwelling of those who lie not: thou art the maintainer of those who lie not. With thee hath Verethraghna, made by Ahura, contracted the best of all friendships, and thus it is how so many men who have lied unto Mithra, even privily, lie smitten down on the ground.*
"For his brightness and glory, I will offer him a sacrifice worth being heard. . . .

XXI.

81. *"We sacrifice unto Mithra, the lord of wide pastures, . . . sleepless, and ever awake;*
"Who made a dwelling for Rashnu, and to whom Rashnu gave all his soul for long friendship;

82. "To whom Ahura Mazda gave a thousand senses and ten thousand eyes
to see. With those eyes and those senses, he watches the man who
injures Mithra, the man who lies unto Mithra. Through those eyes
and those senses, he is, undeceivable, he, of the ten thousand spies,
the powerful, all-knowing, undeceivable god.
"For his brightness and glory, I will offer him a sacrifice worth being
heard. . . .

XXII.

83. "We sacrifice unto Mithra, the lord of wide pastures, . . . sleepless, and
ever awake;
"Whom the lord of the country invokes for help, with hands uplifted;
"Whom the lord of the town invokes for help, with hands uplifted;

84. "Whom the lord of the borough invokes for help, with hands uplifted;
"Whom the master of the house invokes for help, with hands uplifted;
"Whom the . . . in danger of death invokes for help, with hands uplifted;
"Whom the poor man, who follows the good law, when wronged and
deprived of his rights, invokes for help, with hands uplifted.

85. "The voice of his wailing reaches up to the sky, it goes over the earth all
around, it goes over the seven Karshvares, whether he utters his
prayer in a low tone of voice or aloud.

86. "The cow driven astray invokes him for help, longing for the stables:
'When will that bull, Mithra, the lord of wide pastures, bring us
back, and make us reach the stables? When wilt he turn us back to
the right way from the den of the Druj where we were driven?'

87. "And to him with whom Mithra, the lord of wide pastures, has been satisfied, he comes with help; and of him with whom Mithra, the lord of
wide pastures, has been offended, he crushes down the house, the
borough, the town, the province, the country.
"For his brightness and glory, I will offer him a sacrifice worth being
heard. . . .

XXIII.

88. "We sacrifice unto Mithra, the lord of wide pastures, . . . sleepless, and
    ever awake;
    "To whom the enlivening, healing, fair, lordly golden-eyed Homa offered up
    a sacrifice on the highest of the heights, on the Haraiti Bareza, he the
    undefiled to one undefiled, with undefiled baresma, undefiled libations,
    and undefiled words;

89. "Whom the holy Ahura Mazda has established as a priest, quick in per-
    forming the sacrifice and loud in song. He performed the sacrifice
    with a loud voice, as a priest quick in sacrifice and loud in song, a
    priest to Ahura Mazda, a priest to the Amesha Spentas. His voice
    reached up to the sky; went over the earth all around, went over the
    seven Karshvares.

90. "Who first lifted up Homas, in a mortar inlaid with stars and made of a
    heavenly substance. Ahura Mazda longed for him, the Amesha
    Spentas longed for him, for the well-shapen body of him whom the
    swift-horsed sun awakes for prayer from afar.

91. "Hail to Mithra, the lord of wide pastures, who has a thousand ears and
    ten thousand eyes! Thou art worthy of sacrifice and prayer: mayest
    thou have sacrifice and prayer in the houses of men! Hail to the man
    who shall offer thee a sacrifice, with the holy wood in his hand, the
    baresma in his hand, the holy meat in his hand, the holy mortar in
    his hand, with his hands well-washed, with the mortar well-washed,
    with the bundles of baresma tied up, the Homa uplifted, and the
    Ahuna Vairya sung through.

92. "The holy Ahura Mazda confessed that religion and so did Vohu Mano,
    so did Asha Vahishta, so did Khshathra Vairya, so did Spenta
    Armaiti, so did Haurvatat and Ameretat; and all the Amesha Spentas
    longed for and confessed his religion. The kind Mazda conferred upon
    him the mastership of the world; and [so did they] who saw thee
    amongst all creatures the right lord and master of the world, the best
    cleanser of these creatures.

93. "So mayest thou in both worlds, mayest thou keep us in both worlds, O
    Mithra, lord of wide pastures! both in this material world and in the
    world of the spirit, from the fiend of Death, from the fiend Aeshma,
    from the fiendish hordes, that lift up the spear of havoc, and from the
    onsets of Aeshma, wherein the evil-doing Aeshma rushes along with
    Vidotu, made by the Daevas.

94. "So mayest thou, O Mithra, lord of wide pastures! give swiftness to our
    teams, strength to our own bodies, and that we may watch with full
    success those who hate us, smite down our foes, and destroy at one
    stroke our adversaries, our enemies and those who hate us.
    "For his brightness and glory, I will offer him a sacrifice worth being
    heard. . . .

XXIV.

95. "We sacrifice unto Mithra, the lord of wide pastures, . . . sleepless, and
    ever awake;
    "Who goes over the earth, all her breadth over, after the setting of the sun,
    touches both ends of this wide, round earth, whose ends tie afar, and
    surveys everything that is between the earth and the heavens,

96. "Swinging in his hands a club with a hundred knots, a hundred edges,
    that rushes forwards and fells men down; a club cast out of red brass,
    of strong, golden brass; the strongest of all weapons, the most victori-
    ous of all weapons;

97. "From whom Angra Mainyu, who is all death, flees away in fear; from
    whom Aeshma, the evil-doing Peshotanu, flees away in fear; from
    whom the long-handed Bushyasta flees away in fear; from whom all
    the Daevas unseen and the Varenya fiends flee away in fear.

98. "Oh! may we never fall across the rush of Mithra, the lord of wide pas-
    tures, when in anger! May Mithra, the lord of wide pastures, never
    smite us in his anger; he who stands up upon this earth as the
    strongest of all gods, the most valiant of all gods, the most energetic
    of all god , the swiftest of all gods, the most fiend-smiting of all gods,
    he, Mithra, the lord of wide pastures.
    "For his brightness and glory, I will offer him a sacrifice worth being
    heard. . . .

XXV.

99. "We sacrifice unto Mithra, the lord of wide pastures, . . . sleepless, and
   ever awake;
   "From whom all the Daevas unseen and the Varenya fiends flee away in fear.
   "The lord of nations, Mithra, the lord of wide pastures, drives forward at
   the right-hand side of this wide, round earth, whose ends lie afar.

100. "At his right hand drives the good, holy Sraosha; at his left hand drives
   the tall and strong Rashnu; on all sides around him drive the waters,
   the plants, and the Fravashis of the faithful.

101. "In his might, he ever brings to them falcon-feathered arrows, and,
   when driving, he himself comes there, where are nations, enemy to
   Mithra, he, first and foremost, strikes blows with his club on the
   horse and his rider; he throws fear and fright upon the horse and his
   rider.
   "For his brightness and glory, I will offer him a sacrifice worth being
   heard. . . .

XXVI.

102. "We sacrifice unto Mithra, the lord of wide pastures, . . . sleepless, and
   ever awake;
   "The warrior of the white horse, of the sharp spear, the tong spear, the
   quick arrows; foreseeing and clever;

103. "Whom Ahura Mazda has established to maintain and look over all this
   moving world, and who maintains and looks over all this moving
   world; who, never sleeping, wakefully guards the creation of Mazda;
   who, never sleeping, wakefully maintains the creation of Mazda;
   "For his brightness and glory, I will offer him a sacrifice worth being
   heard. . . .

XXVII.

104. "We sacrifice unto Mithra, the lord of wide pastures, . . . sleepless, and
   ever awake;
   "Whose long arms, strong with Mithra-strength, encompass what he seizes
   in the easternmost river and what he beats with the westernmost river,

what is by the Sanaka of the Rangha and what is by the boundary of the earth.

105. *"And thou, O Mithra! encompassing all this around, do thou reach it, all over, with thy arms.*

"The man without glory, led astray from the right way, grieves in his heart; the man without glory thinks thus in himself: 'That careless Mithra does not see all the evil that is done, nor all the lies that are told.'

106. *"But I think thus in my heart:*

"'Should the evil thoughts of the earthly man be a hundred times worse, they would not rise so high as the good thoughts of the heavenly Mithra;

"'Should the evil words of the earthly man be a hundred times worse, they would not rise so high as the good words of the heavenly Mithra;

"'Should the evil deeds of the earthly man be a hundred times worse, they would not rise so high as the good deeds of the heavenly Mithra;

107. *"'Should the heavenly wisdom in the earthly man be a hundred times greater, it would not rise so high as the heavenly wisdom in the heavenly Mithra;*

"'And thus, should the ears of the earthly man hear a hundred time better, he would not hear so well as the heavenly Mithra, whose ear hears well who has a thousand senses, and sees every man that tells a lie.'

"Mithra stands up in his strength, he drives in the awfulness of royalty, and sends from his eyes beautiful looks that shine from afar, (saying):

108. *"'Who will offer me a sacrifice? Who will lie unto me? Who thinks me a god worthy of a good sacrifice? Who thinks me worthy only of a bad sacrifice? To whom shall I, in my might, impart brightness and glory? To whom bodily health? To whom shall I, in my might, impart riches and full weal? Whom shall I bless by raising him a virtuous offspring?*

109. *"'To whom shall I give in return, without his thinking of it, the awful sovereignty, beautifully arrayed, with many armies, and most perfect; the sovereignty of an all-powerful tyrant, who fells down heads, valiant, smiting, and unsmitten; who orders chastisement to be done*

and his order is done at once, which he has ordered in his anger?'
"O Mithra! when thou art offended and not satisfied, he soothes thy
mind, and makes Mithra satisfied.

110. "'To whom shall I, in my might, impart sickness and death? To whom
shall I impart poverty and sterility? Of whom shall I at one stroke
cut off the offspring!

111. "'From whom shall I take away, without his thinking of it, the awful
sovereignty, beautifully arrayed, with many armies, and most perfect;
the sovereignty of an all-powerful tyrant, who fells down heads,
valiant, smiting, and unsmitten; who orders chastisement to be done
and his order is done at once, which he has ordered in his anger.'
"O Mithra! while thou art satisfied and not angry, he moves thy heart to
anger, and makes Mithra unsatisfied.
"For his brightness and glory, I will offer him a sacrifice worth being
heard. . . .

XXVIII.

112. "We sacrifice unto Mithra, the lord of wide pastures, . . . sleepless, and
ever awake;
"A warrior with a silver helm, a golden cuirass, who kills with the
poniard, strong, valiant, lord of the borough. Bright are the ways of
Mithra, by which he goes towards the country, when, wishing well,
he turns its plains and vales to pasture grounds,

113. "And then cattle and males come to graze, as many as he wants.
"May Mithra and Ahura, the high gods, come to us for help, when the
poniard lifts up its voice aloud, when the nostrils of the horses quiver,
when the poniards . . . when the strings of the bows whistle and shoot
sharp arrows; then the brood of those whose libations are hated fall
smitten to the ground, with their hair torn off.

114. "So mayest thou, O Mithra, lord of wide pastures! give swiftness to our
teams, strength to our own bodies, and that we may watch with full
success those who hate us, smite down our foes, and destroy at one
stroke our adversaries, our enemies, and those who hate us.
"For his brightness and glory, I will offer him a sacrifice worth being
heard. . . .

XXIX.

115. "We sacrifice unto Mithra, the lord of wide pastures, . . . sleepless, and
    ever awake.
    "O Mithra, lord of wide pastures! thou master of the house, of the borough,
        of the town, of the country, thou Zarathushtrotema!

116. "Mithra is twentyfold between two friends or two relations;
    "Mithra is thirtyfold between two men of the same group;
    "Mithra is fortyfold between two partners;
    "Mithra is fiftyfold between wife and husband;
    "Mithra is sixtyfold between two pupils (of the same master);
    "Mithra is seventyfold between the pupil and his master;
    "Mithra is eightyfold between the son-in-law and his father-in-law;
    "Mithra is ninetyfold between two brothers;

117. "Mithra is a hundredfold between the father and the son;
    "Mithra is a thousandfold between two nations;
    "Mithra is ten thousandfold when connected with the Law of Mazda,
        and then he will be every day of victorious strength.

118. "May I come unto thee with a prayer that goes lowly or goes highly! As
        this sun rises up above the Hara Berezaiti and then fulfills its career,
        so may I, O Spitama! with a prayer that goes lowly or goes highly,
        rise up above the will of the fiend Angra Mainyu!
    "For his brightness and glory, I will offer him a sacrifice worth being
        heard. . . .

XXX.

119. "We sacrifice unto Mithra, the lord of wide pastures, . . . sleepless, and
    ever awake,
    "Offer up a sacrifice unto Mithra, O Spitama! and order thy pupils to do
        the same.
    "Let the worshipper of Mazda sacrifice unto thee with small cattle, with
        black cattle, with flying birds, gliding forward on wings.

120. "To Mithra all the faithful worshippers of Mazda must give strength and energy with offered and proffered Homas, which the Zaotar proffers unto him and gives in sacrifice. Let the faithful man drink of the libations cleanly prepared, which if he does, if he offers them unto Mithra, the lord of wide pastures, Mithra will be pleased with him and without anger."

121. Zarathushtra asked him: "O Ahura Mazda! how shall the faithful man drink the libations cleanly prepared, which if he does and he offers them unto Mithra, the lord of wide pastures, Mithra will be pleased with him and without anger?"

122. Ahura Mazda answered: "Let them wash their bodies three days and three nights; let them undergo thirty strokes for the sacrifice and prayer unto Mithra, the lord of wide pastures. Let them wash their bodies two days and two nights; let them undergo twenty strokes for the sacrifice and prayer unto Mithra, the lord of wide pastures. Let no man drink of these libations who does not know the staota yesnya: Vispe ratavo."

"For his brightness and glory, I will offer him a sacrifice worth being heard. . . .

XXXI.

123. "We sacrifice unto Mithra, the lord of wide pastures, . . . sleepless, and ever awake;

"To whom Ahura Mazda offered up a sacrifice in the shining Garo-nmana.

124. "With his arms lifted up towards Immortality, Mithra, the lord of wide pastures, drives forward from the shining Garo-nmana, in a beautiful chariot that drives on, ever-swift, adorned with all sorts of ornaments, and made of gold.

125. "Four stallions draw that chariot, all of the same white color, living on heavenly food and undying. The hoofs of their fore-feet are shod with gold, the hoofs of their hind-feet are shod with silver; all are yoked to the same pole, and wear the yoke and the cross-beams of the yoke, fastened with hooks of Khshathra vairya to a beautiful . . .

126. "At his right hand drives Rashnu-Razishta, the most beneficent and
      most well-shapen.
      "At his left hand drives the most upright Chista, the holy one, bearing
      libations in her hands, clothed with white clothes, and white her-
      self; and the cursing thought of the Law of Mazda.

127. "Close by him drives the strong cursing thought of the wise man, oppos-
      ing foes in the shape of a boar, a sharp-toothed he-boar, a sharp-
      jawed boar, that kills at one stroke, pursuing, wrathful, with a
      dripping face, strong and swift to run, and rushing all around.
      "Behind him drives Atar, all in a blaze, and the awful kingly Glory.

128. "On a side of the chariot of Mithra, the lord of wide pastures, stand a
      thousand bows well-made, with a string of cowgut; they go through
      the heavenly space, they fall through the heavenly space upon the
      skulls of the Daevas.

129. "On a side of the chariot of Mithra, the lord of wide pastures, stand a
      thousand vulture-feathered arrows, with a golden mouth, with a horn
      shaft, with a brass tail, and well-made. They go through the heav-
      enly space, they fall through the heavenly space upon the skulls of
      the Daevas.

130. "On a side of the chariot of Mithra, the lord of wide pastures, stand a
      thousand spears well-made and sharp-piercing. They go through the
      heavenly space, they fall through the heavenly space upon the skulls
      of the Daevas.
      "On a side of the chariot of Mithra, the lord of wide pastures, stand a thou-
      sand steel-hammers, two-edged, well-made. They go through the heav-
      enly space, they fall through the heavenly space upon the skulls of the
      Daevas.

131. "On a side of the chariot of Mithra, the lord of wide pastures, stand a
      thousand swords, two-edged and well-made. They go through the
      heavenly space, they fall through the heavenly space upon the skulls
      of the Daevas.
      "On a side of the chariot of Mithra, the lord of wide pastures, stand a
      thousand maces of iron, well-made. They go through the heavenly
      space, they fall through the heavenly space upon the skulls of the
      Daevas.

132. "On a side of the chariot of Mithra, the lord of wide pastures, stands a beautiful well-falling club, with a hundred knots, a hundred edges, that rushes forward and fells men down; a club cast out of red brass, of strong, golden brass; the strongest of all weapons, the most victorious of all weapons. It goes through the heavenly space, it falls through the heavenly space upon the skulls of the Daevas.

133. "After he has smitten the Daevas, after he has smitten down the men who lied unto Mithra, Mithra, the lord of wide pastures, drives forward through Arezahe and Savahe, through Fradadhafshu and Vidadhafshu, through Vourubareshti and Vouru-jareshti, through this our Karshvare, the bright Hvaniratha.

134. "Angra Mainyu, who is all death, flees away in fear; Aeshma, the evil-doing Peshotanu, flees away in fear; the long-handed Bushyasta flees away in fear; all the Daevas unseen and the Varenya fiends flee away in fear.

135. "Oh! may we never fall across the rush of Mithra, the lord of wide pastures, when in anger! May Mithra, the lord of wide pastures, never smite us in his anger; he who stands up upon this earth as the strongest of all gods, the most valiant of all gods, the most energetic of all gods, the swiftest of all gods, the most fiend-smiting of all gods, he, Mithra, the lord of wide pastures.
"For his brightness and glory, I will offer him a sacrifice worth being heard. . . .

XXXII.

136. "We sacrifice unto Mithra, the lord of wide pastures, . . . sleepless, and ever awake;
"For whom white stallions, yoked to his chariot, draw it, on one golden wheel, with a full shining axle.

137. "If Mithra takes his libations to his own dwelling, 'Happy that man, I think,' said Ahura Mazda,—'O holy Zarathushtra! for whom a holy priest, as pious as any in the world, who is the Word incarnate, offers up a sacrifice unto Mithra with bundles of baresma and with the [proper] words.

"'Straight to that man, I think, will Mithra come, to visit his dwelling,

138. "'When Mithra's boons will come to him, as he follows God's teaching, and thinks according to God's teaching.
"'Woe to that man, I think,' said Ahura Mazda, 'O holy Zarathushtra! for whom an unholy priest, not pious, who is not the Word incarnate, stands behind the baresma, however full may be the bundles of baresma he ties, however long may be the sacrifice he performs.'

139. "He does not delight Ahura Mazda, nor the other Amesha Spentas, nor Mithra, the lord of wide pastures, he who thus scorns Mazda, and the other Amesha Spentas, and Mithra, the lord of wide pastures, and the Law, and Rashnu, and Arstat, who makes the world grow, who makes the world increase.
"For his brightness and glory, I will offer him a sacrifice worth being heard. . . .

XXXIII.

140. "We sacrifice unto Mithra, the lord of wide pastures, . . . sleepless, and ever awake.
"I will offer up a sacrifice unto the good Mithra, O Spitama! unto the strong, heavenly god, who is foremost, highly merciful, and peerless; whose house is above, a stout and strong warrior;

141. "Victorious and armed with a well-fashioned weapon, watchful in darkness and undeceivable. He is the stoutest of the stoutest, he is the strongest of the strongest, he is the most intelligent of the gods, he is victorious and endowed with Glory: he, of the ten thousand eyes, of the ten thousand spies, the powerful, all-knowing, undeceivable god.
"For his brightness and glory, I will offer him a sacrifice worth being heard. . . .

XXXIV.

142. "We sacrifice unto Mithra, the lord of wide pastures, . . . sleepless, and ever awake;
"Who, with his manifold knowledge, powerfully increases the creation of

Spenta Mainyu, and is a well-created and most great Yazata, self-shining like the moon, when he makes his own body shine;

143. "Whose face is flashing with light like the face of the star Tistrya; whose chariot is embraced by that goddess who is foremost amongst those who have no deceit in them, O Spitama! who is fairer than any creature in the world, and full of light to shine. I will worship that chariot, wrought by the Maker, Ahura Mazda, inlaid with stars and made of a heavenly substance; (the chariot) of Mithra, who has ten thousand spies, the powerful, all-knowing, undeceivable god.
"For his brightness and glory, I will offer him a sacrifice worth being heard. . . .

XXXV.

144. "We sacrifice unto Mithra, the lord of wide pastures, who is truth-speaking, a chief in assemblies, with a thousand ears, well-shapen, with a thousand eyes, high, with full knowledge, strong, sleepless, and ever awake.
"We sacrifice unto the Mithra around countries;
"We sacrifice unto the Mithra within countries;
"We sacrifice unto the Mithra in this country;*
"We sacrifice unto the Mithra above countries;
"We sacrifice unto the Mithra under countries;
"We sacrifice unto the Mithra before countries;
"We sacrifice unto the Mithra behind countries.

145. "We sacrifice unto Mithra and Ahura, the two great, imperishable, holy gods; and unto the stars, and the moon, and the sun, with the trees that yield up baresma. We sacrifice unto Mithra, the lord of all countries.
"For his brightness and glory, I will offer unto him a sacrifice worth being heard, namely, unto Mithra, the lord of wide pastures.

146.†"Yatha ahu vairyo: The will of the Lord is the law of holiness. . . . I bless the sacrifice and prayer, and the strength and vigour of Mithra, the

---

* This line is not in all the Farsi editions.
†Number 146 is missing in the "Sacred Books of the East" 1898 edition, however some of the text is present. In the Farsi edition, there is a "146" and the text is longer, hence I have translated and extended it here.

lord of wide pastures, who has a thousand ears, ten thousand eyes, a Yazata invoked by his own name; and that of Rama Hvastra.

"Ashem Vohu: Holiness is the best of all good. . . .

"[Give] unto that man brightness and glory, . . . give him the bright, all-happy, blissful abode of the holy Ones!

"To one who worships you, you grant glory and splendour, good health and a strong body, a victorious body and a peaceful state, graceful children, a long life, a shining paradise, and all kinds of peace-giving illuminations."

ZOROASTRIAN HYMN TO ANAHITA (ABAN YASHT 5)

This translation from the Avesta by James Darmesteter was first published in *Sacred Books of the East*, American Edition, 1898, part of Oxford University Press's Sacred Books of the East (SBE) series. Copyright permission has been kindly given by Joseph H. Peterson. I have corrected here some typos that appeared in the 1898 SBE edition. The original hymn is found in the Yasht section of the Avesta and is estimated to be from around 500 B.C.E., though as with the Mithra hymn, some parts are probably much older than that.

> *May Ahura Mazda be rejoiced! . . .*
> *Ashem Vohu: Holiness is the best of all good. . . .*
> *I confess myself a worshipper of Mazda, a follower of*
>   *Zarathushtra, one who hates the Daevas and obeys the laws of*
>   *Ahura;*
> *For sacrifice, prayer, propitiation, and glorification unto [Havani],*
>   *the holy and master of holiness. . . .*
> *Unto the good Waters, made by Mazda; unto the holy water-spring*
>   *ARDVI ANAHITA; unto all waters, made by Mazda; unto all*
>   *plants, made by Mazda,*
> *Be propitiation, with sacrifice, prayer, propitiation, and*
>   *glorification.*
> *Yatha ahu vairyo: The will of the Lord is the law of holiness. . . .*

I.

1. *Ahura Mazda spake unto Spitama Zarathushtra, saying: "Offer up a sacrifice, O Spitama Zarathushtra! unto this spring of mine, Ardvi Sura Anahita, the wide-expanding and health-giving, who hates the Daevas and obeys the laws of Ahura, who is worthy of sacrifice in the material world, worthy of prayer in the material world; the life-increasing and holy, the herd-increasing and holy, the fold-increasing and holy, the wealth-increasing and holy, the country-increasing and holy;*

2. *"Who makes the seed of all males pure, who makes the womb of all females pure for bringing forth, who makes all females bring forth in safety, who puts milk into the breasts of all females in the right measure and the right quality;*

3. *"The large river, known afar, that is as large as the whole of the waters that run along the earth; that runs powerfully from the height Hukairya down to the sea Vouru-Kasha.*

4. *"All the shores of the sea Vouru-Kasha are boiling over, all the middle of it is boiling over, when she runs down there, when she streams down there, she, Ardvi Sura Anahita, who has a thousand cells and a thousand channels: the extent of each of those cells, of each of those channels is as much as a man can ride in forty days, riding on a good horse.*

5. *"From this river of mine alone flow all the waters that spread all over the seven Karshvares; this river of mine alone goes on bringing waters, both in summer and in winter. This river of mine purifies the seed in males, the womb in females, the milk in females' breasts.*

6. *"I, Ahura Mazda, brought it down with mighty vigor, for the increase of the house, of the borough, of the town, of the country, to keep them, to maintain them, to look over them, to keep and maintain them close.*

7. *"Then Ardvi Sura Anahita, O Spitama Zarathushtra! proceeded forth from the Maker Mazda. Beautiful were her white arms, thick as a horse's shoulder or still thicker; beautiful was her . . . , and thus came she, strong, with thick arms, thinking thus in her heart:*

8. "'Who will praise me? Who will offer me a sacrifice, with libations cleanly prepared and well-strained, together with the Homa and meat? To whom shall I cleave, who cleaves unto me, and thinks with me, and bestows gifts upon me, and is of good will unto me?'

9. "For her brightness and glory, I will offer her a sacrifice worth being heard; I will offer up unto the holy Ardvi Sura Anahita a good sacrifice with an offering of libations; thus mayest thou advise us when thou art appealed to! Mayest thou be most fully worshipped, O Ardvi Sura Anahita! with the Homa and meat, with the baresma, with the wisdom of the tongue, with the holy spells, with the words, with the deeds, with the libations, and with the rightly-spoken words.
"Yenhe hatam: All those beings of whom Ahura Mazda . . .

II.

10. "Offer up a sacrifice, O Spitama Zarathushtra! unto this spring of mine, Ardvi Sura Anahita, the wide-expanding and health-giving, who hates the Daevas and obeys the laws of Ahura, who is worthy of sacrifice in the material world, worthy of prayer in the material world; the life-increasing and holy, the herd-increasing and holy, the fold-increasing and holy, the wealth-increasing and holy, the country-increasing and holy;

11. "Who drives forwards on her chariot, holding the reins of the chariot. She goes, driving, on this chariot, longing for men and thinking thus in her heart: 'Who will praise me? Who will offer me a sacrifice, with libations cleanly prepared and well strained, together with the Homa and meat? To whom shall I cleave, who cleaves unto me, and thinks with me, and bestows gifts unto me, and is of good will unto me?'
"For her brightness and glory, I will offer her a sacrifice, worth being heard. . . .

III.

12. "Offer up a sacrifice, O Spitama Zarathushtra! unto this spring of mine, Ardvi Sura Anahita. . . .

13. "Whom four horses carry, all white, of one and the same color, of the same blood, tall, crushing down the hates of all haters, of the Daevas

and men, of the Yatus and Pairikas, of the oppressors, of the blind and of the deaf.
"For her brightness and glory, I will offer her a sacrifice. . . .

IV.

14. "Offer up a sacrifice, O Spitama Zarathushtra! unto this spring of mine, Ardvi Sura Anahita. . . .

15. "Strong and bright, tall and beautiful of form, who sends down by day and by night a flow of motherly waters as large as the whole of the waters that run along the earth, and who runs powerfully.
"For her brightness and glory, I will offer her a sacrifice. . . .

V.

16. "Offer up a sacrifice, O Spitama Zarathushtra! unto this spring of mine, Ardvi Sura Anahita. . . .

17. "To her did the Maker Ahura Mazda offer up a sacrifice to the Airyana Vaejah, by the good river Daitya; with the Homa and meat, with the baresma, with the wisdom of the tongue, with the holy spells, with the words, with the deeds, with the libations, and with the rightly-spoken words.

18. "He begged of her a boon, saying: 'Grant me this, O good, most benefi-cent Ardvi Sura Anahita! that I may bring the son of Pourushaspa, the holy Zarathushtra, to think after my law, to speak after my law, to do after my law!'

19. "Ardvi Sura Anahita granted him that boon, as he was offering liba-tions, giving gifts, sacrificing, and begging that she would grant him that boon.
"For her brightness and glory, I will offer her a sacrifice. . . .

VI.

20. "Offer up a sacrifice, O Spitama Zarathushtra! unto this spring of mine, Ardvi Sura Anahita. . . .

21. "To her did Haoshyangha, the Paradhata, offer up a sacrifice on the enclosure of the Hara, with a hundred male horses, a thousand oxen, and ten thousand lambs.

22. "He begged of her a boon, saying: 'Grant me this, O good, most benefi-cent Ardvi Sura Anahita, that I may become the sovereign lord of all countries, of the Daevas and men, of the Yatus and Pairikas, of the oppressors, the blind and the deaf; and that I may smite down two thirds of the Daevas of Mazana and of the fiends of Varena.'

23. "Ardvi Sura Anahita granted him that boon, as he was offering liba-tions, giving gifts, sacrificing, and entreating that she would grant him that boon.
"For her brightness and glory, I will offer her a sacrifice . . .

VII.

24. "Offer up a sacrifice, O Spitama Zarathushtra! unto this spring of mine, Ardvi Sura Anahita. . . .

25. "To her did Yima Khshaeta, the good shepherd, offer up a sacrifice from the height Hukairya, with a hundred male horses, a thousand oxen, ten thousand lambs.

26. "He begged of her a boon, saying: 'Grant me this, O good, most benefi-cent Ardvi Sura Anahita! that I may become the sovereign lord of all countries, of the Daevas and men, of the Yatus and Pairikas, of the oppressors, the blind and the deaf; and that I may take from the Daevas both riches and welfare, both fatness and flocks, both weal and Glory.'

27. "Ardvi Sura Anahita granted him that boon, as he was offering liba-tions, giving gifts, sacrificing, and entreating that she would grant him that boon.
"For her brightness and glory, I will offer her a sacrifice. . . .

VIII.

28. "Offer up a sacrifice, O Spitama Zarathushtra! unto this spring of mine, Ardvi Sura Anahita. . . .

29. "To her did Azi Dahaka, the three-mouthed, offer up a sacrifice in the land of Bawri, with a hundred male horses, a thousand oxen, and ten thousand lambs.

30. "He begged of her a boon, saying: 'Grant me this boon, O good, most beneficent Ardvi Sura Anahita! that I may make all the seven Karshvares of the earth empty of men.'

31. "Ardvi Sura Anahita did not grant him that boon, although he was offering libations, giving gifts, sacrificing, and entreating her that she would grant him that boon.
"For her brightness and glory, I will offer her a sacrifice. . . .

IX.

32. "Offer up a sacrifice, O Spitama Zarathushtra! unto Ardvi Sura Anahita. . . .

33. "To her did Thraetaona, the heir of the valiant Athwya clan, offer up a sacrifice in the four-cornered Varena, with a hundred male horses, a thousand oxen, ten thousand lambs.

34. "He begged of her a boon, saying: 'Grant me this, O good, most beneficent Ardvi Sura Anahita! that I may overcome Azi Dahaka, the three-mouthed, the three-headed, the six-eyed, who has a thousand senses, that most powerful, fiendish Druj, that demon, baleful to the world, the strongest Druj that Angra Mainyu created against the material world, to destroy the world of the good principle; and that I may deliver his two wives, Savanghavach and Erenavach, who are the fairest of body amongst women, and the most wonderful creatures in the world.'

35. "Ardvi Sura Anahita granted him that boon, as he was offering libations, giving gifts, sacrificing, and entreating that she would grant him that boon.
"For her brightness and glory, I will offer her a sacrifice. . . .

X.

36. "Offer up a sacrifice, O Spitama Zarathushtra! unto Ardvi Sura Anahita. . . .

37. "To her did Keresaspa, the manly-hearted, offer up a sacrifice behind the Vairi Pisanah, with a hundred male horses, a thousand oxen, ten thousand lambs.

38. "He begged of her a boon, saying: 'Grant me this, O good, most beneficent Ardvi Sura Anahita! that I may overcome the golden-heeled Gandarewa, though all the shores of the sea Vouru-Kasha are boiling over; and that I may run up to the stronghold of the fiend on the wide, round earth, whose ends lie afar.'

39. "Ardvi Sura Anahita granted him that boon, as he was offering libations, giving gifts, sacrificing, and entreating that she would grant him that boon.
"For her brightness and glory, I will offer her a sacrifice. . . .

XI.

40. "Offer up a sacrifice, O Spitama Zarathushtra! unto this spring of mine, Ardvi Sura Anahita. . . .

41. "To her did the Turanian murderer, Frangrasyan, offer up a sacrifice in his cave under the earth, with a hundred male horses, a thousand oxen, ten thousand lambs.

42. "He begged of her a boon, saying: 'Grant me this, O good, most beneficent Ardvi Sura Anahita! that I may seize hold of that Glory, that is waving in the middle of the sea Vouru-Kasha and that belongs to the Aryan people, to those born and to those not yet born, and to the holy Zarathushtra.'

43. "Ardvi Sura Anahita did not grant him that boon.
"For her brightness and glory, I will offer her a sacrifice . . .

XII.

44. "Offer up a sacrifice, O Spitama Zarathushtra! unto this spring of mine,
Ardvi Sura Anahita.

45. "To her did the great, most wise Kavi Usa offer up a sacrifice from
Mount Erezifya, with a hundred male horses, a thousand oxen, ten
thousand lambs.

46. "He begged of her a boon, saying: 'Grant me, this, O good, most beneficent Ardvi Sura Anahita! that I may become the sovereign lord of all
countries, of the Daevas and men, of the Yatus and Pairikas, of the
oppressors, the blind and the deaf.'

47. "Ardvi Sura Anahita granted him that boon, as he was offering libations, giving gifts, sacrificing, and entreating that she would grant
him that boon.
"For her brightness and glory, I will offer her a sacrifice. . . .

XIII.

48. "Offer up a sacrifice, O Spitama Zarathushtra! unto this spring of mine,
Ardvi Sura Anahita. . . .

49. "To her did the gallant Husravah, he who united the Aryan nations into
one kingdom, offer up a sacrifice behind the Chaechasta lake, the
deep lake, of salt waters, with a hundred male horses, a thousand
oxen, ten thousand lambs.

50. "He begged of her a boon, saying: 'Grant me this, O good, most beneficent Ardvi Sura Anahita! that I may become the sovereign lord of all
countries, of Daevas and men, of the Yatus and Pairikas, of the
oppressors, the blind and the deaf; and that I may have the lead in
front of all the teams and that he may not pass through the forest, he,
the murderer, who now is fiercely striving against me on horseback.'

51. "Ardvi Sura Anahita granted him that boon, as he was offering libations, giving gifts, sacrificing, and entreating that she would grant
him that boon.
"For her brightness and glory, I will offer her a sacrifice. . . .

XIV.

52. "Offer up a sacrifice, O Spitama Zarathushtra! unto this spring of mine, Ardvi Sura Anahita. . . .

53. "To her did the valiant warrior Tusa offer worship on the back of his horse, begging swiftness for his teams, health for his own body, and that he might watch with full success those who hated him, smite down his foes, and destroy at one stroke his adversaries, his enemies, and those who hated him.

54. "He begged of her a boon, saying: 'Grant me this, O good, most beneficent Ardvi Sura Anahita! that I may overcome the gallant sons of Vaesaka, by the castle Khshathro-saoka, that stands high up on the lofty, holy Kangha; that I may smite of the Turanian people their fifties and their hundreds, their hundreds and their thousands, their thousands and their tens of thousands, their tens of thousands and their myriads of myriads.'

55. "Ardvi Sura Anahita granted him that boon, as he was offering libations, giving gifts, sacrificing, and entreating that she would grant him that boon.
"For her brightness and glory, I will offer her a sacrifice. . . .

XV.

56. "Offer up a sacrifice, O Spitama Zarathushtra! unto this spring of mine, Ardvi Sura Anahita. . . .

57. "To her did the gallant sons of Vaesaka offer up a sacrifice in the castle Khshathro-saoka, that stands high up on the lofty, holy Kangha, with a hundred male horses, a thousand oxen, ten thousand lambs.

58. "They begged of her a boon, saying: 'Grant us this, O good, most beneficent Ardvi Sura Anahita! that we may overcome the valiant warrior Tusa, and that we may smite of the Aryan people their fifties and their hundreds, their hundreds and their thousands, their thousands and their tens of thousands, their tens of thousands and their myriads of myriads.'

59. "Ardvi Sura Anahita did not grant them that boon.
"For her brightness and glory, I will offer her a sacrifice. . . .

XVI.

60. "Offer up a sacrifice, O Spitama Zarathushtra! unto this spring of mine, Ardvi Sura Anahita. . . .

61. "The old Vafra Navaza worshipped her when the strong fiend-smiter, Thraetaona, flung him up in the air in the shape of a bird, of a vulture.

62. "He went on flying, for three days and three nights, towards his own house; but he could not, he could not turn down. At the end of the third night, when the beneficent dawn came dawning up, then he prayed unto Ardvi Sura Anahita, saying:

63. "'Ardvi Sura Anahita! do thou quickly hasten helpfully and bring me assistance at once. I will offer thee a thousand libations, cleanly prepared and well strained, along with Homas and meat, by the brink of the river Rangha, if I reach alive the earth made by Ahura and my own house.'

64. "Ardvi Sura Anahita hastened unto him in the shape of a maid, fair of body, most strong, tall-formed, high-girdled, pure, nobly born of a glorious race, wearing shoes up to the ankle, wearing a golden . . . , and radiant.

65. "She seized him by the arm: quickly was it done, nor was it long till, speeding, he arrived at the earth made by Mazda and at his own house, safe, unhurt, unwounded, just as he was before.

66. "Ardvi Sura Anahita granted him that boon, as he was offering up libations, giving gifts, sacrificing, entreating that she would grant him that boon.
"For her brightness and glory, I will offer her a sacrifice. . . .

XVII.

67. "Offer up a sacrifice, O Spitama Zarathushtra! unto this spring of mine, Ardvi Sura Anahita. . . .

68. "To her did Jamaspa offer up a sacrifice, with a hundred horses, a thousand oxen, ten thousand lambs, when he saw the army of the wicked, of the worshippers of the Daevas, coming from afar in battle array.

69. "He asked of her a boon, saying: 'Grant me this, O good, most beneficent Ardvi Sura Anahita! that I may be as constantly victorious as any one of all the Aryans.'

70. "Ardvi Sura Anahita granted him that boon, as he was offering up libations, giving gifts, sacrificing, and entreating that she would grant him that boon.
"For her brightness and glory, I will offer her a sacrifice. . . .

XVIII.

71. "Offer up a sacrifice, O Spitama Zarathushtra! unto this spring of mine, Ardvi Sura Anahita. . . .

72. "To her did Ashavazdah, the son of Pouru-dhakhshti, and Ashavazdah and Thrita, the sons of Sayuzhdri, offer up a sacrifice, with a hundred horses, a thousand oxen, ten thousand lambs, by Apam Napat, the tall lord, the lord of the females, the bright and swift-horsed.

73. "They begged of her a boon, saying: 'Grant us this, O good, most beneficent Ardvi Sura Anahita! that we may overcome the assemblers of the Turanian Danus, Kara Asabana, and Vara Asabana, and the most mighty Duraekaeta, in the battles of this world.'

74. "Ardvi Sura Anahita granted them that boon, as they were offering up libations, giving gifts, sacrificing, and entreating that she would grant them that boon.
"For her brightness and glory, l will offer her a sacrifice. . . .

XIX.

75. *"Offer up a sacrifice, O Spitama Zarathushtra! unto this spring of mine, Ardvi Sura Anahita. . . .*

76. *"Vistauru, the son of Naotara, worshipped her by the brink of the river Vitanghuhaiti, with well-spoken words, speaking thus:*

77. *"'This is true, this is truly spoken, that I have smitten as many of the worshippers of the Daevas as the hairs I bear on my head. Do thou then, O Ardvi Sura Anahita! leave me a dry passage, to pass over the good Vitanghuhaiti.'*

78. *"Ardvi Sura Anahita hastened unto him in the shape of a maid, fair of body, most strong, tall-formed, high-girded, pure, nobly born of a glorious race, wearing shoes up to the ankle, with all sorts of ornaments and radiant. A part of the waters she made stand still, a part of the waters she made flow forward, and she left him a dry passage to pass over the good Vitanghuhaiti.*

79. *"Ardvi Sura Anahita granted him that boon, as he was offering up libations, giving gifts, sacrificing, and entreating that she would grant him that boon.*
"For her brightness and glory, I will offer her a sacrifice. . . .

XX.

80. *"Offer up a sacrifice, O Spitama Zarathushtra! unto this spring of mine, Ardvi Sura Anahita. . . .*

81. *"To her did Yoishta, one of the Fryanas, offer up a sacrifice with a hundred horses, a thousand oxen, ten thousand lambs on the Pedvaepa of the Rangha.*

82. *"He begged of her a boon, saying: 'Grant me this, O good, most beneficent Ardvi Sura Anahita! that I may overcome the evil-doing Akhtya, the offspring of darkness, and that I may answer the ninety-nine hard riddles that he asks me maliciously, the evil-doing Akhtya, the offspring of darkness.'*

83. "Ardvi Sura Anahita granted him that boon, as he was offering up libations, giving gifts, sacrificing, and entreating that she would grant him that boon. ‹

"For her brightness and glory, I will offer her a sacrifice. . . .

XXI.

84. "Offer up a sacrifice, O Spitama Zarathushtra! unto this spring of mine, Ardvi Sura Anahita. . . .

85. "Whom Ahura Mazda the merciful ordered thus, saying: 'Come, O Ardvi Sura Anahita, come from those stars down to the earth made by Ahura, that the great lords may worship thee, the masters of the countries, and their sons.

86. "'The men of strength will beg of thee swift horses and supremacy of Glory.

"'The Athravans who read and the pupils of the Athravans will beg of thee knowledge and prosperity, the Victory made by Ahura, and the crushing Ascendant.

87. "'The maids of barren womb, longing for a lord, will beg of thee a strong husband;

"'Women, on the point of bringing forth, will beg of thee a good delivery.

"'All this wilt thou grant unto them, as it lies in thy power, O Ardvi Sura Anahita!'

88. "Then Ardvi Sura Anahita came forth, O Zarathushtra! down from those stars to the earth made by Mazda; and Ardvi Sura Anahita spake thus:

89. "'O pure, holy Zarathushtra! Ahura Mazda has established thee as the master of the material world: Ahura Mazda has established me to keep the whole of the holy creation.

"'Through my brightness and glory flocks and herds and two-legged men go on, upon the earth: I, forsooth, keep all good things, made by Mazda, the offspring of the holy principle, just as a shepherd keeps his flock.'

90. "Zarathushtra asked Ardvi Sura Anahita: 'O Ardvi Sura Anahita! With
    what manner of sacrifice shall I worship thee? With what manner of
    sacrifice shall I worship and forward thee? So that Mazda may make
    thee run down (to the earth), that he may not make thee run up into
    the heavens, above the sun; and that the Serpent may not injure thee
    with . . . , with . . . , with . . . , and . . . poisons.'

91. "Ardvi Sura Anahita answered: 'O pure, holy Spitama! this is the sacri-
    fice wherewith thou shalt worship me, this is the sacrifice wherewith
    thou shalt worship and forward me, from the time when the sun is
    rising to the time when the sun is setting.
    "'Of this libation of mine thou shalt drink, thou who art an Athravan, who
    hast asked and learnt the revealed law, who art wise, clever, and the
    Word incarnate.

92. "'Of this libation of mine let no foe drink, no man fever-sick, no liar, no
    coward, no jealous one, no woman, no faithful one who does not sing
    the Gathas, no leper to be confined.

93. "'I do not accept those libations that are drunk in my honor by the
    blind, by the deaf, by the wicked, by the destroyers, by the niggards,
    by the . . . , nor any of those stamped with those characters which
    have no strength for the holy Word.
    "'Let no one drink of these my libations who is hump-backed or bulged
    forward; no fiend with decayed teeth.'

94. "Then Zarathushtra asked Ardvi Sura Anahita: 'O Ardvi Sura Anahita!
    What becomes of those libations which the wicked worshippers of the
    Daevas bring unto thee after the sun has set?'

95. "Ardvi Sura Anahita answered: 'O pure, holy Spitama Zarathushtra!
    howling, clapping, hopping, and shouting, six hundred and a thou-
    sand Daevas, who ought not to receive that sacrifice, receive those
    libations that men bring unto me after [the sun has set].'

96. "I will worship the height Hukairya, of the deep precipices, made of
    gold, wherefrom this mine Ardvi Sura Anahita leaps, from a hun-
    dred times the height of a man, while she is possessed of as much

Glory as the whole of the waters that run along the earth, and she
runs powerfully.
"For her brightness and glory, I will offer her a sacrifice. . . .

XXII.

97. "Offer up a sacrifice, O Spitama Zarathushtra! unto this spring of mine,
Ardvi Sura Anahita. . . .

98. "Before whom the worshippers of Mazda stand with baresma in their
hands: the Hvovas did worship her, the Naotaras did worship her; the
Hvovas asked for riches, the Naotaras asked for swift horses.
Quickly was Hvova blessed with riches and full prosperity; quickly
became Vishtaspa, the Naotaride, the lord of the swiftest horses in
these countries.

99. "Ardvi Sura Anahita granted them that boon, as they were offering up
libations, giving gifts, sacrificing, and entreating that she would
grant them that boon.
"For her brightness and glory, I will offer her a sacrifice. . . .

XXIII.

100. "Offer up a sacrifice, O Spitama Zarathushtra! unto this spring of mine,
Ardvi Sura Anahita. . . .

101. "Who has a thousand cells and a thousand channels: the extent of each of
those cells, of each of those channels, is as much as a man can ride in
forty days, riding on a good horse. In each channel there stands a
palace, well founded, shining with a hundred windows, with a thousand columns, well built, with ten thousand balconies, and mighty.

102. "In each of those palaces there lies a well-laid, well-scented bed, covered
with pillows, and Ardvi Sura Anahita, O Zarathushtra! runs down
there from a thousand times the height of a man, and she is possessed
of as much Glory as the whole of the waters that run along the earth,
and she runs powerfully.

XXIV.

103. *"Offer up a sacrifice, O Spitama Zarathushtra! unto this spring of mine, Ardvi Sura Anahita. . . .*

104. *"Unto her did the holy Zarathushtra offer up a sacrifice in the Airyana Vaejah, by the good river Daitya; with the Homa and meat, with the baresma, with the wisdom of the tongue, with the holy spells, with the speech, with the deeds, with the libations, and with the rightly-spoken words.*

105. *"He begged of her a boon, saying: 'Grant me this, O good, most benefi-cent Ardvi Sura Anahita! that I may bring the son of Aurvat-aspa, the valiant Kavi Vistaspa, to think according to the law, to speak according to the law, to do according to the law.'*

106. *"Ardvi Sura Anahita granted him that boon, as he was offering up liba-tions, giving gifts, sacrificing, and entreating that she would grant him that boon.*
"For her brightness and glory, I will offer her a sacrifice. . . .

XXV.

107. *"Offer up a sacrifice, O Spitama Zarathushtra! unto this spring of mine, Ardvi Sura Anahita. . . .*

108. *"Unto her did the tall Kavi Vishtaspa offer up a sacrifice behind Lake Frazdanava, with a hundred male horses, a thousand oxen, ten thou-sand lambs.*

109. *"He begged of her a boon, saying: 'Grant me this, O good, most benefi-cent Ardvi Sura Anahita! that I may overcome Tathravant, of the bad law, and Peshana, the worshipper of the Daevas and the wicked Arejat-aspa, in the battles of this world!'*

110. *"Ardvi Sura Anahita granted him that boon, as he was offering up liba-tions, giving gifts, sacrificing, and entreating that she would grant him that boon.*
"For her brightness and glory, I will offer her a sacrifice. . . .

XXVI.

111. "Offer up a sacrifice, O Spitama Zarathushtra! unto this spring of mine, Ardvi Sura Anahita. . . .

112. "Unto her did Zairi-vairi, who fought on horseback, offer up a sacrifice behind the river Daitya, with a hundred male horses, a thousand oxen, ten thousand lambs.

113. "He begged of her a boon, saying: 'Grant me this, O good, most beneficent Ardvi Sura Anahita! that I may overcome Pesho-Changha the corpse-burier, Humayaka the worshipper of the Daevas, and the wicked Arejat-aspa, in the battles of this world.'

114. "Ardvi Sura Anahita granted him that boon, as he was offering up libations, giving gifts, sacrificing, and entreating that she would grant him that boon.
"For her brightness and glory, I will offer her a sacrifice. . . .

XXVII.

115. "Offer up a sacrifice, O Spitama Zarathushtra! unto this spring of mine, Ardvi Sura Anahita. . . .

116. "Unto her did Arejat-aspa and Vandaremaini offer up a sacrifice by the sea Vouru-Kasha, with a hundred male horses, a thousand oxen, ten thousand lambs.

117. "They begged of her a boon, saying: 'Grant us this, O good, most beneficent Ardvi Sura Anahita! that we may conquer the valiant Kavi Vishtaspa and Zairi-vairi who fights on horseback, and that we may smite of the Aryan people their fifties and their hundreds, their hundreds and their thousands, their thousands and their tens of thousands, their tens of thousands and their myriads of myriads.'

118. "Ardvi Sura Anahita did not grant them that favor, though they were offering up libations, giving gifts, sacrificing, and entreating that she should grant them that favor.
"For her brightness and glory, I will offer her a sacrifice. . . .

XXVIII.

119. *"Offer up a sacrifice, O Spitama Zarathushtra! unto this spring of mine, Ardvi Sura Anahita. . . .*

120. *"For whom Ahura Mazda has made four horses—the wind, the rain, the cloud, and the sleet—and thus ever upon the earth it is raining, snowing, hailing, and sleeting; and whose armies are so many and numbered by nine-hundreds and thousands.*

121. *"I will worship the height Hukairya, of the deep precipices, made of gold, wherefrom this mine Ardvi Sura Anahita leaps, from a hundred times the height of a man, while she is possessed of as much Glory as the whole of the waters that run along the earth, and she runs powerfully.*
"For her brightness and glory, I will offer her a sacrifice. . . .

XXIX.

122. *"Offer up a sacrifice, O Spitama Zarathushtra! unto this spring of mine, Ardvi Sura Anahita. . . .*

123. *"She stands, the good Ardvi Sura Anahita, wearing a golden mantle, waiting for a man who shall offer her libations and prayers, and thinking thus in her heart:*

124. *"'Who will praise me? Who will offer me a sacrifice, with libations cleanly prepared and well-strained, together with the Homa and meat? To whom shall I cleave, who cleaves unto me, and thinks with me, and bestows gifts upon, me, and is of good will unto me?'*
"For her brightness and glory, I will offer her a sacrifice. . . .

XXX.

125. *"Offer up a sacrifice, O Spitama Zarathushtra! unto this spring of mine, Ardvi Sura Anahita. . . .*

126. *"Ardvi Sura Anahita, who stands carried forth in the shape of a maid, fair of body, most strong, tall-formed, high-girded, pure, nobly born of a glorious race, wearing along her . . . a mantle fully embroidered with gold;*

127. "Ever holding the baresma in her hand, according to the rules, she wears square golden earrings on her ears bored, and a golden necklace around her beautiful neck, she, the nobly born Ardvi Sura Anahita; and she girded her waist tightly, so that her breasts may be well-shaped, that they may be tightly pressed.

128. "Upon her head Ardvi Sura Anahita bound a golden crown, with a hundred stars, with eight rays, a fine . . . , a well-made crown, in the shape of a . . . , with fillets streaming down.

129. "She is clothed with garments of beaver, Ardvi Sura Anahita; with the skin of thirty beavers of those that bear four young ones, that are the finest kind of beavers; for the skin of the beaver that lives in water is the finest-colored of all skins, and when worked at the right time it shines to the eye with full sheen of silver and gold.

130. "Here, O good, most beneficent Ardvi Sura Anahita! I beg of thee this favor: that I, fully blessed, may conquer large kingdoms, rich in horses, with high tributes, with snorting horses, sounding chariots, flashing swords, rich in aliments, with stores of food, with well-scented beds; that I may have at my wish the fullness of the good things of life and whatever makes a kingdom thrive.

131. "Here, O good, most beneficent Ardvi Sura Anahita! I beg of thee two gallant companions, one two-legged and one four-legged: one two-legged, who is swift, quickly rushing, and clever in turning a chariot round in battle; and one four-legged, who can quickly turn towards either wing of the host with a wide front, towards the right wing or the left, towards the left wing or the right.

132. "Through the strength of this sacrifice, of this invocation, O Ardvi Sura Anahita! come down from those stars, towards the earth made by Ahura, towards the sacrificing priest, towards the full boiling [milk]; come to help him who is offering up libations, giving gifts, sacrificing, and entreating that thou wouldst grant him thy favors; that all those gallant warriors may be strong, like king Vishtaspa.
"For her brightness and glory, I will offer her a sacrifice.

133. "*Yatha ahu vairya: The will of the Lord is the law of holiness. . . .*

  "*I bless the sacrifice and prayer, and the strength and vigor of the holy water-spring Anahita.*

  "*Ashem Vohu: Holiness is the best of all good. . . .*

  "*[Give] unto that man brightness and glory, . . . give him the bright, all-happy, blissful abode of the holy Ones!*"

NOTES

Chapter 1: An Introduction to the Mithraic Mysteries

1. Peter Clark, *Zoroastrianism: An Introduction to an Ancient Faith* (Brighton and Portland, U.K.: Sussex Academic Press, 1998), x.

2. Arthur Cotterell and Rachel Storm, *The Ultimate Encyclopedia of Mythology* (London: Hermes House, 2003), 262–63, 502.

3. Clark, *Zoroastrianism*, 47.

4. Richard N. Frye, *The Heritage of Persia* (Costa Mesa, Calif.: Mazda, 1993), 84.

5. David Fingrut, *Mithraism: The Legacy of the Roman Empire's Final Pagan State Religion* (Toronto: SEED Alternative School, 1993), 7.

6. Mohamad Moghdam, "Mithra." Paper given at the Second International Congress of Mithraic Studies, Tehran, 1975, 1. This paper appears online at Circle of Ancient Iranian Studies at the School of Oriental & African Studies (SOAS), University of London. www.cais-soas.com/CAIS/Religions/iranian/mithra.htm

7. Moghdam, "Mithra," 3.

8. This document can be found at the following Web site: http://hcl.harvard.edu/govdocs/guides/pres_papers_part2_page.html

9. Robert Turcan, *The Cults of the Roman Empire* (Oxford: Blackwell Publishers, 2004), 195.

10. Firmicus Maternus, *The Error of Pagan Religions,* translated by Clarence A. Forbes. In Marvin W. Meyer, ed., *The Ancient Mysteries: A Sourcebook of Sacred Texts* (Philadelphia: University of Pennsylvania Press, 1987), 208.

11. Manfred Clauss, *The Roman Cult of Mithras: The God and His Mysteries* (Edinburgh, Scotland: Edinburgh University Press, 2000), 108–109, 144–45, 168.

12. For more information on the new Mithraeum in Tuscany, see the Web site at www.mithra.it.

Chapter 2: Mithraic Iconography

1. M. P. Speidel, *Mithras-Orion: Greek Hero and Roman Army God* (Leiden, Holland: Brill Academic Publishers, 1980) and David Ulansey, *The Origins of the Mithraic Mysteries: Cosmology and Salvation in the Ancient World* (Oxford: Oxford University Press, 1989).

2. For a virtual tour of a reconstructed Mithraeum at Carrawburgh, visit the Newcastle University Museum Web site at http://museums.ncl.ac.uk/archive/index.html

3. Clauss, *The Roman Cult of Mithras,* 42.

4. David Ulansey, "The Eighth Gate: The Mithraic Lion-Headed Figure and the Platonic World-Soul" paper, forthcoming in *The Ancient World* on the following Web site: www.well.com/user/davidu/eighthgate.html

5. Ibid.

Chapter 3: The Seven Initiatory Rites of Mithras

1. For general information on raven lore see: www.sacredhoop.demon.co.uk/HOOP-37/Ravens.html

2. Tertullian is quoted in Clauss, *The Roman Cult of Mithras,* 134–35.

3. Franz Cumont, *The Mysteries of Mithra* (New York: Dover Publications, 1956), 157. (Originally published in 1903.)

4. Robert Turcan, *The Cults of the Roman Empire* (Oxford: Blackwell Publishers, 2004), 244.

5. Porphyry, quoted in Paul Kriwaczek, *In Search of Zarathustra* (London: Phoenix, 2003), 121.

6. Porphyry, quoted in Clauss, *The Roman Cult of Mithras,* 135.

7. Clauss, *The Roman Cult of Mithras,* 136.

8. Masoud Homayouri, *Origins of Persian Gnosis* (London: Mawlana Centre, 1992), 8.

9. Charles Daniels, *Mithras and His Temples on the Wall* (Tyne and Wear, U.K.: Museum of Antiquities of the University and the Society of Antiquaries of Newcastle upon Tyne, 1989), 8.

10. Javad Nurbakhsh, *The Path: Sufi Practices* (New York and London: Khaniqahi Nimatullahi Publications, 2003), 41.

11. Dastur Firoze, M. Kotwal, and James W. Boyd, *A Persian Offering: The Yasna: A Zoroastrian High Liturgy* (Paris: Association Pour L'avancement Des Etudes Iraniennes, 1991), 6, 10.

12. Ibid., 23.

13. www.avesta.org/ritual/barsom.htm

14. See "Zoroastrian Hymn to Homa" at www.avesta.org/yasna/y9to11s.htm.

15. Christian Rätsch, *The Encyclopedia of Psychoactive Plants*, John R. Baker, trans. (Rochester, Vt.: Park Street Press, 2005), 747–48.

16. Hans Dieter Betz, *The "Mithras Liturgy": Text, Translation and Commentary* (Tubingen, Germany: Mohr Siebeck, 2003), 51. For discussion of the father passing on the ritual to his daughter, who is also a magician, or passing it to an apprentice (with *daughter* as a metaphor), see Betz, *The "Mithras Liturgy": Text, Translation and Commentary*, 96–97.

17. This information from Robin M. Weare can be found at: www.liberalmafia.org/hyenas/hyena.FAQ.html

18. www.liberalmafia.org/hyenas/folklore.html

19. Ranuccio Bianchi, *Rome: The Late Empire, Roman Art A.D. 200–400* (New York: G. Braziller, 1971). Also as quoted on the following Web site by Hannah M. G. Shapero: http://groups.yahoo.com/group/mithras/message/3931

20. M. J. Vermaseren, *Mithras the Secret God* (London: Chatto and Windus, 1963), 162–65.

Chapter 4: Echoes of Mithraism around the World

1. Esme Wynne-Tyson, *Mithras: The Fellow in the Cap* (Fontwell, Sussex, U.K.: Centaur Press, 1972).

2. James G. Frazer, *The Golden Bough* (Hertfordshire, U.K.: Wordsworth Editions, Ltd., 1993), 358. (Originally published in 1890.)

3. *New Catholic Encyclopaedia*, vol. III (New York: The Catholic University of America and McGraw-Hill, 1967), 656.

4. Cumont, *The Mysteries of Mithra*, 193.

5. William R. Harwood, *Mythology's Last Gods: Yahweh and Jesus* (New York: Prometheus Books, 1992).

6. Kriwaczek, *In Search of Zarathustra*, 135.

7. Tyson, *Mithras: The Fellow in the Cap*, 117.

8. Jerome praising *praefectus* Urbi of the year 376 C.E. In Clauss, *The Roman Cult of Mithras*, 170.

9. Paul Kriwaczek, *In Search of Zarathustra*, 133.

10. Michel Pastoureau, *Les Emblemes de la France* (Collection Images et symboles) (Paris: Editions Bonneton, 1998). Online at: http://flagspot.net/flags/xf-cap.html

11. Dave Martucci, as quoted on http://flagspot.net/flags/xf-cap.html

12. Isya Joseph, *The Sacred Books and Traditions of the Yezidiz* (Whitefish, Mont.: Kessinger Publishing, 1997), 133. (Originally published in 1919.)

13. Dr. M. Izady, of Kurdish Worldwide Resources (KWR) at: www.kurdish.com/kurdistan/religion/yezdanism.htm

14. Taufiq Wahby, *The Remnants of Mithraism in Hatra and Iraqi Kurdistan, and Its Traces in Yazidism: The Yazadis Are Not Devil-Worshippers* (London: T. Wahby, 1962), 30–31.

15. Clauss, *The Roman Cult of Mithras*, 77–78.

16. Meyer, *The Ancient Mysteries*, 208.

17. The poem can be found in John Matthews, *Taliesin: The Last Celtic Shaman* (Rochester,Vt.: Inner Traditions, 2002), 321–23. It is reproduced here with the author's kind permission.

18. Matthews, *Taliesin*, 213.

19. Philip Carr-Gomm, *The Druid Tradition* (Shaftesbury, U.K.: Element Books, 1996).

20. Charles Squires, *Mythology of the Celtic People* (London: Bracken Books, 1912), 59.

21. Carr-Gomm, *The Druid Tradition*.

22. Matthews, *Taliesin*, 218–19.

23. Stephen Edred Flowers, ed., *Hermetic Magic: The Postmodern Magickal Papyrus of Abaris* (York Beach, Maine, and Boston: Red Wheel/Weiser, 1995), 122.

24. Ibid., 124.

25. Based on Squires, *Mythology of the Celtic People*.

Chapter 5: Simorgh—A Mithraic Fairy Tale

1. Laleh Bakhtiar, *Sufi Expressions of the Mystic Quest* (Singapore: Thames and Hudson, 1997), 45.

2. Henry Corbin, *The Man of Light in Iranian Sufism* (New Lebanon, N.Y.: Omega, 1994), cover and 45–48.

3. Robert Bly, *Iron John* (Shaftesbury, U.K.: Element, 1994). (Originally published in the United States by Addison-Wesley, 1990.)

4. Farid Ud-Din Attar, *The Conference of Birds*, Afkham Darbandi and Dick Davis, trans. (New York: Penguin Classics, 1984), 218–20. Reproduced by permission of Penguin Books, Ltd.

5. Wiccan prayer "Charge of the Goddess" in Janet Farrar and Stewart Farrar, *Eight Sabbats for Witches* (London: Robert Hale, 1992), 43.

Chapter 6: A Mithraic Liturgy

1. G. R. S. Mead, in *A Mithraic Ritual* (Whitefish, Mont.: Kessinger Publishing, 2001), 18–33. (Originally published in 1907.)

2. Corbin, *Man of Light in Iranian Sufism,* especially Chapter Three, "Midnight Sun and Celestial Pole."

3. John Matthews, ed. *Choirs of the God: Revisioning Masculinity* (London: Mandala, 1991), 148.

Chapter 7: The Goddess Anahita

1. From verses 126–28 of the Aban Yasht 5. For the full text, see appendix B.

2. This description of Anahita is based on her description in Tony Allan, Charles Phillips, and Michael Kerrigan, *Wise Lord of the Sky: Persian Myth,* Myth and Mankind series (London: Time Life Books, 1999), 32.

3. Official entry on Anahita by the Embassy of the Islamic Republic of Iran in Ottawa, Canada on their Web site: www.salamiran.org/Women/General/Women_And_Mythical_Deities.html

4. For the Temple of Anahita at Kangavar, see: www.vohuman.org/SlideShow/Anahita%20Kangavar/Anahita-00.htm

5. For the temple at Pir e Sabz, see: www.vohuman.org/SlideShow/Pir-e-Sabz/Pir-e-Sabz-1.htm

6. For the temples of Pir e Banoo Pars and Pir e Naraki, see: www.sacredsites.com/middle_east/iran/zoroastrian.htm

7. For the Temple of Anahita at Bishapur, see: www.vohuman.org/SlideShow/Anahita%20Bishapur/AnahitaBishapur00.htm

8. Personal communication from Jalil Nozari, August 20, 2003.

9. Martin Gray, www.sacredsites.com/middle_east/iran/zoroastrian.htm

Chapter 8: Meditations and Initiations

1. This version of the prayer comes from the Web site http://www.avesta.org/ka/niyayesh.htm#ni4n

2. For details on this technique see Shaykh Hakim Moinuddin Chishti, *The Book of Sufi Healing* (Rochester, Vt.: Inner Traditions, 1991), 144–46.

3. Ulansey, *The Origins of the Mithraic Mysteries,* 38–39.

4. A. P. Long, *In a Chariot Drawn by Lions: The Search for the Female in Deity* (London: The Women's Press, 1992), cover text.

5. Allan, Phillips, and Kerrigan, *Wise Lord of the Sky,* 32.

6. Ulansey, "The Eighth Gate."

7. Rumi in Reshad Field, *The Last Barrier* (Shaftesbury, U.K.: Element, 1990), 39.

8. Farrar and Farrar, *Eight Sabbats for Witches,* 119 and 43.

Chapter 9: The Four Stations of Mithra

1. www.persianoutpost.com/htdocs/yalda.html

2. www.iranheritage.com/programmes/yalda_back.htm

3. For further details on Chehar Shainbeh Suri see:
www.caissoas.com/CAIS/Celebrations/fire_festival.htm

4. Payam Nabarz, "The Seething Cauldron," on the Web site
www.geocities.com/nabarz110/theseethingcauldron

5. For further details about the Nou Roz festival, see the excellent paper by Massumeh Price at:
http://home.btconnect.com/CAIS/Celebrations/norooz.htm

6. For full details of Nou Roz celebrations and photos see:
www.farsinet.com/noruz/

7. Kriwaczek, *In Search of Zarathustra*, 213.

8. For further details about the festival of Tiragan see:
www.avesta.org/tiragan.htm
http://home.btconnect.com/CAIS/Celebrations/tirgan.htm

9. Phaeded Harmani, personal communication about a paper in preparation, entitled, "Manilius, Sirius and the Commagenean Origins of Roman Mithras."

10. Aleister Crowley, *Magick in Theory and Practice* (York Beach, Maine: Samuel Weiser, 1994), 645.

11. Dr. S.H. Taqizadeh, *Old Iranian Calendars* (London: Luzac and Co., 1938) and "The feast of Mithra," an online paper at:
www.avesta.org/mihragan.htm

12. Massumeh Price, an online paper at:
http://oznet.net/iran/mehregan.htm

13. For additional information on the Mehregan festival visit:
www.iranonline.com/festivals/mehregan-english/ and
http://home.btconnect.com/CAIS/Celebrations/mehregan.htm
The Iranonline extract was originally extracted from *Norouz & Other Festivities in Iran,* by Farshid Eghbal & Sandra Mooney (Los Angeles: Eghbal Printing & Publishing, 1996), 75–81.

BIBLIOGRAPHY

Allan, Tony, Charles Phillips, and Michael Kerrigan. *Wise Lord of the Sky: Persian Myth*. London: Duncan Baird Publishers, Time Life Books, 1999.

Attar, Farid Ud-Din. *The Conference of Birds*. Translated by Afkham Darbandi and Dick Davis. New York: Penguin Classics, 1984.

Betz, Hans Dieter, ed. *Mithras Liturgy. PGM IV. 475–829. The Greek Magical Papyri in translation*. 2nd ed. Chicago & London: Chicago Press, 1996.

Betz, Hans Dieter. *The "Mithras Liturgy": Text, Translation, and Commentary*. Tubingen, Germany: Mohr Siebeck, 2003.

Bakhtiar, Laleh. *Sufi Expressions of the Mystic Quest*. Singapore: Thames and Hudson, 1997.

Chishti, Shaykh Hakim Moinuddin. *The Book of Sufi Healing*. Rochester, Vermont: Inner Traditions, 1991.

Clark, Peter. *Zoroastrianism: An Introduction to an Ancient Faith*. Brighton and Portland, U.K.: Sussex Academic Press, 1998.

Clauss, Manfred. *The Roman Cult of Mithras: The God and His Mysteries*. Translated by Richard Gordon. Edinburgh, Scotland: Edinburgh University Press, 2000.

Cooper, D. Jason. *Mithras: Mysteries and Initiation Rediscovered*. York Beach, Maine: Weiser, 1996.

Corbin, Henry. *The Man of Light in Iranian Sufism*. New Lebanon, N.Y.: Omega Publications, 1994.

Cumont, Franz. *The Mysteries of Mithra*. New York: Dover Publications Inc., 1956. (Originally published by Open Court Publishing Company, 1903.)

Daniels, Charles. *Mithras and His Temples on the Wall*. Tyne and Wear, U.K.: Museum of Antiquities of the University and the Society of Antiquaries of Newcastle upon Tyne, 1989.

Frye, Richard N. *The Heritage of Persia*. Costa Mesa, Calif.: Mazda Publishers 1993.

Gaviri, Suzan. *Anahita dar usturah ha-yi Irani*. Tehran, Intisharat-i Jamal al Haqq, year 1372 (1993).

Guthrie, Kenneth Sylvan. *Mithraic Mysteries Restored and Modernized*. Whitefish, Montana: Kessinger Publishing Company. 1993. (Originally published in 1913.)

Homayouri, Masoud. *Origins of Persian Gnosis*. London: Mawlana Centre, 1992.

Joseph, Isya. *The Sacred Books and Traditions of the Yezidiz*. Whitefish, Montana: Kessinger Publishing, 1997. (Originally published in 1919.)

Kashani, Abbas Aryanpur and Manoochehr Aryanpur Kashani, trans. Persian Text collected by Parviz Nilofari. *Persian Folk Songs*. Tehran, Iran: Tehran University Press, 1971.

Kriwaczek, Paul. *In Search of Zarathustra*. London: Phoenix, 2003.

Matthews, John. *Taliesin: The Last Celtic Shaman*. Rochester, Vt.: Inner Traditions, 2002.

Mead, G. R. S. *A Mithraic Ritual*. Whitefish, Montana: Kessinger Publishing Company, 1997. (Originally published in 1907.)

Meyer, Marvin W. *The Ancient Mysteries: A Sourcebook of Sacred Texts*. Philadelphia: University of Pennsylvania Press, 1987.

Mysteria Mithrae Music CD, songs based on the mysteries of Mithras, exclusive tracks by various artists. Digipack with 20-page full-color booklet, many rare and never seen photos of Mithraic temples and altars. For details see: http://arsregia.free.fr/pages/mithra/mithra.htm

OTO seventh degree is a rite to Mithras. For details: www.mysunrise.ch/users/prkoenig/html/rit7.htm

Turcan, Robert. *The Cults of the Roman Empire*. Oxford: Blackwell Publishers, 2004.

Wahby, Taufiq. *The Remnants of Mithraism in Hatra and Iraqi Kurdistan, and Its Traces in Yazidism: The Yazidis Are Not Devil-Worshipers*. London: T. Wahby, 1962.

Wynne-Tyson, Esme. *Mithras: The Fellow in the Cap*. London: Rider & Company, 1958 or Fontwell Sussex, U.K.: Centaur Press, 1972.

Ulansey, David. *The Origins of the Mithraic Mysteries: Cosmology and Salvation in the Ancient World*. Oxford: Oxford University Press, 1989.

FURTHER READING

The best current academic book is:
The Roman Cult of Mithras: The God and His Mysteries by Manfred Clauss.
Translated by Richard Gordon. Edinburgh, Scotland: Edinburgh University
Press, 2000.

Another excellent academic book, which includes a detailed analysis of the
meaning of the bull slaying as star map and spells out the Mithras-Perseus
connection:
*The Origins of the Mithraic Mysteries: Cosmology and Salvation in the Ancient
World* by David Ulansey. Oxford: Oxford University Press, 1989.

This recent extended academic commentary on the Mithras Liturgy is highly
useful:
The "Mithras Liturgy": Text, Translation, and Commentary by Hans Dieter Betz.
Tubingen, Germany: Mohr Siebeck, 2003.

The following contains many original sources and texts that refer to Roman
Mithras.
The Ancient Mysteries: A Sourcebook of Sacred Texts by Marvin W. Meyer.
Philadelphia: University of Pennsylvania Press, 1987.

The following is a great two-volume catalogue of all Mithraic sites and findings.
Corpus Inscriptionum Et Monumentorum Religionis Mithriacae, I, II by M. J.
Vermaseren. The Hague: Aspen Publishers, Inc. 1956, 1960.

A summary of the Vermaseren CIMRM great work listed above:
Mithras the Secret God by M. J. Vermaseren. London: Chatto and Windus, 1963.

For the Mithras and Christ connection:
Mithras: The Fellow in the Cap by Esme Wynne-Tyson. Fontwell Sussex, U.K.:
Centaur Press, 1972. (Originally published by Rider & Company, 1958.)

A classic, and one of the first academic books on the subject—though originally
written in 1903, a number of recent reprints have been published. I have listed
the edition that I referenced for this book:
The Mysteries of Mithra by Franz Cumont. New York: Dover Publications, 1956.

Originally written in 1907, recent reprints are available for this book as well:
A Mithraic Ritual by G. R. S. Mead. Whitefish, Montana: Kessinger Publishing
    Company, 1997.

A book in Farsi with great deal of material on all of the Persian seasonal festivals—Mehergan, Yalda, and so forth. Also contains lots of material on Mithra.
Jahan Farvari: bakhshi az farhang–Irani Kuhan by Dr. Bahram Farahvashi.
    Anteshrat Karyan, year 1364 (1985).

A book in Farsi with great deal of info on the Persian goddess Anahita:
Anahita dar usturah ha-yi Irani by Suzan Gaviri. Tehran: Intisharat-i Jamal al
    Haqq, year 1372 (1993).

On the influence of Mithraism on other religions:
A paper entitled "Mithraism" by W. J. Phythian-Adams. London: Constable &
    Company, Ltd., 1915.

S. G. F. Brandon, "Mithraism and its Challenge to Christianity," Hibbert Journal
    53 (1954–1955), 107–14.

S. Laeuchli, "Christ and Mithra" in Mithraism in Ostia, edited by idem, 85–105.

G. Lease, "Mithraism and Christianity: Borrowings and Transformation," ANRW
    II, 23.2 (1980), 1306–32.

D. Ulansey, The Other Christ: The Mysteries of Mithras and the Origins of
    Christianity. Forthcoming book, based on its title should also be of great
    interest. Oxford University Press, 2005.

Taufiq Wahby, The Remnants of Mithraism in Hatra and Iraqi Kurdistan, and Its
    Traces in Yazidism: The Yazadis Are Not Devil-Worshippers. London: T.
    Wahby, 1962.

A modern Occult and Neo-Pagan book, with lots of detailed photos:
Mithras: Mysteries and Initiation Rediscovered by D. Jason Cooper. York Beach,
    Maine: Weiser, 1996.

This first completely Mithraic revivalist book was originally written in 1913.
Mithraic Mysteries, Restored and Modernized by Kenneth Sylvan Guthrie. Has
    recently been reprinted by Kessinger Publishing Company of Whitefish
    Montana, 1993.

For the original unaltered translation of the "Mithras Liturgy":
The Greek Magical Papyri in Translation, 2nd edition. Edited by Hans Dieter Betz.
    PGM IV. 475–829. University of Chicago Press, 1996.

MITHRAIC GROUPS AND INTERNET RESOURCES

The following are examples of some Mithraic groups and Web sites from around the world.

Mithras groups:

Mithraeum—A religious organization dedicated to the worship of Mithras, and the revival of Mithraism & The Mithraic Mysteries. Based in U.S.A. www.mithraeum.org

"Sun Centre" Mithra group, based in Italy. www.mithra.it/

"Temple of Mithras," based in England. Dedicated to Mithras. www.bizstore.f9.co.uk/indexmithras.htm http://www.geocities.com/nabarz110/Mithras.doc Email: nabarz@hotmail.com

Adoradores de Mithra Página de los Adoradores de Mithra en Catalunya, based in France and Spain. http://iditxa.free.fr/mithra/

Orden del Dios Mithra, based in Spain. http://OrdenDelDiosMithra.iespana.es http://es.groups.yahoo.com/group/ForoDelDiosMithra

Mithras—The Cult Revived, based in Germany. www.datacomm.ch/olhaenzi/roem.civ13.html

Useful Web sites:

The Electronic Journal of Mithraic Studies (EJMS) is a revival of the Journal of Mithraic Studies edited by Dr. Richard Gordon. www.uhu.es/ejms/

There are a number of very interesting papers at Circle of Ancient Iranian Studies at the School of Oriental & African Studies (SOAS), University of London. www.cais-soas.com/CAIS/Religions/iranian/mithraism.htm

Museum of Antiquities' Virtual Mithraeum
http://museums.ncl.ac.uk/archive/mithras/intro.htm

MITHRAISM: The Cosmic Mysteries of Mithras, by David Ulansey
www.well.com/user/davidu/mithras.html

Mithras. www.iranvision.com/mithras.html

Ancient Sources on the Magi and Mithraism. www.thedyinggod.com/magi.htm

Procolita Fort Mithraeum at Hadrian's Wall.
http://museums.ncl.ac.uk/archive/mithras/text.htm

The Legacy of the Roman Empire's Final Pagan State Religion, by David Fingrut
SEED Alternative School, Toronto, 1993
http://penelope.uchicago.edu/Thayer/E/Gazetteer/Periods/Roman/Topics/
Religion/Mithraism/David_Fingrut**.html

Vohuman.org—A Zoroastrian educational institute providing a Web journal on
Zoroastrian heritage
http://www.vohuman.org

E-lists:

THE MITHRAS LIST—The original public discussion forum for Mithraic
subjects. http://groups.yahoo.com/group/mithras/

THE MITHRAEUM LIST—A specifically religious list for those interested in the
worship of Mithras as a spiritual path.
http://groups.yahoo.com/group/Mithraeum/

ABOUT THE AUTHOR

Payam Nabarz is Persian born. He is a Sufi and a practicing Dervish, and has spent much time as a wandering Dervish walking the land. In England he studied British Neo-Paganism among many other spiritual traditions; while most people were heading east in search of enlightenment, he went west. The grass is always greener on the other side! Nabarz is a Druid in the Grove of the "Order of Bards, Ovates and Druids," a member of Golden Dawn Occult Society, founder of Oxford Pagan Circle, and a revivalist of the Temple of Mithras. He was also a Pagan Federation Regional Coordinator for several years. He is the founder of Spirit of Peace, a charitable organization that aids various charities (in the past, Amnesty International and Adopt a Minefield). Spirit of Peace is dedicated to personal inner peace and world peace via interfaith dialogue among different spiritual paths. Nabarz's numerous writings have appeared in many esoteric magazines including *The Sufi, Touchstone* (journal of OBOD), *Pagan Dawn* (journal of Pagan Federation), *Stone Circle, The Little Red Book, Pentacle,* and *White Dragon.*

INDEX